ROBERT LOWELL

Edited by Michael London
and Robert Boyers

DAVID LEWIS   NEW YORK

ROBERT LOWELL:
A Portrait of the Artist in His Time

Library of Congress Catalog card number: 71–107885.

SBN number: 912012-00-5.

Manufactured in the United States of America by Haddon
Craftsmen, Inc.

Designed by Edward Aho.

First Printing.

Contents

Introduction
The Unfinished Portrait

With the publication of his first book, *Land of Unlikeness,* in 1944,
Robert Lowell initiated a career which to date encompasses six books
of poetry, two books of translations, two plays, and the
autobiographical *Life Studies.* During this twenty-five-year period,
Lowell's reputation has grown steadily and Lowell has become
perhaps the most controversial and envied American poet of his
generation. His often difficult personal life and his political activities
are part of the controversy, and it is to his credit that he has not
allowed himself to be transformed into just another public performer.

The aim of the editors of this book has been to present the most
important and interesting criticism of Robert Lowell's work. We have
not hesitated to reprint articles which have been reprinted elsewhere
when we feel the article to be important historically.

In all, we have assembled a rather diverse collection of articles and
reviews, first impressions and considered impressions; a collection
punctuated by a few broad, comparative essays, and a crucial interview.
Many of the selections are superb of their kind, demonstrating just
how effectively Lowell has managed to engage the enthusiasm and
the wit of our gifted writers. Some of the pieces are interesting not
so much for what they reveal about Lowell or his work, but for what
they tell us about the critical propensities of a given period, the
atmosphere in which a poet like Lowell had to make his way.

Obviously, even in a collection of this breadth, one is forced to
omit certain pieces one would in some ways have liked to include.
The literature on Lowell is already extensive, and growing rapidly
every year, as one can see by consulting Jerome Mazzaro's checklist.
The editors have attempted to avoid overlap wherever possible and

what ought ideally to emerge from a reasonably consecutive reading of the book is an understanding of the dynamics of what we might call "The Robert Lowell Phenomenon in American Letters." Part of this phenomenon has been the hostile reception of Lowell's books by people with no genuine reason to dispute his success, who are simply engaged in fighting literary wars having very little to do with literature itself. The editors have left this problem to future historians of the period.

This is not to suggest, of course, that there has not been intelligent criticism of the negative sort. This we have represented in proportion as it has been characteristic of Lowell criticism, and in proportion as we have felt it useful to a proper evaluation of the man and his work. We have included controversies where these have been instructive and we have tried to juxtapose contrasting views in such a way that they would heighten the reader's awareness of crucial issues, rather than simply enforce his inclination to retreat into relativism.

All those who feel Robert Lowell's importance in our culture, and who are deeply interested in his poetry, owe a debt of gratitude to the late Randall Jarrell, who early recognized Lowell's immense gifts, and helped us all to see them more clearly than we could have hoped to without him. One must also remind readers that there has been no more consistent champion of Lowell's work in recent years than M. L. Rosenthal, whose book The New Poets (*Oxford University Press, 1967*) contains an excellent discussion of much that is crucial in Lowell. And of course, there is none who knows more about Robert Lowell's poetry than Jerome Mazzaro, whose book *The Poetic Themes of Robert Lowell* is a distinguished contribution. It is owing to his diligence and generosity, moreover, that students of Robert Lowell's poetry can now have use of a thorough bibliography in which diverse sources can easily be located.

Our "portrait," then, is definitely a personal one which may not please all interested parties. However, we hope it will prove stimulating to both admirers and critics of Robert Lowell's work.

ROBERT BOYERS
Saratoga Springs, N.Y.

POET

Allen Tate
Introduction to
Land of Unlikeness

There is no other poetry today quite like this. T. S. Eliot's recent prediction that we should soon see a return to formal and even intricate metres and stanzas was coming true, before he made it, in the verse of Robert Lowell. Every poem in this book has a formal pattern, either the poet's own or one borrowed, as the stanza of "Satan's Confession" is borrowed from Drayton's "The Virginian Voyage," adapted to a personal rhythm of the poet's own.

But this is not, I think, a mere love of external form. Lowell is consciously a Catholic poet, and it is possible to see a close connection between his style and the formal pattern. The style is bold and powerful, and the symbolic language often has the effect of being *willed;* for it is an intellectual style compounded of brilliant puns and shifts of tone; and the willed effect is strengthened by the formal stanzas, to which the language is forced to conform.

A close reader of these poems will be able to see two general types, or extremes which it is the problem of the poet to unite, but which I believe are not yet united: this is not a fault, it merely defines the kind of poet that Lowell, at this early stage, seems to be. On the one hand, the Christian symbolism is intellectualized and frequently given a savage satirical direction; it points to the disappearance of the Christian experience from the modern world, and stands, perhaps, for the poet's own effort to recover it. On the other hand, certain shorter poems, like "A Suicidal Nightmare" and "Death from Cancer," are richer in immediate experience than the explicitly religious poems; they are more dramatic, the references being personal and historical and the symbolism less willed and explicit.

The history of poetry shows that good verse does not inevitably make its way; but unless, after the war, the small public for poetry shall exclude all except the democratic poets who enthusiastically greet the advent of the slave-society, Robert Lowell will have to be reckoned with. Christopher Dawson has shown in long historical perspective that material progress may mask social and spiritual decay. But the spiritual decay is not universal, and in a young man like Lowell, whether we like his Catholicism or not, there is at least a memory of the spiritual dignity of man, now sacrificed to mere secularization and a craving for mechanical order.

R. P. Blackmur
"Nothing Loved"

Robert Lowell's *Land of Unlikeness* ... shows, not examples of high
formal organization achieved, but poems that are deliberately moving
in that direction and that have things put in to give the appearance of
the movement of form when the movement itself was not secured.
In fact, Lowell's verse is a beautiful case of citation in any argument in
support of the belief in the formal inextricability of the various elements
of poetry: metre is not metre by itself, any more than attitude or
anecdote or perception, though any one of them can be practised by
itself at the expense of the others, when the tensions become mere
fanaticism of spirit and of form: conditions, one would suppose,
mutually mutilating. Something of that sort seems to be happening in
Lowell's verse. It is as if he demanded to *know* (to judge, to master)
both the substance apart from the forms with which he handles it and
the form apart from the substance handled in order to set them
fighting. . . . Lowell is distraught about religion; he does not seem to
have decided whether his Roman Catholic belief is the form of a force
or the sentiment of a form. The result seems to be that in dealing with
men his faith compels him to be fractiously vindictive, and in dealing
with faith his experience of men compels him to be nearly blasphemous.
By contrast, Dante loved his living Florence and the Florence to come
and loved much that he was compelled to envisage in hell, and he

From "Notes on Seven Poets" in *Language as Gesture*. By permission of
Harcourt, Brace & World, Inc., and George Allen & Unwin, Ltd. Copyright 1945
by R. P. Blackmur

wrote throughout in loving metres. In Lowell's *Land of Unlikeness* there is nothing loved unless it be its repellence; and there is not a loving metre in the book. What is thought of as Boston in him fights with what is thought of as Catholic; and the fight produces not a tension but a gritting. It is not the violence, the rage, the denial of this world that grits, but the failure of these to find *in verse* a tension of necessity; necessity has, when recognised, the quality of conflict accepted, not hated. To put a thing, or a quality, or an intimation, *in verse,* is for the poet the same job as for the man not a poet the job of putting or holding a thing *in mind*. Mind and verse are mediums of response. If Lowell, like St. Bernard whom he quotes on his title page, conceives the world only as a place of banishment, and poetry (or theology) only as a means of calling up memories of life before banishment, he has the special problem of maturing a medium, both of mind and verse, in which vision and logic combine; and it is no wonder he has gone no further. *Inde anima dissimilis deo inde dissimilis est et sibi.* His title and his motto suggest that the problem is actual to him; the poems themselves suggest, at least to an alien mind, that he has so far been able to express only the violence of its difficulty. As it is now, logic lacerates the vision and vision turns logic to zealotry.

Marius Bewley
from *The Complex Fate*

The 'technicians' among modern American poets may be divided into several categories, but perhaps those who take religion as their theme, no doubt seeing in the order of their verse a correspondence to the order of their theology, are the most important. To this group the young American poet belongs . . . as the one poet whose verse I should consider with some care in this paper: I mean Mr. Robert Lowell.* There are several reasons for selecting Lowell's verse in preference to that of other writers of his generation (Mr. Lowell was born in 1917). First of all, he has received a degree of recognition far beyond that accorded any other new writer during the 'forties, and the tributes have ranged from publicity in *Time* to accolades from T. S. Eliot and Santayana. From the first the most distinguished American critics appeared to enter a conspiracy for the purpose of establishing Lowell's literary reputation on as sound a base in as short a time as possible. The enthusiasm of his admirers has been equalled on this side of the Atlantic only by the boosters of Dylan Thomas. And undeniably Lowell's verse has a great deal of intrinsic interest. It is integrated with the American background and the New England tradition to a degree unique among contemporary poets; while traditional, it also represents something new, though not perhaps quite as new as critics have claimed; and it is intensely serious—sometimes over-reachingly so.

* *Poems:* 1938–1949. Faber and Faber.

In its own distinctive way it is alive with that sense of responsibility and function I have predicated of American poets in general.

But since my own criticism of Lowell's poetry will be considerably less enthusiastic than the prevailing view, I should like to say at once what I believe its virtues are. In several of his poems there is an immediacy of relation between his sensibility and the old New England of shipping and the sea that comes off with great distinction. 'The Quaker Graveyard in Nantucket' which begins,

> A brackish reach of shoal off Madaket,—
> The sea was still breaking violently and night
> Had steamed into our North Atlantic Fleet,

is as original and fine a poem as America has lately produced. There is a kind of enduring newness in the evocations of the poetry that assert themselves more solidly with time. Speaking of a burial at sea,

> We weight the body, close
> Its eyes and heave it seaward whence it came,
> Where the heel-headed dogfish barks its nose
> On Ahab's void and forehead . . .

But it is difficult to quote piecemeal from such a poem.

An important element in Mr. Lowell's poetry is his feeling for Puritan New England. At the time most, if not all, of these poems were written, Lowell was a convert to the Catholic Church, and the Church forms a large part of their subject matter; but Lowell is not, as Mr. John Berryman has called him, 'the master of the Catholic subject without peer since Hopkins'. The quality of Lowell's sensibility depends almost entirely on its intractable Protestant puritanism, and it is never at its ease in Catholic images. The very structure of his sensibility is centred in considerations that were of overwhelming importance to the early New Englanders, but which are alien to Catholic feeling—ideas of innate depravity, the utter corruption of human nature and creation, regeneration, damnation of the non-Elect, and a habit of tortuous introspection to test the validity of grace in the soul. All these doctrines have in Lowell's poetry professedly undergone conversion to Rome, but on the face of it they still look very much their old Protestant selves. One critic wrote of Lowell's poetry that it exposed 'the full force of the collision between a long heritage of New England Calvinism and the tenets of the Roman Catholic Church'. Although the critic did not use the description in an unfavourable sense, it remains a very good one of what happens in Lowell's verse. A head-on collision between the Catholic tradition and an Apocalyptic Protestant sensibility is exactly what occurs in a verse like the following from 'Where the Rainbow Ends':

> In Boston serpents whistle at the cold.
> The victim climbs the altar stair and sings:
> 'Hosannah to the lion, lamb, and beast
> Who fans the furnace face of IS with wings:
> I breathe the ether of my marriage feast.'
> At the high altar, gold
> And a fair cloth. I kneel and the wings beat
> My cheek. What can the dove of Jesus give
> You now but wisdom, exile? Stand and live,
> The dove has brought an olive branch to eat.

The poem of which this is the third verse has a certain impressiveness, but it is characteristically reluctant to yield up its meaning. It contains some extremely awkward images which need not be examined here as this quality of awkwardness can be better studied in some other verses, and a good many of the lines are far from being inevitably precise in their meaning. For example, the first line above may mean that in Boston sin is non-sensuous and chillblained, being the result mainly of the more frigid spiritual vices. But I should hesitate to stake anything of value on such a reading being the correct one. As for the remainder of this verse, it appears likely that the poet has just received Holy Communion, but if so, he celebrates it in an Apocalyptic terminology that seems unsuitable for such a subject. In this poem the two traditions collide, but it is a collision only—the metaphorical impact of staunchly opposed opposites. Mr. Lowell himself seems not even to be aware of the polarity involved, and none of the struggle of the opposing traditions get through into the texture of his verse.

The Puritan saints, so far from resting on assurances of their election, gave themselves up to some of the most agonizing soul probing ever encouraged by any religion. They examined endlessly the nature of the grace they felt in their souls that they might be sure it was authentic and not a temptation from the Devil; they searched the Scriptures for confirmation, and analysed endlessly the movements of their hearts. All this developed a tone, an attitude—and despite the Catholic gesturing, it is an attitude one finds in Lowell's poetry. This attitude or tone sometimes becomes feverishly tortuous, and leads Lowell into attenuations so rarefied, and through logical transitions so slippery and concealed, that it is frequently impossible to follow him all the way. The poem 'Colloquy in Black Rock' is an example of one of these dialogues between Lowell and his own heart as a preparation for its fuller possession by Christ. It is a dull poem, but nevertheless it is worth considering as a way of approaching his most serious defect—the conviction that he is being, not only intelligible, but highly ordered and logical in the disposition of his images and the structure of his thought when, in reality, his experience is claustrophobically private and subjective. Despite the rigorous appearance of an objective framework of logic 'The Ferris Wheel' is such a poem, and it could be duplicated in this quality by many other of Lowell's verses.

A number of Lowell's poems can be interpreted in purely Protestant terms—for example, 'The Drunken Fisherman', which is one of his best pieces. And no doubt it would be fairer to Lowell if one were to concentrate on these. But Lowell was specifically acclaimed as a Catholic poet, and to this fact he no doubt owes a good deal of his recognition. But whenever the subject is pointedly Catholic there is something disturbing in the tone. Turning to 'A Prayer for My Grandfather to Our Lady', Lowell's uncertainty or awkwardness is unmistakable under the boldness of feeling in a passage like this one addressed to the Blessed Virgin:

> O Mother, I implore
> Your scorched blue thunderbreasts of love to pour
> Buckets of blessings on my burning head
> Until I rise like Lazarus from the dead:
> *Lavabis nos et super nivem delabor.*

This is a network of conflicting connotations that operates at cross-purposes. 'Thunderbreasts', I presume, is meant to suggest the mythical Thunderbird of various Indian tribes, which was supposed to bring rain, and so the word may imply the life-giving qualities of Our Lady's love. But Our Lady and the Thunderbird (if it *is* intended, and I don't see what else could be meant here) belong to traditions too remote from each other to coalesce imaginatively at the low pressure to which they are submitted. Blue, of course, is Mary's colour. And perhaps 'blue thunderbreasts' is meant to emphasize the blue heavens from which rain and grace come. But the quality of Lowell's sensibility is such (and I am thinking of the poem in the full context of the volume) that the word seems likely to start a train of disease images. 'Buckets of blessings on my burning head' is breath-takingly infelicitous. Apart from the ugly sound of it, and the almost Gilbert and Sullivan visual image it presents, it suggests that Our Lady is dousing a halo, which can hardly be what is meant. I am not merely trying to be difficult, but I find this passage typical in the awkward qualities I have mentioned. It frequently happens that when Mr. Lowell is dealing with a religious subject something seems to go wrong with his verse—not inevitably so, for 'The Holy Innocents' is a very good poem. But a religious theme is usually a signal for intolerable strain.

This strain is not lessened when Mr. Lowell relates human action to religious significance. His sequence of four poems, 'Between the Porch and the Altar', is a melodramatic narration of a man who deserts his wife and two children for another woman, gets killed in a motor accident, and goes to Hell. At any rate, that is the action as far as I can follow it, but the character of the seducer seems strangely uneven. In the first poem he is a son with a mother fixation. In the second he is a

Concord farmer who, in the closing image, is identified with Adam
in the act of committing Original Sin. In the fourth poem he turns up,
rather sportily, in a night club shortly before his fatal mishap. Here is
the opening of the fourth poem, and it illustrates the recurrence of that
strain or awkwardness that I have just noted elsewhere:

> I sit at a gold table with my girl
> Whose eyelids burn with brandy. What a whirl
> Of Easter eggs is coloured by the lights,
> As the Norwegian dancer's crystalled tights
> Flash with her naked leg's high-booted skate,
> Like Northern Lights upon my watching plate.
> The twinkling steel above me is a star;
> I am a fallen Christmas tree. Our car
> Races through seven red lights—then the road
> Is unpatrolled and empty, and a load
> Of ply-wood with a tail-light makes us slow.
> I turn and whisper in her ear. You know
> I want to leave my mother and my wife,
> You wouldn't have me tied to them for life. . . .

Apparently at that moment the accident occurs which, in view of the
sentiments he is expressing just then, sends him straight to the Devil.

The first thing one notices about this passage is a characteristic
wooden ugliness that is related to the rhythm—particularly to Mr.
Lowell's flattening habit of placing a cæsura just before the last foot of
every line. It is a common practice with him, and can be better observed
in a poem like 'After the Surprising Conversions':

> I preached one morning on a text from Kings;
> He showed concernment for his soul. Some things
> In his experience were hopeful. He
> Would sit and watch the wind knocking a tree. . . .

But to return to the earlier quotation—the rhythmical flatness is
matched by an unsatisfactoriness in the images themselves. Anticipating

the descent into Hell in the last part of the poem, the second line strains too hard to get as much sordidness as possible out of a few glasses of brandy, and the sense of strain is not reduced by the absurd image of the Easter eggs, which is obviously introduced for the purpose of recalling the Redemption, quite as if by accident. Again, I wonder why the nationality of the fancy skater is insisted on since the only purpose that particular exactness can serve is to start the American reader thinking of Sonja Henie. Nor can I understand in what relevant sense the speaker's plate may be said to be 'watching', unless, indeed, he is speaking, not of the plate on the gold table, but of his retina which he compares to a photographic plate. In the next line it is extremely difficult to know what the twinkling steel is. It may possibly mean that a sword is hanging above the poet's head, and that the consequent feeling of uncertainty which it engenders is a warning which might, if heeded, save him, and which for that reason he compares to the star of Bethlehem. But it is asking more than reasonable co-operation from any reader to put any very precise sense in the lines at all. The same kind of muzziness attends the next image into which the figure of the twinkling star naturally moves, 'I am a fallen Christmas tree'. This could, no doubt, mean a number of things, but it hardly seems to mean anything with much certainty. The action which is recorded in the last lines is handled laboriously and jerkily, and the closing bit of 'wickedness' is blurted out in an extremely youthful way.

Most critics have referred to Mr. Eliot as among Lowell's chief influences, but he seems to be much nearer Edwin Arlington Robinson. Both poets are disconcertingly fond of classic allusions, and they both present little tin-types of unusual American characters and episodes. And both have a disastrously 'literary' taste for the more romantic and ancient themes. We find Mr. Lowell writing exotic little set pieces (but on the surface quite 'modern' and difficult to read): 'Napoleon Crosses the Berezina', 'Charles the Fifth and the Peasant', or 'The Fens' (after Cobbett). As for Mr. Lowell's rhythm, a passage like the following from Robinson is much nearer a good deal of Lowell's verse than anything in Eliot:

Now I call that as curious a dream
As ever Meleager's mother had—
Æneas, Alcibiades, or Jacob.
I'll not except the scientist who dreamed
That he was Adam or that he was Eve
At the same time; or yet that other man
Who dreamed that he was Æschylus, reborn
To clutch, combine, compensate, and adjust
The plunging and unfathomable chorus
Wherein we catch, like a bacchanale through thunder,
The chanting of the new Eumenides,
Implacable, renacent, farcical,
Triumphant, and American.

I should find myself hard-pressed if I were asked to put a particular passage from Lowell against that to demonstrate my point, but with the exception of several poems that seem to me highly distinguished, the volume as a whole is alive with echoes of that kind of writing. Yet Lowell's two or three really successful poems are strikingly original; but original also is a peculiar kind of ugliness which runs through much of his verse. Some of his lines remain in the memory as classic examples of verbal and visual infelicity, for example:

Her Irish maids could never spoon out mush
Or orange juice enough . . .

In the most literal sense Lowell's world is astonishingly without colour. His images are nearly all grey or black or white, and they gravitate towards such unpleasant items as snow, ice, snakes choking ducklings, melted lard, dead cats, rats, coke barrels, iron tubs, fish, mud, Satan, rubble, stones, smoke, coke-fumes, hammers, the diseases of old age, and every possible variation on the most depressing aspects of winter. Except in a few poems I cannot see that Lowell transcends the dreary materials he builds them with. On the few occasions he achieves beauty in his poetry the sea is likely to be beating coldly and sombrely in the background.

And yet, under these disagreeable surfaces, Lowell's poetry does give evidence of an unusual integrity. It proves, I think, that the sense of function . . . of the American poet, is not wholly, and in all cases, a product of America's material activity. Among its deeper historical roots one may point to the New England puritanism of the seventeenth century, which regarded logic and rhetoric as a means of knowing and communicating Divine Truth. It is under the banners of logic and rhetoric, although these are subsumed in the name of poet, that Mr. Lowell undertakes his work. And it makes little difference from the viewpoint of his intention that the logic is often elusive and the rhetoric unappealing. No poet could well conceive of a greater function than this religious onslaught on Truth, and it is, as I have tried to indicate, a function made wholly valid by the tradition from which Mr. Lowell emerges.

Leslie Fiedler
The Believing Poet
and the Infidel Reader

The critical comment on Robert Lowell's latest book [*Lord Weary's Castle*] has made me more acutely aware of a discrepancy I have long felt at the center of the relationship between many recent poets and their readers. To the reader, this discrepancy means that his deepest poetic satisfactions have come to be sought in works with whose underlying structure of belief he profoundly disagrees. While this sort of ambiguous allegiance is frequently the pattern of our relation with poets of the past, it is, I think, a new and disturbing aspect of the connection between a practising poet and his most enthusiastic advocates in his own generation.

For the reader, there is something treacherous in this appropriation of the specific insights, organization of sensibility and experience inherent in an *Anschauung* he does not share; in the case of Lowell, the reader has, without the disquieting necessity of coming to terms with difficult institutions and dogmas, the benefit of seeing his world in terms of original sin and grace. He is perhaps aware that something in him ordinarily starved is being satisfied obliquely and by proxy, but he does not confess it. It is the poet's skills, he will insist, his music or his honest eye that is the source of his pleasure; or, a trifle condescendingly, the unbelieving reader will confide that a particular "false and partial" view is, at the moment, "useful." At worst, he will pretend to discover

From *The New Leader* Vol. XXX, No. 12 (May 10, 1947). By permission of Leslie Fiedler. Copyright 1947 by the American Labor Conference on International Affairs, Inc.

"heresies" that have slipped past the poet's orthodoxy and that only the properly heterodox can relish.

Such hi-jacking of spiritual goods eventuates in more than a contempt for belief and a moral uneasiness; it confirms a centrifugal tendency in recent response to poetry. The reader, embarrassed at the poet's belief, retreats to the periphery of texture and technique, and never quite makes it back from there to a total reaction to the poem; never responds to the poet with his whole political, moral, sensuous self.

For the poet, it means a special variation of his by now familiar alienation. At the creative center of his fantasy and belief, he is aware of no division; but that *felt* unity seems to him a lie when he turns outward where the applauders of his art deplore his faith and the sharers of his faith ignore his art. Refusing the logical poles of silence or conformity, he chooses the dangerous uses of ambiguity: the ambiguities of translation and satire, the ambiguities of the dramatic and the baroque, that will at once confess and conceal his awareness of his distance in both worlds from those who are closest. Yet the very choice of ambiguity means a kind of complexity; it is a device with which the literary infidel feels at home, and I do not know how the believing poet can feel quite guiltless of connivance in such a situation.

The anomaly of readers and critics, whose majority refuses to treat religion in any terms other than the "failure of nerve" or, at best, "the myth," touting poets committed to belief, of course, does not begin with Lowell. Before him there is the whole history of the "kidnapping" of Hopkins, the reception of the quasi-beliefs of a Rilke or a Yeats, and the case of such writers as Eliot and Auden, whose talents extort admiration from those to whom their Anglican or Kierkegaardian orthodoxies seem unconvincing or repellent. But the latter two introduced their voices, their manner in the service of secular attitudes fashionable at the time: a self-depreciating ennui, or Marxism qualified by Freudian tropes. Later when they moved toward beliefs not quite so chic, those that did not scream "betrayal" or make aesthetic pseudo-conversions learned to praise their work as performance or partial insight. Lowell, by virtue of his generation and temperament, is peculiarly the precise symbol of the diffuse social fact at its moment of crisis. He presents singly, once and for all, the believer's uncongenial doctrine in a manner available only to a group (one has, I think, to say clique) that has not made his leap to belief.

We must see him in the total context of the paradox: the *Nation* in praise of *Lord Weary's Castle* (with reservations as above), the *New Leader* applauding Péguy (with the assurance, of course, that only death prevented an open break with the Church), *Partisan Review* broadcasting the *Four Quarters* (but reserving its prose for scourging the "failure of nerve")—an institutionalized schizophrenia. Why this discrepancy exists I find it impossible to say; questions of genesis are of secondary importance; what is important is to *recognize* the discrepancy, and to see how precisely, in particular cases, the tension between the poet's surfaces and the inwardness of his belief is worked out. This I propose to do very briefly for Lowell, who is so extraordinarily rich, impassioned and resourceful as a poet, that any partial insight (and this claims to be no more) into his work might well be profitable.

Techniques are always, to a certain extent, *given*. The poet must be published, heard; an apostle to the never quite converted gentiles (they are having the best of this world vicariously and they want their own, too), he must in some degree speak the expected language, endure the charge of being all things to all men, abide enthusiasm which misrepresents him, applause that depreciates his center. This situation compels a special sort of defensive ambiguity—as if one were forced to describe the flora and fauna of a new country with only the terms on a list prepared by one who had never been there. This I call the Ambiguity of Translation, the invisible sort of translation that goes on underground where a common language is used by an atomized society. "When the ruined farmer knocked out Abel's brains, Our Father laid great cities on his soul . . ." is this sort of attempt, much admired, often, I think, for the wrong reasons. The infidel reader's response is as likely to be that Cain's world is, after all his (the myth profaned), as that his world is Cain's (the myth translated). An effort to transfer

a context of value from the past can be misread as a kind of superior
debunking, like Mann's three-volume proof that Joseph is really—
Henry Wallace.

A special instance of this general approach is the Ambiguity of Satire.
In simple satire, where the reader and poet are secure in a shared set
of values from which they may fall but which they can never despise,
the use of distortion and epithet turns into Grotesques for laughter
and despite—error and evil that in life may be confusingly attractive.
For the poet aware that there is no shared common ground of doctrines
with his reader, there is the device of *double* satire. Not what is to be
despised, but what is to be accepted at last is distorted: "Christ the
Drunkard," "Dirty Saint Francis"; solemn references are made in tones
of glibness "Nick bends the tree/ The woman takes the Fall."
Sometimes the proper reaction is made; one is shocked back from the
extremes he, half-aware, was approaching, into an acceptance of
evaluations that he would have refused at a less complex level. But
there is a danger always of turning all to Vaudeville, of leaving us at
the level of the garish and the absurd. And where the intent is not
underlined, the reader may be stranded at the simpler level. This was
Jarrell's fate, when he read the phrase "St. Peter, the distorted key"
as a kind of revelatory, unorthodox slip.

These devices of ambiguity and evasion predominate in Lowell's
first book; in *Lord Weary's Castle* he tends to slough them along with
the rough and ready manner they imply, to lean more on the Dramatic
and the Baroque as his essential stratagems.

The direct use of the dramatic device in the lyric is to evade
responsibility; almost all popular songs, for instance, presume a mask
to whom the trivial feelings of the song properly belong; we never take
their words for the genuine sentiment of the author. In more serious
lyric verse we have come more and more to expect the poet's personal
voice, to demand that he really subscribe to what he avows. But Lowell
shies away from the intimate confession he senses may be unwelcome,
welcomes the obliquity of the dramatic, and especially its illusion of
objectivity. Just as the business of his constant specific reference, the

clutter of *things* in his verse is to create the impression that we are presented with no arbitrary construction but the world as it is, so the deliberate detachment of "Mary Winslow," the shift from the fisherman's voice to impersonal, third person commentary in "The Drunken Fisherman," and the complete immersion in the fictional "I" of "Katherine's Dream" reinforce our sense of recognition, persuade us it is the things in themselves, not Lowell, that impel us to Catholic conclusions. The peril of such a method is the uncertainty of the poet's control, the possibility of stopping at the fiction.

The Baroque has been the traditional expression of Catholic faith in a broken environment: the disjunction of center and surface it makes a rationale; its shrill assertion that complication is the essence of pattern, *will* the spring of creation, its profusion of free detail all inform Lowell's verse. Such a style is the natural habitat of an oceanic imagery of storm, smashed heads and blood, but this very volupté of violence disturbs, and the intrinsic conflict of whole and part mars the peace the poet's faith invokes. We are made uneasy when we discover that the rich, startling explosion of "Where Mary twists the warlock with her flowers—/ Her soul a bridal chamber fresh with flowers/ And her whole body an ecstatic womb,/ As through the trellis peers the sudden Bridegroom." has been moved from one poem to another when the first was scrapped. The tension of periphery and center, of a whole faith and a partial belonging are fixed, not solved in the baroque—and it is interesting to note in Lowell beside it, the development of another style, chiefly in the elegiac pieces, whose leitmotif is the river rather than the sea, and whose motion bears us to the quiet focus of two worlds where the Charles becomes the Acheron and "the wide waters and their voyager are one."

In the solution of our ultimate disjunction, all others are subsumed; but the poem, by definition, compromises the vision for publication in the latest review and the poet, renders to the little magazine those things which are the little magazine's.

Randall Jarrell
From the Kingdom
of Necessity

Many of the people who reviewed *Lord Weary's Castle* felt that it was
as much of an event as Auden's first book; no one younger than Auden
has writter better poetry than the best of Robert Lowell's, it seems to
me. Anyone who reads contemporary poetry will read it; perhaps
people will understand the poetry more easily, and find it more
congenial, if they see what the poems have developed out of, how they
are related to each other, and why they say what they say.

Underneath all these poems "there is one story and one story only";
when this essential theme or subject is understood, the unity of attitudes
and judgments underlying the variety of the poems becomes startlingly
explicit. The poems understand the world as a sort of conflict of
opposites. In this struggle one opposite is that cake of custom in which
all of us lie embedded like lungfish—the stasis or inertia of the stubborn
self, the obstinate persistence in evil that is damnation. Into this realm
of necessity the poems push everything that is closed, turned inward,
incestuous, that blinds or binds: the Old Law, imperialism, militarism,
capitalism, Calvinism, Authority, the Father, the "proper Bostonians,"
the rich who will "do everything for the poor except get off their
backs." But struggling within this like leaven, falling to it like light,
is everything that is free or open, that grows or is willing to change:
here is the generosity or openness or willingness that is itself salvation;
here is "accessibility to experience"; this is the realm of freedom, of

the Grace that has replaced the Law, of the perfect liberator whom **the** poet calls Christ.

Consequently the poems can have two possible movements or organizations: they can move from what is closed to what is open, or from what is open to what is closed. The second of these organizations —which corresponds to an "unhappy ending"—is less common, though there are many good examples of it: "The Exile's Return," with its menacing *Voi ch'entrate* that transforms the exile's old home into a place where even hope must be abandoned; the harsh and extraordinary "Between the Porch and the Altar," with its four parts each ending in constriction and frustration, and its hero who cannot get free of his mother, her punishments, and her world even by dying, but who sees both life and death in terms of her, and thinks at the end that, sword in hand, the Lord "watches me for Mother, and will turn/ The bier and baby-carriage where I burn."

But normally the poems move into liberation. Even death is seen as liberation, a widening into darkness: that old closed system Grandfather Arthur Winslow, dying of cancer in his adjusted bed, at the last is the child Arthur whom the swanboats once rode through the Public Garden, whom now "the ghost of risen Jesus walks the waves to run/ Upon a trumpeting black swan/ Beyond Charles River and the Acheron/ Where the wide waters and their voyager are one." (Compare the endings of "The Drunken Fisherman" and "Dea Roma.") "The Death of the Sheriff" moves from closure—the "ordered darkness" of the homicidal sheriff, the "loved sightless smother" of the incestuous lovers, the "unsearchable quicksilver heart/ Where spiders stare their eyes out at their own/ Spitting and knotted likeness"—up into the open sky, to those "light wanderers" the planets, to the "thirsty Dipper on the arc of night." Just so the cold, blundering, iron confusion of "Christmas Eve Under Hooker's Statue" ends in flowers, the wild fields, a Christ "once again turned wanderer and child." In "Rebellion" the son seals "an everlasting pact/ With Dives to *contract*/ The world that *spreads* in pain"; but at last he rebels against his father and his father's New England commercial theocracy, and "the world *spread/*

When the clubbed flintlock broke in my father's brain." The italicized words ought to demonstrate how explicitly, at times, these poems formulate the world in the terms that I have used.

"Where the Rainbow Ends" describes in apocalyptic terms the wintry, Calvinist, capitalist—Mr. Lowell has Weber's unconvincing belief in the necessary connection between capitalism and Calvinism—dead end of God's covenant with man, a frozen Boston where even the cold-blooded serpents "whistle at the cold." (The poems often use cold as a plain and physically correct symbol for what is constricted or static.) There "the scythers, Time and Death,/ Helmed locusts, move upon the tree of breath," of the spirit of man; a bridge curves over Charles River like an ironic parody of the rainbow's covenant; both "the wild ingrafted olive and its root/ Are withered" [these are Paul's terms for the Judaism of the Old Law and the Gentile Christianity grafted upon it]; "every dove [the Holy Ghost, the bringer of the olive leaf to the Ark] is sold" for a commercialized, legalized sacrifice. The whole system seems an abstract, rationalized "graph of Revelations," of the last accusation and judgment brought against man now that "the Chapel's sharp-shinned eagle shifts its hold/ On serpent-Time, the rainbow's epitaph." This last line means what the last line in "The Quaker Graveyard"—"The Lord survives the rainbow of His will"— means; both are inexpressibly menacing, since they show the covenant as something that binds only us, as something abrogated merely by the passage of time, as a closed system opening not into liberation but into infinite and overwhelming possibility; they have something of the terror, but none of the pity, of Blake's "Time is the mercy of Eternity."

Then the worshipper, like a victim, climbs to the altar of the terrible I AM, to breathe there the rarefied and intolerable ether of his union with the divinity of the Apocalypse; he despairs even of the wings that beat against his cheek: "What can the dove of Jesus give/ You now but wisdom, exile?" When the poem has reached this point of the most extreme closure, when the infinite grace that atones and liberates is seen as no more than the acid and useless wisdom of the exile, it opens with a rush of acceptant joy into: "Stand and live,/ The dove has brought an olive branch to eat." The dove of Jesus brings to the worshipper the olive branch that shows him that the flood has receded, opening the whole earth for him; it is the olive branch of peace and reconciliation, the olive branch that he is "to eat" as a symbol of the eaten flesh of Christ, of atonement, identification, and liberation. Both the old covenant and the new still hold, nothing has changed: here as they were and will be—says the poem—are life and salvation.

Mr. Lowell's Christianity . . . is a kind of photographic negative of the faith of the usual Catholic convert, who distrusts freedom as much as he needs bondage, and who sees the world as a liberal chaos which can be ordered and redeemed only by that rigid and final Authority to Whom men submit without question. Lowell reminds one of those heretical enthusiasts, often disciplined and occasionally sanctified or excommunicated, who are more at home in the Church Triumphant than in the church of this world, which is one more state. A phrase like Mr. Lowell's "St. Peter, the distorted key" is likely to be appreciated outside the church and overlooked inside it, *ad maiorem gloriam* of Catholic poetry. . . . Freedom is something that he has wished to escape into, by a very strange route. In his poems the Son is pure liberation from the incestuous, complacent, inveterate evil of established society, of which the Law is a part—although the Father, Jehovah, has retained both the violence necessary to break up this inertia and a good deal of the menacing sternness of Authority as such, just as the problems themselves have. It is interesting to compare the figure of the Uncle in early Auden, who sanctifies rebellion by his authority; the authority of Mr. Lowell's Christ is sanctified by his rebellion or liberation.

Anyone who compares Mr. Lowell's earlier and later poems will see this movement from constriction to liberation as his work's ruling principle of growth. The grim, violent, sordid constriction of his earliest poems—most of them omitted from *Lord Weary's Castle*—seems to be tempermental, the Old Adam which the poet grew from and only partially transcends; and a good deal of what is excessive in the extraordinary rhetorical machine of a poem like "The Quaker Graveyard at Nantucket," which first traps and then wrings to pieces the helpless reader—who rather enjoys it—is gone from some of his later poems, or else dramatically justified and no longer excessive. "The Quaker Graveyard" is a baroque work, like *Paradise Lost,* but all the *extase* of baroque has disappeared—the coiling violence of its rhetoric, the harsh and stubborn intensity that accompanies all its verbs and verbals, the clustering stresses learned from accentual verse, come from a man contracting every muscle, grinding his teeth together till his shut eyes ache. Some of Mr. Lowell's later work moved, for a while, in the direction of the poem's quiet contrast-section, "Walsingham"; the denunciatory prophetic tone disappeared, along with the savagely satiric effects that were one of the poet's weaknesses. Some of the later poems depend less on rhetorical description and more on dramatic speech; their wholes have escaped from the hypnotic bondage of the details. Often the elaborate stanzas have changed into a novel sort of dramatic or narrative couplet, run-on but with heavily stressed rhymes. A girl's nightmare, in the late "Katherine's Dream," is clear, open, and speech-like, compared to the poet's own descriptive meditation in an earlier work like "Christmas at Black Rock."

Mr. Lowell has a completely unscientific but thoroughly historical mind. It is literary and traditional as well; he can use the past so effectively because he thinks so much as it did. He seems to be condemned both to read history and to repeat it. His present contains the past—especially Rome, the late Middle Ages, and a couple of centuries of New England—as an operative skeleton just under the skin. (This is rare among contemporary poets, who look at the past more as Blücher is supposed to have looked at London: "What a city to sack!") War, Trade, and Jehovah march side by side through all Mr. Lowell's ages: it is the fundamental likeness of the past and present, and not their disparity, which is insisted upon. "Cold/ Snaps the bronze toes and fingers of the Christ/ My father fetched from Florence, and the dead/ Chatters to nothing in the thankless ground/ His father screwed from Charlie Stark and sold/ To the select-men." Here is a good deal of the history of New England's nineteenth century in a sentence. . . .

Mr. Lowell's period pieces are notable partly for their details—which are sometimes magically and professionally illusionary—and partly for the empathy, the historical identification, that underlie the details. These period pieces are intimately related to his adaptations of poems from other languages; both are valuable as ways of getting a varied, extensive, and alien experience into his work. Dismissing these adaptations as misguided "translations" is like dismissing "To Celia" or *Cathay,* and betrays an odd dislike or ignorance of an important and traditional procedure of poets.

Mr. Lowell is a thoroughly professional poet, and the degree of intensity of his poems is equalled by their degree of organization. Inside its elaborate stanzas the poem is put together like a mosaic: the shifts of movement, the varied pauses, the alternation in the length of sentences, and the counterpoint lines and sentences are the outer form of a subject matter that has been given a dramatic, dialectical internal organization; and it is hard to exaggerate the strength and life, the constant richness and surprise of metaphor and sound and motion, of the language itself. The organization of the poems resembles that of a great deal of traditional English poetry—especially when compared to that type of semi-imagist modern organization in which the things of a poem seem to marshal themselves like Dryden's atoms—but often this is complicated by stream-of-consciousness, dream, or dramatic-monologue types of structure. This makes the poems more difficult, but it is worth the price—many of the most valuable dramatic effects can hardly be attained inside a more logical or abstract organization. Mr. Lowell's poetry is a unique fusion of modernist and traditional poetry, and there exist side by side in it certain effects that one would have thought mutually exclusive; but it is essentially a post- or anti-modernist poetry, and as such is certain to be influential.

This poet is wonderfully good at discovering powerful, homely, grotesque, but exactly appropriate particulars for his poems. "Actuality is something brute," said Peirce. "There is no reason in it. I instance putting your shoulder against a door and trying to force it open against an unseen, silent, and unknown resistance." The things in Mr. Lowell's poems have, necessarily, been wrenched into formal shape, organized under terrific pressure, but they keep to an extraordinary degree their stubborn, unmoved toughness, their senseless originality and contingency: no poet is more notable for what, I have read, Duns Scotus calls *haeccitas*—the contrary, persisting, and singular thinginess of every being in the world; but this detailed factuality is particularly effective because it sets off, or is set off by, the elevation and rhetorical sweep characteristic of much earlier English poetry. Mr. Lowell is obviously a haptic rather than a visual type: a poem like "Colloquy in Black Rock" has some of the most successful kinaesthetic effects in English. It is impossible not to notice the weight and power of his lines, a strength that is sometimes mechanical or exaggerated, and sometimes overwhelming. But because of this strength the smooth, calm, and flowing ease of a few passages, the flat and colloquial ease of others, have even more effectiveness than they ordinarily would have: the dead mistress of Propertius, a black nail dangling from a finger, Lethe oozing from her nether lip, in the end can murmur to the "apple-sweetened Anio":

> . . . Anio, you will please
> Me if you whisper upon sliding knees:
> "Propertius, Cynthia is here:
> She shakes her blossoms when my waters clear."

Mr. Lowell, at his best and latest, is a dramatic poet: the poet's generalizations are usually implied, and the poem's explicit generalizations are there primarily because they are dramatically necessary—it is not simply the poet who means them. He does not present themes or generalizations but a world; the differences and similarities between it and ours bring home to us themes, generalizations, and the poet himself. It is partly because of this that atheists are vexed by his Catholic views (and Catholics by his heretical ones) considerably less than they normally would be.

But there are other reasons. The poet's rather odd and imaginative Catholicism is thoroughly suitable to his mind, which is so traditional, theocentric, and anthropomorphic that no images from the sciences, next to none from philosophy, occur in his poems. Such a Catholicism is thoroughly suited to literature, since it *is* essentially literary, anthropomorphic, emotional. It is an advantage to a poet to have a frame of reference, terms of generalization, which are themselves human, affective, and effective as literature. *Bodily Changes in Fear, Rage, Pain, and Hunger* may let the poet know more about the anger of Achilles, but it is hard for him to have to talk about adrenalin and the thalamus; and when the arrows of Apollo are transformed into a "lack of adequate sanitary facilities," everything is lost but understanding. (This helps to explain the dependence of contemporary poetry on particulars, emotions, things—its generalizations, where they are most effective, are fantastic, though often traditionally so.) Naturally the terms of scientific explanation cannot have these poetic and emotional effects, since it is precisely by the exclusion of such effects that science has developed. (Many of the conclusions of the sciences are as poetic as anything in the world, but they have been of little use to poets—how can you use something you are delighted never to have heard of?) Mr. Lowell's Catholicism represents effective realities of human behavior and desire, regardless of whether it is true, false, or absurd; and, as everyone must realize, it is possible to tell part of the truth about the world in terms that are false, limited, and fantastic—else how should we have told it? There is admittedly no "correct" or "scientific" view of a great many things that a poet writes about, and he has to deal with them in dramatic and particular terms, if he has foregone the advantage of pre-scientific ideologies like Christianity or Marxism. Of course it seems to me an advantage that he can well forego; I remember writing about contemporary religious poems, "It is hard to enjoy the ambergris for thinking of all those suffering whales," and most people will feel this when they encounter a passage in Mr. Lowell's poetry telling them how Bernadette's miraculous vision of Our Lady "puts out reason's eyes." It does indeed.

It is unusually difficult to say which are the best poems in *Lord Weary's Castle:* several are realized past changing, successes that vary only in scope and intensity—others are poems that almost any living poet would be pleased to have written. But certainly some of the best things in the book are "Colloquy in Black Rock," "Between the Porch and the Altar," the first of the two poems that compose "The Death of the Sheriff," and "Where the Rainbow Ends"; "The Quaker Graveyard at Nantucket" and "At the Indian-Killer's Grave" have extremely good parts; some other moving, powerful, and unusual poems are "Death from Cancer," "The Exile's Return," "Mr. Edwards and the Spider," and "Mary Winslow"—and I hate to leave entirely unmentioned poems like "After the Surprising Conversions," "The Blind Leading the Blind," "The Drunken Fisherman," and "New Year's Day."

When I reviewed Mr. Lowell's first book I finished by saying, "Some of the best poems of the next years ought to be written by him." The appearance of *Lord Weary's Castle* makes me feel less like Adams or Leverrier than like a rain-maker who predicts rain and gets a flood which drowns everyone in the country. One or two of these poems, I think, will be read as long as men remember English.

Richard Eberhart
"The Gold Standard"

Lowell's new collection has the long title poem and six others. It would be impossible in a review to try to show all the changes Lowell has made in the long poem "The Mills of the Kavanaughs" from its publication in this magazine. His habit of changing his work goes back to the beginning, as I took some pains to adumbrate in reviewing his second book. The version printed in this journal differs markedly in lines, phrases and whole stanzas (the book version is one stanza longer); he has rewritten the poem for book publication and we may assume that this last version is what he considers best. I think it is superior in many places, although extraordinary lines are lost by omission; the ending is better-written in the book version, although there is a fusion of parts of stanzas with others. A close scrutiny should be made, line by line, of both versions to get the whole gamut of action and meaning.

Most of Lowell's qualities show up in this ambitious poem of major complexity. It is not my purpose to tell the story, or to point out the "beauties." The poem should be considered as a part of his whole output and outlook; there is a great deal of unity and sameness in his work.

Much has been said about his new direction for modern poetry. We know that he has gone back to a Browning type of rhymed dramatic monologue, pouring the richness of his mind into a strictness of form which he has mastered with an intensely personal style and flavor. We know that his example in some way, and to an extent not yet known, alters the general direction of our verse; that his complexities in thought and attitude toward love, politics, and religion have made for a dense, close-packed, gnarled, intense, and savage kind of poetry.

Lowell is a traditionalist. He is not going to overthrow the iamb or anything of that sort. He has a rich understanding of the resources of the language; he can bring up almost at will sparkling and exciting images. He can direct a poetical narrative so that it never flags, is always fascinating, and produces continuously new tropes which, upon repeated rereadings, stand solid and inevitable. Masculine would be a term for his work. Yet he is not difficult in a contorted, ambiguous sense; his meanings are available to the eye and the ear, his tone is steady and his attitudes are serious.

"Mother Maria Theresa" is a beautiful piece, sonorous yet gentle when he reads it. He does not print translations but again in this book writes a poem "after" some one, in this instance Werfel, with "The Fat Man in the Mirror." This shows his light side, the deft and playful touch.

Reading the title poem yet again, trying to think of it from the point of view of a general, educated reader as distinguished from one professionally involved in letters, I would report as that reader that the narrative cannot be understood at once. Is this good or bad? This posited reader would have no trouble in understanding the narratives of Robinson. Further, the rhymed couplets sometimes get in the way, even though they are occasionally varied, diverting the attention from the sense with a heavy clump-clump pointing, and there is something more than puzzling, challenging if one wishes to worry it out, in the somehow undigested shooting back and forth between centuries and decades and events. A careful collation of the changes made in the poem will substantiate this point, for Lowell has tried to lighten obtuse usages and has often made the narrative sense more readily comprehensible by alterations.

Lowell's work fascinates with the problem of what is, or ought to be, American. He represents the oldest of New England strains, yet after

our boast of three centuries on this continent there does not seem
any poetic speech purely or exclusively American, certainly not in
Lowell. He studied his Latin hard, and he felt the genius of Pope; his
verse owes much to such sources. Likewise Robinson, from the same
region, found it necessary to follow Tennyson. Lowell imposes his own
kind of classical style upon his New England or New England-like
scenes: maybe the roughness, the turgidity, the boxer-like brilliance
is the American thing?

"Thanksgiving Over" is notable for an opening up of his style, a
directness of thrust. "Her Dead Brother" sends up trails and whorls of
contemplation somewhat as does a Jarrell poem. Maybe "David and
Bathsheba in the Public Garden" opens up a little too.

Lowell re-educates taste in a hard way, and that is good. He is
uncompromising, an attitude which has its own justice. It is probably
like picking away at a mine of pure gold; the gold is embedded in
schist; you handle real schist while baring veins of pure imagination;
you bring out a valuable and malleable metal. He puts you on a gold
standard and if that is not apt, it was no fault of his, it was nature's
fault where the gold was.

William Arrowsmith
"A Monotony of Violence"

The poetry of Robert Lowell has been saluted with much critical
extravagance; but for good reason. For Lowell is a genuine poet of very
great strength, and *Lord Weary's Castle* had the hardness of
extraordinary achievement and hence the full promise. Its strength and
its brilliance were, if anything, more than self-evident, and on these
good grounds many critics—myself included— judged that Lowell's
was the promise of the major poet. The promise remains; but *The Mills
of the Kavanaughs* has done nothing to keep it and something to
weaken it. *As yet* Lowell shows himself incapable of extending his
strength—rather he concentrates even further what was already too
concentrated; and he seems to be unaware of his weakness. Yet his
performance within his habitual range is always exciting and sometimes
perfect. By this I think I am saying that Lowell's verse is already
assured minor poetry and that *The Mills of the Kavanaughs* is an
unsuccessful attempt to extend his range—but without modulation—
from minor to major.

Lowell's greatest virtue is his strength of line, rhythm and language;
this virtue, pushed to extremes or overextended, characteristically
generates a vice. God knows, *Lord Weary's Castle* was nothing if not
strong. That strength was achieved, like most strengths, at a necessary
cost: a loss of delicacy, a forcing of effect, a monotony of violence in

From "Five Poets" by William Arrowsmith. By permission of *The Hudson
Review,* Vol. IV, No. 4, (Winter, 1952). Copyright © 1952 by
William Arrowsmith.

both language and subject. The cost was less apparent at the time, because *Lord Weary's Castle* was worth it; *The Mills of the Kavanaughs* raises the question. To understand why, we have to see that the sources of Lowell's strength are the beginnings of a characteristic weakness when the poet moves from a short lyric or ode to an extended narrative or revery.

His most obvious strength is one of diction, a harsh slamming language, heaped up by alliteration, assonance and blunt rhyming, by ruthless enjambing, and by substitutions for strength, particularly in the first foot. Liberal spondees from jagged, generally repulsive, compounds: *coke-barrel, fungus-eyeballs, nigger-brass, mud-flat, broom-pole butt, mole-tide,* etc. Add to this a breath-sweep so tasking it deserves comparison to Milton's; a bold disregard for logical or metrical pause; and, finally, a savageness of subject grafted to a savage language. These qualities are at least the more obvious sources of Lowell's strength; within the framework of a twenty- or thirty-line poem, they made a kind of explosion on the page, more consistently violent, it seems to me, than any "lyric" poetry of which I know. What Lowell had done was to take almost every device by which, normally, long poetry is protected from monotony—the enjambement, the substitutions, the breath-sweep, clause-piling and rhyme-roughening —and compress them within a shorter frame. It worked; magnificently so.

When he came to compose a long poem—*The Mills of the Kavanaughs* is over 600 lines—he seems never to have doubted that the same devices would work just as well. And they might have worked in any poetry less characteristically violent and effected. But in *The Mills of the Kavanaughs* one gets—no paradox—what can only be called a monotony of violence. Yet a different strategy would seem to be indicated. If you are going to compress the anti-monotony devices of long poetry into a smaller frame, it stands to reason that you cannot merely expand your compressed lyric—*at the same compression.* The risk of doing so is that your devices may boomerang; my guess is that they have boomeranged in Lowell's long poem. *The Mills of the*

Kavanaughs is, for all its extraordinary verse- or stanzaic brilliance, when taken at its length, a monotonous poem. Even explosions can become monotonous, after all. What I miss, technically, is the strophic and antistrophic balance which might have offset the characteristic slamming of his lines. For instance, in terms of linegroups: the basic pattern of the poem is heroic couplets; some rhyme-variation is clearly intended to irregularize the pattern; but his variations serve no other purpose. Yet economy and a sense of balance in big poetry might have suggested a tonal contrast between end-stopped couplets and enjambed verses. To my mind the four most nearly perfect lines of the poem—they are perfect—are the closing four. First, however, the run-ons:

> For neither conscience nor omniscience warned
> Him from his folly, when the virgin scorned
> His courtship, and the quaking earth revealed
> Death's desperation to the Thracian field.

And the end-stopped (I read a pause after "gave") lines which perfect their predecessors:

> And yet we think the virgin took no harm:
> She gave herself because her blood was warm—
> And for no other reason, Love, I gave
> Whatever brought me gladness to the grave.

This seems to me achievement of the real thing, and I am far from wanting to ascribe its success to a balancing device alone, however successful. It is meant to crown the whole poem, and not merely the preceding enjambement. But I think its contrast, even as a crown, with the rest of the poem is indicative of the extent to which something has been lost because too great attention has been paid to strength. Item: somewhere Lowell says "A beer can filled/ With fishkins marks the dingle where they died." The *dingles* down Maine? Or the *dingles* in which you can alliteratively die, drown, diddle or dally? It is not a common kind of flaw, but indicative: *almost* anything for strength. But the strength of a narrative is not identical with the strength of the shorter poem, and no one but a lyricist could have thought that it was.

Emphatically, I should like to avoid giving the impression that Lowell's poetry is not one of the most remarkable poetries in America. It is at least that. Line by line, *The Mills of The Kavanaughs* would provide twenty poets with their best verses, their hardest hits, their surest whatevers. It is just that temptation that strength will make—a temptation to make more—that is the peril. It is easy to say, transform it, less easy to see how it would be done, where the mastery is so great that the merest misstep may mean the bog.

More important or less important than these technical points and their balancing flourish—I can't be sure—I wish I understood the poem. I don't, in any satisfactory, even early, way, understand it. And this might mean: wait till it works itself out, or, what six readings without success might suggest, speak up.

The Mills of the Kavanaughs looks like a narrative or an extended narrative revery. It is spoken by Anne Kavanaugh, the widow of a naval officer disgraced at Pearl Harbor and the impotent heir of an old Catholic logging fortune in Maine. The tenor of the narrative is a "revery of her childhood and marriage, addressed to her husband," and supported by the symbolism of the story of the rape of Persephone by Hades. Presumably supported, for it is just this symbolism that to me makes the narrative so difficult. In an ordinary way, it is of course all very clear, but the narrative seems to turn on it in a manner which finishes by blurring. I can see, with the intended force, I think, the resurrection carry-over into Red Kavanaugh's ring:

> *Cut down we flourish,* on his signet ring.

But what am I to make of "marriage by drowning," or is it even related? And yet it seems to be, for it is followed by some play upon Cinderella and then the analogue of Hades' offer to Persephone in the Hymn to Demeter: "Anne, my whole/ House is your serf." And again, in some lines magnificent in themselves, but obscure in relation:

> This was Avernus. There, about this time,
> Demeter's daughter first reviewed the dead—
> Most doomed and pompous, while the maples shed

> There martyr's rubric. . . .
> There, hearing how she'd come to little good,
> She took a husband to dispirit hell.

Fall, yes. But "to little good"? Why should she come to little good? And since this is the motive offered for the marriage, isn't the question an important one for a narrative poem? But I can find no answer elsewhere, unless it is the point of her stressed poverty. In his preface to the poem, Lowell in a way gives a point to his symbols by a kind of phrasing: ". . . a marble statue of Persephone, the goddess who becomes a queen by becoming queen of the dead." And in the first stanza: "Harry, not a thing/ Was missing: we were children of a king." In itself this is quite unobjectionable; but Persephone and Hades are rich enough symbols in themselves that they must be carefully controlled if they are not to become obscure, and it seems to me that *The Mills of the Kavanaughs* does not even attempt control. The danger of eschatologies is their very richness; they are so imbedded in language and thought that they tend to keep their own directions; Lowell ignores this, and proceeds, characteristically, to pack his symbols so that his simplicities assume a complexity which wrecks them. And in narrative, or dramatic, poetry, symbols have to be given a different kind of life than in lyric poetry; they have to bear the weight of motives, completions and pace. Lowell's poem does not have pace, and, I am afraid, in both technique and content long Lowell looks just like short Lowell. This is not to damn him; not by a long shot: *The Mills* is magnificent poetry, but not a narrative poem. Not yet, anyhow.

William Carlos Williams
In a Mood of Tragedy:
The Mills of the Kavanaughs

In his new book Robert Lowell gives us six first-rate poems of which we may well be proud. As usual he has taken the rhyme-track for his effects. We shall now have rhyme again for a while, rhymes completely missing the incentive. The rhymes are necessary to Mr. Lowell. He must, to his mind, appear to surmount them.

An unwonted sense of tragedy coupled with a formal fixation of the line, together constitute the outstanding character of the title poem. It is as though, could he break through, he might surmount the disaster.

When he does, when he does under stress of emotion break through the monotony of the line, it never goes far, it is as though he had at last wakened to breathe freely again, you can feel the lines breathing, the poem rouses as though from a trance. Certainly Mr. Lowell gets his effects with admirable economy of means.

In this title poem, a dramatic narrative played out in a Maine village, Mr. Lowell appears to be restrained by the lines; he appears to *want* to break them. And when the break comes, tentatively, it is toward some happy recollection, the tragedy intervening when this is snatched away and the lines close in once more—as does the story: the woman playing solitaire in the garden by her husband's flag-draped grave. She dreams of the past, of the Abnaki Indians, the aborigines, and of how, lying prone in bed beside her husband, she was ravished in a dream.

Of the remaining five poems, "Her Dead Brother" is most succinct in the tragic mood that governs them all, while the lyric, "The Fat Man in the Mirror" (after Werfel) lifts the mood to what playfulness there is—as much as the mode permits: a tragic realization of time lost, peopled by "this pursey terror" that is "not I." The man is torn between a wish and a discipline. It is a violently sensual and innocent ego that without achievement (the poem) must end in nothing but despair.

Is the poet New England—or what otherwise is his heresy (of loves possessed only in dreams) that so bedevils him? At the precise moment of enjoyment she hears "My husband's Packard crunching up the drive." It is the poet's struggle to ride over the tragedy to a successful assertion—or is it his failure?—that gives the work its undoubted force.

Shall I say I prefer a poet of broader range of feeling? Is it when the restraints of the rhyme make the man restless and he drives through, elbows the restrictions out of the way that he becomes distinguished or when he fails?

It is to assert love, not to win it that the poem exists. If the poet is defeated it is then that he most triumphs, love is most proclaimed! the Abnakis are justified, their land repossessed in dreams. Kavanaugh, waking his wife from her passionate embraces, attempts to strangle her, that she, like Persephone, may die to be queen. He doesn't kill her, the tragedy lying elsewhere.

The tragedy is that the loss is poignantly felt, come what may: dream, sisterhood, sainthood—the violence in "Falling Asleep Over the Aeneid"; "Mother Maria Theresa"; "David and Bathsheba in the Public Garden," excellent work. What can one wish more?

Randall Jarrell
The Mills of the Kavanaughs

Since Robert Lowell's *The Mills of the Kavanaughs* consists of only seven poems—one tremendously long, four quite sizeable—I can treat them one by one. "The Fat Man in the Mirror" makes a better impression on you if you haven't read the strange and beautiful Werfel poem on which it is based; this "imitation after Werfel"—never was anything less imitative!—is a baroque, febrile, Horowitz-Variations-on-*The-Stars-and-Stripes-Forever* affair. Part I of "Her Dead Brother" is a restrained, sinister, and extremely effective poem; the suicide-by-gas-stove Part II is effective in some portions, but is mannered and violent—Part I seems better off as the separate poem that it originally was.
It would be hard to write, read, or imagine a more nightmarish poem than "Thanksgiving's Over." On one level it is a complete success, and it is almost with a sigh of relief that one concludes that it does not quite succeed on another level, that all this is the possible with which art does not have to deal, nor the probable with which it must. Still, it is a frightening and impressive—and in parts very moving—poem which anybody will want to read. The organization and whole conception of "David and Bathsheba in the Public Garden" are so mannered and idiosyncratic, so peculiar to Mr. Lowell, that the poem is spoiled, in spite of parts as beautiful as that about the harvest moon. Someone is sure to say about this poem that you can't tell David from Bathsheba without a program: they both (like the majority of Mr. Lowell's characters) talk just like Mr. Lowell.

From "Three Books" in *Poetry and the Age*. By permission of Alfred A. Knopf, Inc. Copyright 1953 by Randall Jarrell.

I cannot think of any objection at all to "Mother Marie Therese" and "Falling Asleep over the Aeneid," and if I could I would be too overawed to make it. "Mother Marie Therese" is the best poem Mr. Lowell has ever written, and "Falling Asleep over the Aeneid" is—is better; *very* few living poets have written poems that surpass these. "Mother Marie Therese" is the most human and tender, the least specialized, of all Mr. Lowell's poems; it is warped neither by Doctrine nor by that doctrine which each of us becomes for himself; in it, for once, Mr. Lowell really gets out of himself. Sometimes the New Brunswick nun who is talking does sound like a not-too-distant connection of the Lowells, but generally she seems as much herself as porpoise-bellied Father Turbot, "his bald spot tapestried by colored glass," seems himself when he squeaks: "N-n-nothing is so d-dead/ As a dead S-s-sister." Certainly Father Turbot is real; the drowned Mother Superior ("reading Rabelais from her chaise./ Or parroting the *Action Française*"; she who "half-renounced by Candle, Book, and Bell./ Her flowers and fowling-pieces for the church"; she who saw that our world is passing, but "whose trust/ Was in its princes") is real; and the sixty-year-old nun who speaks the poem in grief for her is most real of all. One can judge something of her reality and of the quality of the poem simply by looking at the long passage with which the poem ends:

> The bell-buoy, whom she called the Cardinal,
> Dances upon her, If she hears at all,
> She only hears it tolling to this shore,
> Where our frost-bitten sisters know the roar
> Of water, inching, always on the move
> For virgins, when they wish the times were love,
> And their hysterical hosannahs rouse
> The loveless harems of the buck ruffed grouse
> Who drums, untroubled now, beside the sea—
> As if he found our stern virginity
> *Contra naturam*. We are ruinous;
> God's Providence through time has mastered us:

> Now all the bells are tongueless, now we freeze,
> A later Advent, pruner of warped trees,
> Whistles about our nunnery slabs, and yells,
> And water oozes from us into wells;
> A new year swells and stirs. Our narrow Bay
> Freezes itself and us. We cannot say
> Christ even sees us, when the ice floes toss
> His statue, made by Hurons, on the cross
> That Father Turbot sank on Mother's mound—
> A whirligig! Mother, we must give ground,
> Little by little; but it does no good.
> Tonight, while I am piling on more driftwood,
> And stooping with the poker, you are here,
> Telling your beads; and breathing in my ear,
> You watch your orphan swording at her fears.
> I feel you twitch my shoulder. No one hears
> Us mock the sisters, as we used to, years
> And years behind us, when we heard the spheres
> Whirring *venite;* and we held our ears.
> My mother's hollow sockets fill with tears.

"Falling Asleep over the Aeneid" is as good—and as thoroughly and surprisingly organized—a poem about power and the self as any I can recall. Its subject matter and peculiar circumstances justify the harshness and violence, the barbarous immediacy, that often seem arbitrary in Mr. Lowell's poems; and these are set off by passages as tender and beautiful as this description of the dead Pallas:

> Face of snow,
> You are the flower that country girls have caught,
> A wild bee-pillaged honey-suckle brought
> To the returning bridegroom—the design
> Has not yet left it, and the petals shine;
> The earth, its mother, has, at last, no help:
> It is itself.

I have rarely had more of a sense of the terrible continuity of the world (and of the ego that learns neither from itself nor from the world what the dead face is made to tell Aeneas: "Brother, try,/ A child of Aphrodite, try to die:/ To die is life") than when I read the conclusion into which all the terms of the poem coalesce:

> Church is over, and its bell
> Frightens the yellowhammers, as I wake
> And watch the whitecaps wrinkle up the lake.
> Mother's great-aunt, who died when I was eight,
> Stands by our parlor sabre. "Boy, it's late.
> Vergil must keep the Sabbath." Eighty years!
> It all comes back. My Uncle Charles appears,
> Blue-capped and bird-like. Phillips Brooks and Grant
> Are frowning at his coffin, and my aunt,
> Hearing his colored volunteers parade
> Through Concord, laughs, and tells her English maid
> To clip his yellow nostril hairs, and fold
> His colors on him. . . . It is I, I hold
> His sword to keep from falling, for the dust
> On the stuffed birds is breathless, for the bust
> Of young Augustus weighs on Vergil's shelf:
> It scowls into my glasses at itself.

I am not sure how good this passage will seem in isolation; as the ending of this poem, an ending with every term prepared for, every symbol established, it is as magnificent as it is final.

"The Mills of the Kavanaughs," the long narrative poem that fills half the book, is an interesting and powerful poem; but in spite of having wonderful lines and sections—many of both—it does not seem to me successful as a unified work of art, a narrative poem that makes the same sort of sense a novel or story makes. It is too much a succession of nightmares and daydreams that are half-nightmare; one counts with amusement and disbelief the number of times the poem becomes a nightmare-vision or its equivalent. And these are only too successfully nightmarish, so that there is a sort of monotonous violence and extremity about the poem, as if it were a piece of music that consisted of nothing but climaxes. The people too often seem to be acting *in the manner of* Robert Lowell, rather than plausibly as real people act (or implausibly as real people act). I doubt that many readers will think them real; the husband of the heroine never seems so, and the heroine is first of all a sort of symbiotic state of the poet. (You feel, "Yes, Robert Lowell would act like this if he were a girl"; but whoever saw a girl like Robert Lowell?)

Occasionally, for a few lines, the poem becomes so academic and clumsy that one is astonished: "My husband was a fool/ To run out from the Navy when disgrace/ Still wanted zeal to look him in the face." I do not believe that even Cotton Mather ever managed to think in the style of that last line. If I quote a similar passage—"Soon enough we saw/ Death like the Bourbon after Waterloo,/ Who learning and forgetting nothing, knew/ Nothing but ruin. Why must we mistrust/ Ourselves with Death who takes the world on trust?/ Although God's brother, and himself a god,/ Death whipped his horses through the startled sod;/ For neither conscience nor omniscience warned/ Him from his folly, when the virgin scorned/ His courtship, and the quaking earth revealed/ Death's desperation to the Thracian field"— and then tell the reader that these rather labored and academic lines are three-fourths of the *last stanza* of the poem, I won't blame him for looking unbelieving.

The poem is hurt very much by being a sort of anthology of favorite Lowell effects—situations are repeated, there is even a passage adapted from an earlier poem; the reader gets confused and thinks, "Am I in 'Her Dead Brother' now? Here's the stove, but where's the suicide? Isn't this 'David and Bathsheba' now?" What Mr. Lowell is attempting to do in this poem is often beyond his powers and knowledge (where narrative verse is concerned everybody alive is an amateur, though Frost was a professional thirty years ago); usually the poet is having to try much too hard, so that one does not feel very often in this poem the spontaneity, the live half-accidental half-providential rightness, that some of the best poetry has or seems to have. Sometimes Mr. Lowell is having great difficulties, and sometimes he is seeking refuge from them in some of the effects that he has produced so well and so often before.

He is a poet of both Will and Imagination, but his Will is always seizing his Imagination by the shoulders and saying to it in a grating voice: "Don't sit there fooling around; *get to work!*"—and his poor Imagination gets tense all over and begins to revolve determinedly and familiarly, like a squirrel in a squirrel-cage. Goethe talked about the half-somnambulistic state of the poet; but Mr. Lowell too often is either having a nightmare or else is wide awake gritting his teeth and working away at All The Things He Does Best. Cocteau said to poets: *Learn what you can do and then don't do it;* and this is so—we do it enough without trying. As a poet Mr. Lowell sometimes doesn't have enough trust in God and tries to do everything himself: he proposes and disposes—and this helps to give a certain monotony to his work. But probably the reader will want to say to me, by now, what Lincoln said about the drunkard Grant: "If I knew his brand I would order my other generals a barrel." And I have put my objections to his long poem rather too strongly; it is a powerful and impressive poem, with a good many beautiful or touching passages and a great many overwhelming ones, one of the better poems of one of the best of living poets.

M. L. Rosenthal
Robert Lowell and the
Poetry of Confession

A reluctance to destroy himself any more rapidly than he was already doing may have been one of the causes of Dylan Thomas's refusal to look steadily into the abyss in his poetry. But in the most powerful work of the modern period the great push is often precisely in that direction. Eliot's interest in the "inexpressibly horrible," Pound's violence, Crane's suicidal symbolism, and the psychological self-probings of younger poets all point the same way. "I get the feeling," one of them has written me, "that the madhouse is not far away from many poets writing now. I think there is something wrong in both my feeling that this should become accepted as part of the state of affairs and my feeling that this should be countered consciously and fiercely. . . . I think too that this kind of writing . . . will hurl poetry up a tree it can't descend from. . . . Where will it go? *Can* it make a 'return,' can it reaccept the culture that after all fed it and flung it on its way?"

No one can really answer these questions, although my correspondent supplied *his* answer to the last of them: "No." Emily Dickinson once called publication "the auction of the mind," but today many of our writers seem to regard it as soul's therapy. We are now far from the great Romantics who, it is true, spoke directly of their emotions but did not give the game away even to themselves. They found, instead,

From "Exquisite Chaos: Thomas and Others," in *The Modern Poets*. By permission of M. L. Rosenthal and Oxford University Press, Inc. Copyright 1960 by M. L. Rosenthal.

cosmic equations and symbols, transcendental reconciliations with "this lime-tree bower my prison," or titanic melancholia in the course of which, merging a sense of tragic fatality with the evocations of the nightingale's song, the poet lost his personal complaint in the music of universal forlornness. Later, Whitman took American poetry to the very edge of the confessional in his *Calamus* poems and in the quivering avowal of his helplessness before the seductions of "blind loving wrestling touch, sheath'd hooded sharp-tooth'd touch." More recently, under the influence of the Symbolists, Eliot and Pound brought us into the forbidden realm itself, although a certain indirection in their work masks the poet's actual face and psyche from greedy eyes.

Robert Lowell's poetry has been a long struggle to remove the mask, to make his speaker unequivocally himself. As with Thomas, whose style Lowell's sometimes (especially in a few earlier poems) resembles, his chief mask has been that of the "crucified" man, overwhelmed by compassion and at the same time a boisterous participant in the human ordeal. He departs from Thomas in the specific meaning of the mask: for him it is a mask of moral guilt, like Eliot's, for the present decadence of values and the crash of a great tradition. He is after all a *Lowell,* and he charges himself with all the meanness of contemporary New England as he sees it—sunken in commercialist degradation, the net result of the nastiness behind its long history going back to the repressive Puritanism and to the heartless extermination of the Indians. A Catholic convert for a number of years, Lowell worked this perspective into his poetry as Eliot had done with his Anglicanism, but with a "jackhammer" passion (to use a figure from his savagely depressed poem "Colloquy in Black Rock"). He is also a social critic as uncompromising in his strictures as any Marxist. So his mask is a composite one, as his "Children of Light" shows:

> Our fathers wrung their bread from stocks and stones
> And fenced their gardens with the Redman's bones;
> Embarking from the Nether Land of Holland,

> Pilgrims unhouseled by Geneva's night,
> They planted here the serpent's seed of light;
> And here the pivoting searchlight probe to shock
> The riotous glass houses built on rock,
> And candles gutter by an empty altar,
> And light is where the landless blood of Cain
> Is burning, burning the unburied grain.

The driving rhymes and indignant irony in this poem and such others as "The Drunken Fisherman" and "As a Plane Tree by the Water" demonstrate Lowell's power even while they induce certain reservations. The feeling is genuine; it smashes home. And there is no question of its moral bearing. But in these poems from *Lord Weary's Castle* (1946), as in many of the pieces comprising Lowell's first volume, *Land of Unlikeness* (1944), the emotion is stronger and more immediate than the literal content. The level of *thought,* as opposed to that of *feeling* and *statement,* is a bit stale—even juvenile. He is shocked to realize what "our fathers" did to the Indians and embittered by the unconscious hypocrisy of Puritanism and its historical results. While Lowell handles these set themes beautifully, we have here an instance of the problem Eliot long ago raised of finding an objective correlative for an emotion not directly expressible, an emotion "in *excess* of the facts as they appear." Lines 4 and 5 of "Children of Light" will illustrate:

> Pilgrims unhouseled by Geneva's night,
> They planted here the serpent's seeds of light . . .

As an intellectual proposition these lines are merely a hedging comment on a knotty point of doctrine of little interest to anyone now except theological apologists or historians. On the other hand, if we inquire into the emotional connotations of that paradoxical image "the serpent's seeds of light" we find that again and again in his writings Lowell uses snake and serpent images to suggest sly and furtive guilt, evil that *will* assert itself, and very often guilt or evil of a sexual character. The related meaning of "seeds" is obvious, and "light" suggests, if only ironically, that something not only desirable but valuable is associated with the guilt of the serpent's seeds. These implications are fully worked out in other poems. In "Between the Porch and the Altar," two guilty lovers, an unfaithful husband and his mistress, *become* snakes (in the husband's eyes) whenever they gratify themselves in the way that means "light" for them:

> . . . When we try to kiss,
> Our eyes are slits and cringing, and we hiss;
> Scales glitter on our bodies as we fall. . . .

If Lowell's lovers were not so oppressed by guilt, this would be exactly like the hissing end of Lawrence's "River Roses":

> . . . We whispered: "No one knows us.
> Let it be as the snake disposes
> Here in this simmering marsh."

"Between the Porch and the Altar" helped prepare the way for the maskless confessions of his most recent poems. Its adulterous, mother-dominated hero is first described in the third person, and its serpent imagery helps us see his pathological state:

> Meeting his mother makes him lose ten years,
> Or is it twenty? Time, no doubt, has ears
> That listen to the swallowed serpent, wound
> Into its bowels, but he thinks no sound
> Is possible before her, he thinks the past
> Is settled. . . .
> Nothing shames
> Him more than this uncoiling, counterfeit
> Body presented as an idol. . . .

Throughout "Between the Porch and the Altar" the sense of sin, rather than sin itself, is clearly the protagonist's main problem. He is sick with the burden of his mother and of the crushing family traditions and "New England Conscience" associated with her, and he must throw the burden off even if it means, as his equally guilt-ridden sweetheart puts it, to "ruin" his two children and his wife. The Roman Catholic framework hardly solves the moral problems behind all this, but poetically it separates the protagonist's viewpoint sufficiently from that of the poem as a whole to enable us to see the difference. The speaker in Lowell's poems needs most of all the strength to "cast off remorse," as Yeats demanded. "Between the Porch and the Altar" begins to get at this need, and away from the half-relevant abstractions of other poems. Even "The Dead in Europe," with its picture of the bombed civilians who fell "hugger-mugger in the jellied fire," is marred by arbitrary and generalized religious rhetoric (whereas the later "A Mad Negro Soldier Confined at Munich" is not), and the magnificent elegy "The Quaker Graveyard in Nantucket" is almost betrayed by it. What saves the latter poem is the least pretentious thing about it, the crowded, sensuous concreteness of its description:

> A brackish reach of shoal off Madaket,—
> The sea was still breaking violently and night
> Had steamed into our North Atlantic Fleet,
> When the drowned sailor clutched the drag-net. Light
> Flashed from his matted head and marble feet,
> He grappled at the net
> With the coiled, hurdling muscles of his thighs. . . .

and

> . . . Sea-gulls blink their heavy lids
> Seaward. The winds' wings beat upon the stones,
> Cousin, and scream for you and the claws rush
> At the sea's throat and wring it in the slush
> Of this old Quaker Graveyard. . . .

or

> . . . a gaff
> Bobs on the untimely stroke
> Of the greased wash exploding on a shoal-bell
> In the old mouth of the Atlantic. It's well;
> Atlantic, you are fouled with the blue sailors. . . .

Lowell introduces into this elegy for his drowned cousin, Warren Winslow, motifs from *Moby Dick* and from Christian worship. (Section VI, entitled "Our Lady of Walsingham," is intended to suggest the ultimate calm confidence of true faith; the statue of Our Lady, "Expressionless, expresses God.") These motifs swell the organ music of the poem, enabling the poet to identify the death of young Winslow with that of Ahab and the *Pequod's* crew and providing a specific religious and literary context for his contemplation of the ironies and the intransigence of existence, of "is, the whited monster." Though Lowell relates them skillfully to his theme of one specific death and to his sea music, they are nevertheless extraneous to the essential elegy. For this reason the poem lacks the piercing emotional authority of "Between the Porch and the Altar" and of some less elaborate poems (for instance, "The Slough of Despond," "The Death of the Sheriff," and "Rebellion"). Nor does it convey the terror of "is" as effectively as the less expansive "After the Surprising Conversions," "Mr. Edwards and the Spider," "Colloquy in Black Rock," and "The Ghost" (adapted from Propertius).

Lowell's 1951 volume, *The Mills of the Kavanaughs,* moves into the foreground themes more or less suppressed previously. In these poems, Lowell gives freer play to his driving motives of distorted and blocked love, mental exacerbation verging into insanity, and symbolic and actual homicide and suicide. The title sequence takes us into the mind of an elderly woman remembering her impoverished and loveless childhood and compensatory self-love, her unsatisfactory marriage and the later breakdown of her husband, a wartime naval officer, his homicidal jealousy after his return, and her own burning but unsatisfied sexual need. She thinks of herself in terms of the myth of Persephone, as one who has given "whatever brought me gladness" to death and the grave. "Her Dead Brother," with its theme of incest, and "Thanksgiving's Over," with its sexual cruelty, would-be suicide, and madness, and other poems in this volume show how Lowell is approaching the revolutionary breakthrough of *Life Studies.*

In this book he rips off the mask entirely. *The Mills of the Kavanaughs* had one ludicrous aspect, the circumstances of the protagonists cumbersomely devised to account for their pressing psychological despair. In most of *Life Studies* there is one protagonist only—Robert Lowell. Through what he has to say about himself we discover the real, essential bearing of most of the earlier work. As a result, it is hard not to think of *Life Studies* as a series of personal confidences, rather shameful, that one is honor-bound not to reveal. About half the book, the prose section called "91 Revere Street," is essentially a public discrediting of his father's manliness and character, as well as of the family and social milieu of his childhood. Another section, the concluding sequence of poems grouped under the heading "Life Studies," reinforces and even repeats these motifs, bringing them to bear on the poet's psychological problems as an adult. The father, naval officer *manqué* and then businessman and speculator *manqué,* becomes a humiliating symbol of the failure of a class and of a kind of personality. Lowell's contempt for him is at last mitigated by adult compassion, though I wonder if a man can allow himself this kind of operation on his father without doing his own spirit incalculable damage. But the damage has clearly been in the making a long time, and Lowell knows very well that he is doing violence to himself most of all:

> . . . I hear
> my ill-spirit sob in each blood cell,
> as if my hand were at its throat. . . .
>
> ("Skunk Hour")

He does not spare himself in these poems, at least two of which have to do with sojourns in mental hospitals and his return home from them. We have grotesque glimpses into his marital life. "Man and Wife," for instance, begins: "Tamed by *Milton,* we lie on Mother's bed." It later tells how

> All night I've held your hand,
> as if you had
> a fourth time faced the kingdom of the mad—
> its hackneyed speech, its homicidal eye—

"My mind's not right," says the speaker in "Skunk Hour," the poem which ends the book. It is partly Lowell's apology for what he has been saying in these pieces, like Geronition's mumbling that he is only "an old man, a dull head among windy spaces." And it is partly his assertion that he cannot breathe without these confessions, however rank they may be, and that the things he has been talking about are too stubbornly alive to be ignored:

> I stand on top
> of our back steps and breathe the rich air—
> a mother skunk with her column of kittens swills the
>   garbage pail.
> She jabs her wedge-head in a cup
> of sour cream, drops her ostrich tail,
> and will not scare.

It will be clear that the first impression given by *Life Studies* is that it is impure art, magnificently stated but unpleasantly egocentric, somehow resembling the triumph of the skunks over the garbage cans. Since its self-therapeutic motive is so obvious and persistent, something of this impression sticks all the way. But as the whole work floods into view the balance shifts decisively. Lowell is still the wonderful poet of "The Quaker Graveyard in Nantucket," the poet of power and passion whose driving aesthetic of anguish belies the "frizzled, stale and small" condition he attributes to himself. He may be wrong in believing that what has happened to New England's elite is necessarily an embodiment of the state of American culture, the whole maggoty character of which he feels he carries about in his own person. But he is not wrong in looking at the culture through the window of psychological breakdown. Too many other American poets, no matter what their social class and family history, have reached the same point in recent years. Lowell is foremost among them in the energy of his uncompromising honesty.

Furthermore, *Life Studies* is not merely a collection of small moment-by-moment victories over hysteria and self-concealment. It is also a beautifully articulated sequence. I say "articulated," but the impact of the sequence is of four intensifying waves of movement that smash at the reader's feelings and break repeatedly over his mind. The poems that make up the opening movement are not personal in the sense of the rest of the book. They are poems of violent contradiction, a historical overture to define the disintegration of a world. In the first a train journeys from Rome to Paris at mid-century. The "querulous hush-hush" of its wheels passes over the Alps and beyond them, but nowhere in the altitudes to which it rises does it touch the sanely brilliant heights of ancient myth and thought. For its riders there are, at one terminal, the hysteria of *bella Roma,* where "the crowds at San Pietro screamed *Papa*" at the pronouncement of the dogma of Mary's assumption and where "the Duce's lynched, bare, booted skull still spoke"; and at the other terminal, the self-destructive freedom of "Paris, our black classic." The next poem reaches far enough back in time to reveal the welter of grossly sensual, mindlessly grasping egotism that attended the birth of the modern age. Marie de Medici, "the banker's daughter," soliloquizes about "blood and pastime," the struggle between monarchy and the "pilfering, pillaging democracies," the assassination of her husband. The third poem returns from modern Europe and its bloody beginnings to our own American moment. All that turbulence of recent centuries now seems frozen into intellectual and moral death:

> Ice, ice. Our wheels no longer move.
> Look, the fixed stars, all just alike
> as lack-land atoms, split apart,
> and the Republic summons Ike,
> the mausoleum in her heart.

But then the fourth poem hurls at us the monologue of a mad Negro soldier confined at Munich. Here the wit, the audacious intimacy, the acutely bizarre tragic sense of Lowell's language take on jet speed. In this monologue the collapse of traditional meaning and cultural distinctions is dramatized in the frenzy of one contemporary figure. Thus Lowell begins to zero in on his main target, himself as the damned speaking-sensibility of his world. The humiliated, homicidal fury of the Negro soldier throws its premonitory shadow over the disturbed "comedy" of "91 Revere Street" which follows. It helps us to see, beneath the "Jamesian" nuances of relationship in a society of ritual pretensions but no center of gravity, how anguished is this prose section's murderous dissection of the poet's parents and its complaint against a childhood gone awry. In this way it prepares us for the personal horrors with which the book closes.

But before that long, devastating final wave of poems, there is a smaller one, corresponding in gathering force with the first group. This third wave is again made up of four poems, each of them about a modern writer with whom Lowell feels kinship as an embattled and alienated spirit. Following hard upon the prose, these poems clearly say: "This is what the predatory centuries, and the soul-devouring world in which I walked the maze of my childhood, have done to man's creativity." Lowell first portrays Ford Madox Ford, the "mammoth mumbler" cheated out of his earned rewards, scratching along in America, sick and "gagged for air." Then, dear to Lowell's heart, the self-exiled Santayana looms before us, "free-thinking Catholic infidel." The third poem recreates with sentimental bitterness a winter Lowell and Delmore Schwartz spent at Harvard in 1946. Nothing could be more pathetically open about Lowell's state of mind concerning himself and his art than the parts of their conversation he chooses to record and even to italicize:

> . . . "Let Joyce and Freud,
> the Masters of Joy,
> be our guests here," you said. The room was filled
> with cigarette smoke circling the paranoid,
> inert gaze of Coleridge, back
> from Malta—his eyes lost in flesh, lips baked and black. . . .
> You said:
> *"We poets in our youth begin in sadness;*
> *thereof in the end come despondency and madness;*
> Stalin has had two cerebral hemorrhages!"

The ironic facetiousness that so often marks Schwartz's writing and conversation is here absorbed by Lowell into a vision of unrelieved breakdown centered on the image of Coleridge's "paranoid gaze" in the picture. That image, together with the mocking allusion to Stalin as one of "we poets" who came at last to madness, brings past and present, and all political and psychological realities, into a single focus of defeat. Then in the fourth poem, "Words for Hart Crane," the group comes to a climax paralleling that of "A Mad Negro Soldier" in the first group. Crane's brief, self-destructive career is seen as the demand of the creative spirit, deliberately wearing the most loathsome mask it can find, for unquestioning love from the culture that has rejected it. Here, just before he plunges back into his major theme, the "life studies" of himself and his family, Lowell again, at the most savagely committed pitch he can command, presents the monologue of a dramatically suffering figure whose predicament has crucial bearing on his own situation.

In large part, the fourteen poems of the final section echo the prose of "91 Revere Street." But they echo it as a storm echoes the foreboding sultriness of a threatening spell of weather before it. Apart from the obvious differences that verse makes, they break out of the cocoon of childhood mentality that somehow envelopes "91 Revere Street" despite its more sophisticated aspects. Lowell, like Yeats and Thomas, casts over his autobiographical prose a certain whimsey (though often morbid) and childlike half-awareness. But the poems are overborne by sadness first and then by the crash of disaster. Side by side Lowell places memories of his confinement in mental hospitals and a denigration of his great act of defiance as a conscientious objector in World War II which led to his imprisonment for a year:

> I was a fire-breathing Catholic C.O.,
> and made my manic statement,
> telling off the state and president. . . .

The only poem of this group in which he does not talk in his own person, " 'To Speak of Woe That Is in Marriage,' " is a monologue by the wife of a lecherous, "hopped-up" drunkard. It is placed strategically just before the last poem "Skunk Hour," and after "Man and Wife," in which Lowell makes certain we know he is discussing his own marriage, and it is a deliberate plunge into the depths of the theme of degradation at all but the last moment. Finally, "Skunk Hour," full of indirections and nuances that bring the sickness of our world as a whole back into the scene to restore a more universal vision, reaches a climax of self-contempt and of pure symbol-making. This is Lowell's fantastic, terrifying skunk image for the secret self's inescapable drive to assure itself of continued life:

> I myself am hell;
> nobody's here—
> only skunks, that search
> in the moonlight for a bite to eat.
> They march on their soles up Main Street:
> white stripes, moonstuck eyes' red fire
> under the chalk-dry and spar spire
> of the Trinitarian Church

Life Studies brings to culmination one line of development in our poetry of the utmost importance. Technically, it is an experiment in the form of the poetic sequence looser than but comparable to *Mauberley* and *The Bridge*. To build a great poem out of the predicament and horror of the lost Self has been the recurrent effort of the most ambitious poetry of the last century. Lowell's effort is a natural outgrowth of the modern emphasis on the "I" as the crucial poetic symbol, and of the self-analytical monologues of the sensibility which have helped define that emphasis from "The Love Song of J. Alfred Prufrock" to Miss Rukeyser's *Elegies*. It is also an outgrowth of the social criticism that has marked almost the whole sweep of poetry in this century. Thus, Lowell's poems carry the burden of the age within them. From this fact they derive (given Lowell's abilities) an authority not quite present in the post-Byronics of *The True Confession of*

George Barker,* or in other works in which the speaker thrusts himself to the fore mainly as an *interesting* person.

It is important, I think, to remember one implication of what writers like Robert Lowell are doing: that their individual lives have profound meaning and worth, and that therapeutic confession will lead to the realization of these values. In this respect their explorations are very different from the sense of bleakness in some of Hart Crane, or in a poem like Kenneth Fearing's "Green Light" whose predicate sentences (in which the subject is omitted) and half-images suggest a universal irrelevance of experience:

> Bought at the drug store, very cheap; and later pawned.
> After a while, heard on the street; seen in the park.
> Familiar, but not quite recognized.
> Followed and taken home and slept with.
> Traded or sold. Or lost.

To what subject do these predicates belong? Certainly the images are of the commercial world, yet they refer also to love and memory. Later, other images, absurd or fantastic or commonplace, are added: the predicates of human existence. The poet makes the point that all the impressions of daily life and of fantasy, inseparable from the self-centered and brooding mind, are "strange, and yet not extraordinary." A tragic pointlessness of truth is suggested, simultaneously defining the universe as zero and raising the pettiest details, such as the green light of the busy corner, to a level of universal significance. If truth is pointless, then so are the facts of wisdom, morality, desire, and death. They are facts

> Bought at the drug store down the street
> Where the wind blows and the motors go by and it is always
> night, or day;

* George Barker, *The True Confession of George Barker,* Alan Swallow, Denver, 1950.

> Bought to use as a last resort,
> Bought to impress the statuary in the park.

Fearing's poem represents a letting go, while the work of poets with a perspective like Lowell's is an attempt to hold fast to a moral perspective. Such poets, in their way, are carrying on where Yeats left off when he proposed that the time had come to make the literal Self poetry's central redeeming symbol:

> I must lie down where all the ladders start,
> In the foul rag-and-bone shop of the heart.

Joseph Bennett
"Snobbish Memoirs"

Robert Lowell, in his volume . . . does an exercise on the Brunetto
Latini Canto . . . from *Inferno XV* . . . Mr. Lowell's rendition suffers
considerably from its off-hand, journalistic technique. It is carelessly
written, and indifferent. The indifference is in the attitude of the poet
to his materials. The casualness is not deliberate, contrived, the cunning
craft of the artist, but lack of interest. The poem in question is a
memoir of Santayana, and indeed the whole volume is a collection of
lazily recollected and somewhat snobbish memoirs, principally of the
poet's own wealthy and aristocratic family. Only occasionally does a
glint of the old Lowell show through, as at one point in the
Santayana poem,

> that worn arena, where the whirling sand
> and broken-hearted lions lick your hand
> refined by bile as yellow as a lump of gold.

This book does little to add to Lowell's standing as a poet. Lazy and
anecdotal, it is more suited as an appendix to some snobbish society
magazine, to *Town and Country* or *Harper's Bazaar,* rather than as
purposeful work. Fortunately for those of us who have been moved by
what Mr. Lowell has done in the past, one cannot take the book very
seriously; and the rare, maverick rebellious genius which gave us the
extraordinary *tours de force* and startling technical triumphs of *Land*

of Unlikeness and *Lord Weary's Castle* is merely sleeping. *Hic dormit bonus Homerus.*

The prose autobiographical section of the book is the chief offender. Need we recapitulate the grandparents, the aunts, uncles, parents, cousins, all wealthy, all aristocratic, who romp through town mansions, country estates, seaside villas—Beacon Hill, Beverly Farms, Middleboro —*The Proper Bostonians, The Late George Apley*—a mixture of Cleveland Amory and John Marquand: we visit an insane asylum for Porcellian members; our jail in New York reminds us of the soccer court at St. Mark's School; we learn the intricacies of the *pre-*St. Mark's schools; and we seem constantly on the verge of being provided with a Harvard club-ladder. Such remarkable Lowells as Amy and James Russell hover benignly or malevolently in the background to remind us that the family is literary as well; but others, such as A. Lawrence and Ralph, are soft-pedaled (Cotuit and Nahant branches). The whole is topped off with the whipped cream of heirloom furniture and plate, chauffeurs, choremen, Admirals, Pierce-Arrows, hermit heiresses, etc. I am relieved to report, however, that we enter the precincts neither of Myopia nor the Somerset Club.

This disappointing book detracts from but cannot destroy Mr. Lowell's unique, deserved, and very high reputation. One looks forward with a mixture of hope and anxiety to his next volume.

Geoffrey H. Hartman
The Eye of the Storm

The poet, approaching his fiftieth year, has changed his style: there are
freer rhythms, unexpectedly gentle contours, and a partial return to
imagistic reticence. This is a strange turn of events, since the early
Lowell, in curious rivalry with Hart Crane, took Eliot as a point of
departure toward a complete reversal of direction. As thoroughly
accusative as Eliot's poetry is evasive, *Lord Weary's Castle* raised the
image to the power of a direct, admonitory emblem. The needles of a
Christmas tree "nail us to the wall," "Time and the grindstone and the
knife of God" assail us by their overt and cumulative presence, and
verbal flushes learned from Hopkins obtrude: "The search-guns click
and spit and split up timber / And nick. . . ." Lowell's newest poetry,
however, is balanced in tone and elliptical in movement: its energy
is more hidden, its exclamations almost musical.

There are difficulties in evaluating this change of style. Perhaps the
best that can be done is to balance the gain and the loss. To start with
the loss: Lowell had recovered and mechanized an aspect of medieval
style, the "definition poem." Now some of the definiteness is gone.
The strange and splendid harshness, the pointed shards of images, the
aggressive apostrophes—they have given way to a new and casual
compactness. Lowell is also, perhaps, affected by a European or
"international" style which seems to have reached American poetry in
the sixties. The Hopkinsian, or over-energetic, use of language is being

abandoned for a quieter and naiver mode. Has Lowell succumbed to this *dolce stil nuovo* in such poems as "The Lesson"?

> No longer to lie reading *Tess of the d'Urbervilles,*
> while the high mysterious squirrels
> rain small green branches on our sleep!

This, surely, is "imitating," and to the point of parody. But Lowell's earlier stylistic appropriations are at least equally apparent in these new poems, and with ominous rather than whimsical overtones, as in "Beyond the Alps" (from *Life Studies* and expanded here) where a classical dawn comes with unclassical violence:

> the blear-eyed ego kicking in my berth
> lay still, and saw Apollo plant his heels
> on terra firma through the morning's thigh. . . .

This is the Lowell one knows best, who associates birth with labor and violence. Things "bleed with dawn." And because this Lowell remains so essential in *For The Union Dead,* it is hard to consider the muted style as very significant. If Lowell's poetry moves more haltingly between sentiments and stanzas, his images continue to be entries in a doomsday book: they come nearer and nearer to us, threatening our detachment, massing with prophetic intensity. Is the intermingling, then, of a subtler style, purely experimental, purely a technique? "Each drug that numbs," he says in "Soft Wood," "alerts another nerve to pain." Perhaps it is a spice or drug of this kind.

I would argue that the style of *For The Union Dead* reveals a genuine spiritual change, a revision of thought on the deepest and most internal level. Let us begin with what remains constant in Lowell. The major concern of this book is, as ever, pain: pain and anguish at temporality. That "chilling sensation of here and now, of exact contemporaneity" which Elizabeth Bishop had praised is strongly present. Lowell's attitude toward time is paradoxical: time is the accuser, yet time is inauthentic. Time eyes us through objects that loom large, or through "unforgivable" landscapes, yet everything converges to no effect, like waves breaking harmlessly and sight blurring. Time, and also memory, are the "back-track of the screw"; yet their pressure —the pressure essentially of religious expectation—is unremitting. "Even new life is fuel," Lowell says ironically.

> No ease from the eye
> of the sharp-shinned hawk in the birdbook there,
> with reddish brown buffalo hair
> on its shanks, one ascetic talon
> clasping the imperial sky.
> It says:
> an eye for an eye
> a tooth for a tooth.

The *lex talionis* here referred to is an imperative laid by consciousness on itself, and requires us to be perpetually on guard, open to every sight. Our verdict on temporal matters should be that they are "true and insignificant" ("Hawthorne"). Instead, because of an American or Puritan tension between trivia and magnalia, life becomes a restless search for evidence, a satanic "going to and fro" in the earth.

If time is inauthentic, can a poet do more than record or "accuse" this to-and-fro? What genuine visionariness is possible? The question has a bearing on Lowell's development and on his present change of style. His earliest poetry strives for vision, but there is no vision except a methodical *hastening of the end*. In the poetry that precedes *Life Studies,* darkness calls to darkness: Nature appears as a world of portents rising against the dominion of man, and the poet harshly welcomes the suggested reversal. His visionary method is a kind of *temporicide,* and his poetical method sets spiritual symbol against daily event. He is not a reconciling poet. The very grinding together of natural experience and supernatural emblem is part of a harshness directed against temporality.

But in *Life Studies,* and even more so in the present volume, Lowell resists methodical darkness. He is like Faustus at midnight who cries, *"Lente, lente currite noctis equi."* There is a first retreat from darkness, and into life, when poetry becomes more confessional—a sharp-eyed census of the unreconcilable elements in life. The retreat, however, is very imperfect. For realism easily becomes expressionism, while Lowell's indicative mood tends to indite rather than describe. "The man is killing time," he writes in "The Drinker." Or, in the title poem of *For The Union Dead,* which turns on several apocalyptic emblems: "The ditch is nearer." This nearing, this investing of experience with doom, this dark gloating even, this aggressive parody of at-one-ment in the grim images and the massing of the very words ("The Duce's lynched, bare, booted skull still spoke") is the temptation as well as energy of his vision.

It is, however, the special distinction of *For The Union Dead* to retreat even further from darkness by taking this retreat for subject. Here poetry itself, by virtue of its style—that subtler style—holds back the darkening mind. A presumption of restraint is felt at every level. Lowell is more successful in avoiding the intrusive literary or apocalyptic symbol, though whales still rear their blubber and spiders march. A poem like "The Drinker," with its discreet, almost neutral ending, is utterly different from "The Drunken Fisherman" (*Lord Weary's Castle*) which outsped even Donne's imagination of ruin. The new portrait of "Jonathan Edwards" is unusually urbane in tone and meandering. Natural experience and supernatural emblem may even blend, as when Exodus 12 quietly supports the "red ear of Indian maize ... splashed on the door" in "The Old Flame," a poem dealing with the old passing into the new. That Lowell should admit newness is itself new, through an ironic image of "the plow / groaning up hill—/ a red light, then a blue ..." flickers in memory and disturbs the idea of a definitive progress. "Water," another memory study, shows him in the very act of restraining a darkening yet consolatory movement of the mind:

> Remember? We sat on a slab of rock.
> From this distance in time
> it seems the color
> of iris, rotting and turning purpler,

> but it was only
> the usual gray rock
> turning the usual green
> when drenched by the sea.

The greatest of these memory studies, and the most difficult, is the title poem. Its precarious forward motion reflects the problem of the prophetic mind. There is a consistent "drawing back" from certain conclusions or imaginations. I do not like everything in "For the Union Dead"; the continuity, for example, is aggressively casual. Yet its vibrant and vital imprisonment of apocalyptic themes is totally effective in evoking great but repressed powers—powers waiting for "the blessed break." Chief among these is the power of both Negro and white to take the initiative in civil rights, though the rights struggle is in an eccentric rather than central position. The poem centers, if at all, in several "places" (civil rights, Boston, urbanization, the slippage of time) and is held together in Lowell fashion by an elliptical biography and an ideal. The ideal, that of service, finds its clearest expression in Lowell's inversion of a Christian paradox: service, leadership, is to "choose life and die"; and dying into life is what *Life Studies* already taught. The poem ends with a further inversion of a Christian theme, with a parody of Revelation. Servility instead of service and the omen of a monstrous backlash flood the aquarium of memory:

> The Aquarium is gone. Everywhere,
> giant finned cars nose forward like fish;
> a savage servility
> slides by on grease.

This is still the poet of "The Quaker Graveyard," but quietly, consciously, in the eye of the storm.

John Wain
The New Robert Lowell

Robert Lowell is, at the moment, a largely overrated poet; the word
seems to have gone round that he can do no wrong. Thus, confronted
with *Life Studies,* one London reviewer whimpers, "Poetry of this
order needs neither to be justified nor explained; one should simply
be thankful that there is still someone to write it." Come now, a
professional critic shouldn't give up so easily; there is plenty in Lowell's
work that would benefit by explanation, and even an occasional poem
that needs to be "justified." Not that this is Lowell's fault. Like any
poet, he makes his work as good as he can. And he starts with certain
unique advantages.

Lowell's poems are, to begin with, wonderfully flavorful. He gets into
them so many different kinds of sharp tang; Eastern seaboard, Atlantic
spray, Boston family ramifications, ancestral shivers and—binding
the whole bundle together—the strong personal sense of what it is like
to be *him*. Not just a man from the Northeast, not just a Bostonian,
not (even) just a Lowell, but *Robert Lowell*. The personal flavor
somehow caps and confirms all the other flavors. So much in his
sensibility is inherited and shared, and so much is idiosyncratic; the
result is a mind that can deal with the world, cover a wide range, and
yet stand always on its own ground.

Any poetry that is strongly rooted in place, in ancestry, in situation,
is bound to stand out among the machine-turned factory products that

make up so much modern verse. (John Betjeman's success in England is, I think, largely due to his delight in specific places and flavor and texture of the life to be found in them.) Though it is coming back now, any sort of local flavor has been long absent from the mainstream of modern poetry; perhaps because modern poetry grew up in big cities, and big cities resemble each other closely and also nourish a blind contempt for regional life. The result, for almost a hundred years, has been a poetry almost as generalized as that of the Augustans. A movement like surrealism, for instance, directed the poets' attention toward the content of their unconscious minds, which turned out to be interestingly universal but also highly impersonal and anonymous. Even today, this anonymity is still being put forward as the spearhead of poetic achievement. In the August number of *Poetry,* which is devoted to contemporary French poetry, Mr. Wallace Fowlie writes enthusiastically that the founding Fathers, Nerval, Baudelaire, Rimbaud, Corbière and Laforgue, "used poetry as a means of illuminating psychic regions in themselves that would otherwise have been kept concealed." The poetry of this tradition, a tradition already with a century of achievement to its credit, "is concerned ... with the phenomena of man's psychic life that reach far back into the past and far ahead into the future." Precisely. The here and now, the localized, are trivial. The attempt to render the day-to-day quality of life in one place, among one people, can safely be left to the magazine article. And the young French poet, Provençal or Norman, who moves to Paris is expected to become a Parisian. The generalities of "man's psychic life," like the generalities of neo-classical civilization with its insistence on the intelligible and the universal, swamp the flavor of Provence or Normandy, in the interests of a big-city modernity that may well seem, in retrospect, one of the most hampering of literary conventions.

In America, the situation is no better. (I do not, for the moment, speak of England, where our problem seems to be mainly one of incompetence; the typical minor poet in England is bad because he just doesn't *try*.) American poets tend to be taught their craft at universities, and academic life is remarkably homogeneous; hence the production-

line poetry of the last fifteen years with its careful ironies, its standard
literary references, and its general air of having been written with
that part of the mind that writes a PhD thesis. The reaction, when it
came, was into a formless ranting that seems even further from genuine
imaginative creation. Throughout it all, of course, the handful of
genuine poets was at work, and the minor work will mostly blow
away by itself. I bring up the matter only to point out that the bulk
of this minor verse, which fills the Little Magazines and seeps into the
anthologies, has a flavor as standard as sawdust or lunch-counter food.
Even where the poet had grown up in a place full of individuality
and savour, his allegiance to the doctrines of "modernity," as taught by
innumerable English departments, prevented him from bringing this
savour into his work. From Santa Barbara to New Hampshire, the
same poetic lunch counter was open. And the San Francisco
Renaissance, dominated as it was by New York lads, captured nothing
of California except its mid-century silliness.

Set against this a poet like Lowell, strongly rooted, consistently
interested in the locality, the family and (this is the chief interest of his
uneven volume of *Imitations*) the culture that has for four centuries
linked the Eastern seaboard to Europe. Here are a set of preoccupations
which remain unshaken and unbroken. The "phenomena of man's
psychic life" are there too, but the poet knows they can be trusted to
come through without any special coaxing, if the concrete situation
is rendered faithfully and deeply enough.

That, in fact, is the essential nature of Robert Lowell's work. It
starts from the concrete, intensely observed and deeply meditated: and
reverberates outward into a universal relevance. That this can be done
is an old literary discovery, though one that is often forgotten. For
some reason—I have never seen an explanation of it—writers most often
achieve universality by sticking faithfully to the local and particular.
Chekhov, for instance, is utterly and unquestionably a part of the
Russia of his time; his people think, speak, suffer, react, in a way that
is entirely Russian and entirely *fin de siècle;* but no writer is more
universal, more loved by people who have no knowledge of, and no

special interest in, that time and place. Similarly with Lowell. Personally I happen to like and be interested in the Northeastern coast of the United States, but his poetry would be just as real and satisfying to me if I cared nothing for its locality. The important thing is that there should be reality, should be concreteness, a devouring hunger for the particular, so that the poem never loses the hardness and bulk of an object grasped in one's hands. Take (and I quote the whole), the poem "Water."

It was a Maine lobster town—
each morning boatloads of hands
pushed off for granite
quarries on the islands,

and left dozens of bleak
white frame houses stuck
like oyster shells
on a hill of rock,

and below us, the sea lapped
the raw little match-stick
mazes of a weir,
where the fish for bait were trapped.

Remember? We sat on a slab of rock.
From a distance in time,
it seems the color
of iris, rotting and turning purpler,

but it was only
the usual gray rock
turning the usual green
when drenched by the sea.

The sea drenched the rock
at our feet all day,
and kept tearing away
flake after flake.

One night you dreamed
you were a mermaid clinging to a wharf-pile,
and trying to pull
off the barnacles with your hands.

We wished our two souls
might return like gulls
to the rock. In the end,
the water was too cold for us.

This poem is "about" a relationship, perhaps a marriage, which is haunted by tension and insecurity and ultimately breaks up. The pounding of the sea on the rock, and pathetic dream of the mermaid clinging to the pier and trying to get rid of the hard, skin-tearing barnacles, even perhaps the emptiness of the oyster shells which the bleak human habitations bring to mind, all add up to a complete metaphor of this relationship and its failure, till the stabbing pathos of the last stanza brings the poem ending as cold and salt as Atlantic water. This isn't scene painting; it is a poem about a human situation, and human situations happen in definite, sharply visualized settings.

By contrast, it is in those poems that deal with places and atmospheres quite different from those of the Northeast that come closer to being simple water-colors. "July in Washington," for instance, makes the familiar progression from detailed observation to generalized truth; but it seems to me not quite to get there. What stays in one's mind is the landscape; the balance is not fully achieved. Similarly, the very attractive poem "Buenos Aires," which begins

> In my room at the Hotel Continental
> a thousand miles from nowhere,
> I hear
> the bulky, beefy breathing of the herds

remains, despite its brilliance, a framed picture. It does not get down from the wall and move into our lives.

These considerations, I think, explain why the title poem, "For the Union Dead," is one of the most successful in the book. If we approach it with any expectation of solemn rhetoric, the opening of the poem will strike what seems an ironic note.

> The old South Boston Aquarium stands
> in a Sahara of snow now. Its broken windows are boarded.
> The bronze weathervane cod has lost half its scales.
> The airy tanks are dry

So what? Is this one more piece of that studied irony so predictable in modern poetry? When we wish to think solemnly, tenderly, of the dead Union soldiers, must we be detained by the dropped scales of the weathervane cod on the closed-up aquarium? The poem's answer to this kind of question is untroubled, unforced and completely convincing. As a boy, the poet pressed his nose against the glass of the aquarium; he delighted in contemplating the "dark downward and vegetating kingdom of the fish and reptile." Now he presses his middle-aged nose to a pane of glass on a construction site.

> Behind their cage,
> yellow dinosaur steamshovels were grunting
> as they cropped up tons of mush and grass
> to gouge their underworld garage.

The fish and reptiles, however alien, were living; the sinister dinosaurs of yellow-painted metal, which have taken their place, are part of the dehumanization that has overtaken the world and diluted, along with much else, the Yankee values for which Colonel Shaw's soldiers gave their lives. The Negro soldiers have become bronze; Boston has become a gigantic car-park.

> There are no statues for the last war here;
> on Boylston Street, a commercial photograph
> shows Hiroshima boiling
> over a Mosler Safe, the "Rock of Ages"
> that survived the blast. Space is nearer.
> When I crouch to my television set,
> the drained faces of Negro school-children rise like balloons.

There is irony here, certainly, and it is the true irony of poetry, mordant and avenging. The values represented by that faded religious phraseology ("Rock of Ages") are drowned in a swamp of money; the unchanging faces of Negro infantry, sculptured in bronze, are contrasted with the "balloons," liable to be grotesquely inflated or popped to flatness, of the Negro school-children's faces on television. (We don't need to be told what they are doing on television. Only one thing makes a Negro school child into news, and it is not a pretty thing to contemplate.)

All this is brilliant. The lament for the Union Dead is perfectly realized in terms of what has been lost. And Lowell's eye for the universalizing detail is perfectly shown.

Since one of the most famous of modern American poems is Allen Tate's "Ode to the Confederate Dead," Lowell's poem will naturally provoke comparisons. The distance between the two poems is in fact very wide. Tate's poem is orotund, non-ironical, bardic. Its rhythms are slow and rich, its colors gorgeous. Read them one after the other and you might almost be moving from the richness of tobacco-growing country to the hard coast of Maine. The change is positively physical. It would be a mistake, however, to draw any facile conclusions from this. There is not a new Civil War among the poets. In 1946 Lowell published his commemorative poem, "The Quaker Graveyard at Nantucket," which has remained his best-known poem up to the present time; and if we compare this with Tate's poem the differences become smaller. The language of "The Quaker Graveyard" is as rhetorical as Tate's; its rhythms are full of turmoil; emotionally, it is stuffed full to overflowing.

In the great ash-pit of Jehoshaphat
The bones cry for the blood of the white whale,
The fat flukes arch and whack about its ears,
The death-lance churns into the sanctuary, tears
The gun-blue swingle, heaving like a flail
And hacks the coiling like out: it works and drags
And rips the sperm-whale's midriff into rags,
Gobbets of blubber spill to wind and weather.
Sailor, and gulls go round the stoven timbers
Where the morning stars sing out together
And thunder shakes the white surf and dismembers
That red flag hammered in the mast-head. Hide
Our steel, Jonas Messias, in Thy side.

Admittedly this violent verse describes a violent situation—the
butchering of a whale amid Atlantic seas. But the present-day Lowell
has dried out his language and rhythms to a harsh spareness that can
serve for subject-matter just as violent as whaling. "Fall 1961," for
instance, deals with those weeks of frozen horror when we waited for
the rockets to come over; if there is a greater violence than whale-
hunting, this is it; and this is how the poem conveys it:

Our end drifts nearer,
the moon lifts,
radiant with terror.
The state
is a diver under a glass bell.
A father's no shield
for his child.
We are like a lot of wild
spiders crying together,
but without tears.

Already in mid-career, Lowell has come a long distance: from that
crowded, bustling verse to this sharp and yet reposeful lyricism. It will
be interesting to see what further development lies ahead for this
restless, powerful poet, so dedicated to his art and so versed in its secrets.

Robert Bly

Robert Lowell's *For the Union Dead*

The older poets have all died in the last years; the publishing world
feels lonesome without a great poet around. Robert Lowell is being
groomed for this post. The result is evil, especially for Lowell. Mr.
Lowell has written powerful poems in the past, and some good poems
recently, but the last thing we need is another review trying to show
he is a master.

Most of the poems in *For the Union Dead* are bad poems. Everyone
writes bad poems at times, but advice from other poets is often a
great help in keeping the worst of them from being published. Eliot, as
everyone knows, sent *The Wasteland* to Pound. Pound also helped
Yeats. Poets' criticism is harsh. Lowell seems to get none of it. He is
surrounded by flatterers. Moreover, one has the sense that many of the
bad poems in the book were written to satisfy demands—the demands
of people like Jason Epstein, Stephen Marcus, and A. Alvarez, perfect
examples of the alienated establishment intellectual, none of whom
knows anything about poetry. Lowell's vision of himself seems more
and more to be identical with that of the people around him.

As we read *For the Union Dead,* we realize that two intellectual
traditions, both bankrupt, have come together in the book. One is the
entire string of intellectual longings represented by the history of the
Partisan Review. The *Partisan Review* writers never broke through to
any clear view of modern literature or politics. Their insistence on
the value of alienation, their academic notions of modernism, are dead,
like fatigued metal.

Phillip Booth foolishly compared Lowell to Whitman in his review, but Lowell's book embodies exactly what Whitman was fighting against. *For the Union Dead* has a peculiarly stale and cold air, instantly recognizable. It is the air of too many literary conversations, an exhausting involvement with the Establishment.

Since the ideas behind the book are decrepit, Lowell has no choice but to glue the poems together with pointless excitement. The persistence of bodiless excitement derives from a second bankrupt tradition which is centred on the notion that an artist must never be calm, but must be *extreme* at all costs. This destructive notion, a bourgeois notion, flows from both right wing influences on Lowell, like Tate, and left wing influences like the *Partisan Review* writers.

Lowell has always had a poor grasp of the inner unity of a poem. In *Imitations* he inserted violent anal or explosive images into quiet, meditative poems—his translations of Montale for example—without realizing that the sensational images had destroyed the inner balance of the poems. In *For the Union Dead* he does the same thing to his own poems.

The routine violence in Lowell's poems reminds one of Nineteenth Century provincial literature.

> The pitying, brute, doughlike face of Jael
> watched me with sad inertia, as I read—
> Jael hammering and hammering her nail
> through Sisera's idolatrous, nailed head.

For the Union Dead is something rare, a book of poems that is a melodrama.

The attempt to glue the poems together with mere excitement fails. Time after time, Lowell sets out in a poem to live inside a certain emotion, and suddenly a flood of objects buries the whole project. In seven poems, "The Mouth of the Hudson," "The Old Flame," "The Flaw," "For the Union Dead," "Water," "Fall, 1961" and "Night Sweat" the inner and outer worlds hold together, sometimes for only a few lines, sometimes for the whole poem. But the rest of the poems are melodrama; the inner and outer worlds have split apart.

Men write melodrama when the ideas available to them are dead. Lowell tells us that modern life makes everyone nervous, that we shouldn't support South American generals, that gods seem less real as we grow older. The ideas Eliot and Stevens put in their poems had size and vigor; Lowell's ideas are banal and journalistic. They have no life of their own, and are painfully incongruous in poems intended to be on the highest level.

The question we have to ask about the book is not why there are a few good poems—there are good poems because Lowell's talent is very great—but why so many incredibly bad poems appear in the book. Moreover, they are an odd sort of bad poem. When Eliot and Stevens wrote bad poems, these were weaker versions of their good poems, but Lowell's bad poems take on the quality of lies.

> Perseus, David and Judith,
> lords and ladies of the Blood,
> Greek demi-gods of the Cross,
> rise sword in hand
> above the unshaven,
> formless decapitation
> of the monsters, tubs of guts,
> mortifying chunks for the pack.

This is like a bishop lying about the early history of the church to a half-literate audience. If Lowell were to say these transparent pedantries in a more modest tone, it wouldn't be so offensive. It is the air of grandeur he puts on when he writes this empty rhetoric that is so offensive. The passage is coarse and ugly. Even worse, it is unimaginative.

> Horrible the connoisseur tyrant's querulous strut;
> an acorn dances in a girdle of green oak leaves
> up the steps to the scaffold to the block,
> square bastard of an oak.

What Lowell is doing here is counterfeiting. He is counterfeiting intellectual energy, pretending to be saying passionate things about tyrants and hangings, but in fact he gives only a series of violent words set next to each other; the indignation is ersatz, and the passage means nothing at all.

By and large, *For the Union Dead* is a counterfeit book of poetry. Lowell is pretending to be at the center of himself, when he is not. He is pretending to have *poetic* excitement, when all he has to offer is *nervous* excitement. And that is accepted as poetry, for American readers are so far from standing at the center of themselves that they can't tell when a man is counterfeiting and when he isn't.

The people who praised this book so highly did no one a service. Something evil is happening to Lowell: he is being praised for what is not in his books. We and Lowell are being presented with a false vision of his poetry. This cannot help but draw him farther from himself.

Robert Brustein
The Old Glory

Benito Cereno is the third play in the extraordinary theater trilogy by
Robert Lowell called *The Old Glory,* a work in which the renowned
poet has fashioned a dramatic history of the American character.
Held together by the unifying symbol of the flag, *The Old Glory* is
based on stories by Hawthorne and a novella by Melville, but while
Mr. Lowell has managed to adapt these tales with relative fidelity to the
original texts, he has made them wholly and uniquely his own work.
Invested with the author's keen historical sense and marvelous gift
for language, the source materials assume the thickness and authority
of myth; ritual and metaphors abound; traditional literature and
historical events begin to function like Greek mythology, as the source
and reflection of contemporary behavior. Mr. Lowell feels the past
working in his very bones. And it is his subtle achievement not only to
have evoked this past, but also to have superimposed the present upon
it, so that the plays manage to look forward and backward at the
same time. Adopting a style which is purposely chilling, measured and
remote, he has endowed his plays with flinty intelligence and tautened
passion, making them work on the spectator with all the suggestive
power of non-discursive poems.

The three plays examine the American character at three different
points in its historical development. This character the author finds to
be permeated with violence from its beginnings—a violence which
invariably erupts out in moments of panic. In *Endecott and the Red
Cross,* a mild-mannered Puritan military man, faced with high-living

Anglican-Royalists in colonial America, is forced into shedding blood by political-religious expediency; and in *My Kinsman, Major Molineux,* the American Revolution unfolds as a violent nightmare experienced by two Deerfield youths seeking out their British cousin in Boston, "the city of the dead."

In *Benito Cereno,* the third and finest play, Mr. Lowell brings us to the beginning of the 19th century and proceeds to unearth the seeds of our current discords. Based on Herman Melville's novella of the same name, *Benito Cereno* has all the theatrical power of the first two plays, as well as a heavily charged prose style and a strong suspenseful narrative. Melville's story is largely concerned with the shadow cast over a civilized mind by the primitive darkness. Mr. Lowell heightens this theme, examining along the way the ambiguous American attitude towards slavery and servitude.

In the American Place Theatre production, Jonathan Miller, the director, paced this play with an eye to its half-languorous, half-ominous atmosphere, giving it the rhythm of "an ocean undulating in long scoops of swells," but finally letting it explode into a shocking climax, to the accompaniment of discharging muskets. The visual effects of the original production, with its simple set and illustrative costuming, were excellent (the crisp uniforms of the American officers in black cutaway coats and white tights juxtaposed against the shabby-sumptuous attire of Cereno and the rags of the slaves). But it is the acting that was really unusual. In an age of flaccid, self-indulgent histrionics, Mr. Miller evoked performances of extraordinary depth, control and energy. Three actors in particular were superb: Roscoe Lee Browne, alternating between Calypso sunniness and sinister threat as Babu; Lester Rawlins, suave, smug and self-satisfied as Delano; and Frank Langella as Cereno, his eyes continually lowered with shame, his voice morose and rich, a trembling wreck of stateliness and nobility. But it is a violation to single out individuals for praise when the entire cast was functioning with that precision and power that we have come to expect only from long-established repertory companies.

   The Old Glory, certainly, is the first American play to utilize
historical materials in a compelling theatrical manner (just compare it
with those lifeless high-school pageants that Maxwell Anderson used to
grind out), perhaps because it is the first such play to assume a mature
intellect on the part of its audience. After years of prosaic language,
mundane forms and retarded themes—obstacles which only O'Neill
was able to transcend successfully in his last plays, and then only
through sheer doggedness and will—the American drama has finally
developed an important subject and an eloquent voice. *The Old Glory*
may well mark the beginning of a dramatic renaissance in America,
during which our theater—like our fiction and poetry—will be able to
tap the sources of our inmost being, and not just sink us deeper into
narcosis and complacency. *Benito Cereno* is a cultural-poetic
masterpiece, but the entire trilogy is an event of great moment. For it
heralds the arrival not just of a brilliant new dramatist but of one
who may very well come to revolutionize the American theater.

John Simon
Strange Devices on the Banner

There is always joy in certain quarters when a poet starts writing for
the theater. In the glorious ages of the drama, from Aeschylus to
Goethe and Schiller, drama and poetry lived in wedlock. The 19th
century broke up that happy union. But sentimentalists like to see
marriages last, however unviable they have become, and there seems to
be less rejoicing in heaven over a repentant sinner than on earth over
reconciled spouses. So, when Robert Lowell's *The Old Glory* was
produced off-Broadway, when, in other words, a major American poet
was appearing on the stage with verse drama, it was to some—notably
to most of the highbrow critics—as if the world has suddenly become
a better place.

    The Old Glory consists of three one-acters: two shorter ones,
Endecott and the Red Cross and *My Kinsman, Major Molineux,* based
on short stories by Hawthorne, and one longer one, *Benito Cereno,*
from Melville's novella. In *Endecott,* a well-meaning Puritan governor
of Salem in the 1630s discovers, as he quashes mixed Indian-and-white
maypole dancing, that, much as he is against King Charles and the
Church of England and their various worldly and opportunistic
representatives in the New World, he is not really for the more fanatical
aspects of his own Puritans. Yet he is forced into severity against the
revelers because "a statesman can either work with merciless efficiency,
and leave a desert,/ or he can work in a hit and miss fashion/ and

leave a cess-pool." Endecott opts for the desert, but allows for a little bit of cesspool by way of an oasis.

In *Molineux,* a youth from Deerfield arrives in Boston with his little brother just before Tea Party time. He hopes for a career through his powerful kinsman who commands the redcoats in Boston. During a hallucinatory night in which the Bostonians treat the boys with a mixture of hostility and mockery, the Major is always mysteriously alluded to and strangely unseeable—until the boys have to watch him being killed by the anti-English mob, and are even hypnotically drawn into that mob.

The plot of *Benito Cereno* needs no summary, but it should be noted that Lowell has made considerable changes here (as elsewhere), mostly in the direction of showing the contradictions in the American attitude toward Negroes: "In a civilized country," says Lowell's Captain Delano, "everyone disbelieves in slavery and wants slaves." And the play proceeds to show the rights and wrongs of both blacks and whites.

Clearly, Lowell is trying to capture the ironies, cruelties, and inconclusiveness on which America was built: in *Endecott,* the ambiguities are chiefly religious; in *Molineux,* political; in *Cereno,* racial. Beyond that, though, he is concerned with essential human nature, which he sees as paradoxical, untrustworthy, and, above all, tenebrous. But, regrettably, there are three obstacles he cannot quite negotiate: the limitations of the one-acter, the demands of dramatic form, the problem of stage poetry.

Endecott, for example, is an interesting figure who manages to arouse our sympathetic curiosity, but only at the expense of swallowing up most of the playlet: his psyche exacts much more of our attention than do the perfunctory characters and negligible events of the play. In *Cereno,* attempts at writing some sequences in the manner of Genet, Beckett or Kafka rub uneasily against patches of realism and even a Hollywoodish, shoot-'em-up finale. In *Molineux,* the absurdist mode is fairly consistent (though not so witty as in Beckett or Ionesco), but it clashes with stabs at mythologizing—Charon is introduced as ferryman to Boston, "the City of the Dead"!—and, throughout, one feels a certain confusion between symbol and rigmarole.

Again, dramatizing fiction has required such devices as the confidant, but, in *Molineux,* the presence of the kid brother is not only illogical, it also dissipates the harrowing isolation of Hawthorne's solitary youth. In *Cereno,* Lowell must supply Captain Delano with a sidekick, the naive bosun Perkins, whom the poet intended both as butt of Delano's greater insight and wit and as a Prince Hal, who is supposed to end up, as Lowell put it in an interview, "superior to Delano." This superiority is meant to manifest itself. Lowell tells us, in two short and separate speeches, one of which is only six words long and, allegedly, hinges on Perkins' ironic use of the one word "Sir."

Now this sort of thing is all very well in lyric poetry, but it just does not register in performed drama. And it is true of all three plays that, though they are aware of the things that make a play a play— not merely action and conflict, as commonly held, but also diversified verbal texture, humor, pathos, variety of tempo, absorbing talk, and so on—he is unable either to provide enough of them or to marshal them properly. Thus action tends to bunch up in one place, humor to sound forced, and the language to become static or inconsistent. Babu, for example, far from remaining a slave fresh out of Africa, turns into a Calypso cut-up and connoisseur of American and European history and conditions.

Yet the final problem is the poetry itself. Though written in free verse, *The Old Glory* attains to poetry only in Captain Delano's speech beginning "I see an ocean undulating in long scoops and swells . . ." But this passage is only a slight reworking of Melville's third paragraph; and where it departs from Melville's prose, it improves on it only in one participle, "swallows sabering flies." Here now is a typical passage:

> Things aren't really bad,
> but the time will come, the time will surely come,
> I know the King's mind, or rather the mind of his advisers—
> kings can't be said to have minds.
> The rulers of England will revoke our charter,

> they will send us a royal Governor,
> they will quarter soldiers on us,
> they will impose their system of bishops.

What is the point of printing this as verse? Even its most eloquent champion, Robert Brustein, refers to it in the Introduction as a "prose style." True, there is the precedent of Eliot and Fry, but are *The Cocktail Party* and *Venus Observed* worthy of emulation? Verse that is not really verse can add only pretentiousness to a play, confuse the actors, and throw dust in the ears of the audience. It may even deflect the playwright's attention from his primary task.

But could one not write truly poetic plays today? The answer, apparently, is no. By far the best 20th-century poet-playwright, Bertolt Brecht, kept his poetry off the stage. On it, he allowed for song interludes; otherwise, with trifling exceptions, his plays were in prose. Poetry today has, unfortunately, become a minority art, no longer an integral part of the culture as it was in the heyday of verse drama. Reluctantly, we must accept its divorce from the theater, which must at least *seem* to speak the language of the land. The poet, as writer, may still have a place in the theater; poetry, barring a miracle, does not. What history hath put asunder, no man is likely to join together.

Jerome Mazzaro
Lowell After
For the Union Dead

Although it is evident that Robert Lowell's most recent poetry has
entered the contexts of a post-Christian world, it is still asking
teleological questions. It still wishes to know what man's ultimate
purpose is, and it still tends to effect its most jarring evocations by
suggesting possible answers in the juxtapositions of immediate
experience and historical perspectives. Moreover, since man's ultimate
purpose is somehow related or relatable to his origins, it searches out
these origins, aware that once the nature of the origins alters, so, too,
does man's purpose. From these searches, Lowell's concepts of free will
and meaningful action have evolved, and now, as the God-created
universe and Christian experience of the early volumes fade into
sentimentality and man no longer seeks in his actions to know, love,
and serve God, the poetry becomes both the record and moral of their
loss. In the most public poems, it shows man's struggle against first a
scientific, evolutionary universe and then, in turn, a larger and perhaps
more disarming overview of lost religious purpose. Here, as man's
origins are nature and chance, his purpose, unhampered by Christian
charity, is to extend his dominion over nature and chance so as to insure
continued survival. In the more personal poems, where neither origins
nor ends can be determined, absurdism is offered. Man finds himself
consistently confronted with the circumstance that his experience of
things is radically incongruent with the demands that his life have

meaning. But the most persuasive force at work is the will of history, the future, working on the will of what from a Christian point of view is ungracious man. It is the irrational will which Arthur Schopenhauer portrayed as coming like supersensible soapbubbles and which man's reason works on to augment and give rationality. This will, which cares nothing for the individual, cherishes the form or species.

In many respects, the acceptance of this Schopenhauerian, post-Christian world with its rejection of the world as illusion and its investment of value in the ideal is prepared for in *For the Union Dead* (1964). Here Lowell first names the masks of the historical and philosophical perspectives which are to oppose on a time-possessed plane his formerly Christian ideal. Each of these masks is modelled after his own nickname Cal, lending a kind of whimsical congruence to both the elements of the juxtapositions. The personal experiences of one Cal evoke the larger perspectives of other historical "Cals." Lowell's choice for the most pervasive of these larger perspectives, the predetermined, damned "Cal," is John Calvin as viewed in his writings through the writings of Jonathan Edwards. He is ostensibly the sinner caught like the spider in the "hands of the Great God" or Josiah Hawley about to take his own life. Lowell chooses for its evolutionary counterpart, Caliban and Robert Browning, and for the absurd man, the perspective of the Roman Emperor Caligula and Albert Camus. The already established nature and function of the dramatic monologue which Lowell likewise inherits from Browning and his own view of the synthetic nature of the poet's function permit him to speak either as himself or to shift into any of these historical voices with equal integrity and facility.

In *For the Union Dead,* his or his shifting voice reveals at various times the conditions which proclaim that modern man like the predetermined man of Calvinist theology is powerless and foredoomed. There are no worldly answers either to man's isolation or to his problem of suffering. Men die, one poem admits, and they are not happy. All acts of will, like events of physical nature, another insists, are subject to the laws of causation. Because of man's basically passive and mechanical will, a third remarks, once separate laws of man and nature reduce themselves into a single principle. Within the bounds of these combined perspectives, the volume's subject, untouched by grace, becomes the victim of historical determinism, relying upon imagination for the key to his origins and purposes and succumbing compulsively to the same cycles of rot and renewal which have undercut Lowell's once Christian ideal. This ideal, which in its contemplative state identified with Bernard of Clairvaux and which in its active state, with founders of religious societies like Noah and Aeneas, was able once through grace to escape absorption into such compulsive historical cycles. Likewise, within the bounds of these perspectives, Lowell prepares his readers for the subsequent acceptance of the Schopenhauerian belief that "salvation is the victory over, and the annihilation of, the world, which is nothing; of life, which is suffering; and of the individual ego, which is an illusion."

Typical of the poems which establish these perspectives in the volume and which also point the direction of Lowell's most recent work is "The Neo-Classical Urn." The poem on one level recounts the seemingly senseless destruction of turtles by the young Lowell. The turtles are on a historical level kin of the straggler crab with purple spots which in Browning's "Caliban on Setebos; or, Natural Theology in the Island" Caliban threatens to maim by twisting off one pincer, and which in Lowell's "Florence" the ungracious, Florentine children do actually "throw strangling ashore." With them Lowell introduces for investigation the same Calvinistic determinism, the same interest in natural theology, and the same struggle for existence that Browning offers in his poem. Specifically, both poets seem bent on rejecting the idea of moral law as proposed by Charles Darwin in *The Origin of Species* (1859) and the belief of the American Transcendentalist Theodore Parker that at every stage of human development man has produced a theology to express the highest reaches of his spiritual life.

The protagonists of both the Lowell and Browning poems assume the poses of a Calvinistic God working his wrath and caprice upon the helpless world. Knowledge of this God each protagonist assumes by evidences provided in nature, and each expresses him in the humanized or anthropomorphized manner proposed by Parker. The nature over which each rules is Darwinian. In its continuing struggle for existence, only the most cleverly adapted plants and animals survive. They leave offspring, which inherit and in turn improve the genetic endowment they received from their forebears. In the slow changes in bodily form which become necessary for continued survival, they image man's origin as chance and nature and his purpose as survival. For both poets, who draw exaggerations of such images, neither Parker nor Darwin offers a theory so satisfying as Augustine's notion that one's knowledge of God comes from a memory which is different from man's memory of worldly objects or the traditional religious accounts of man's ultimate origin as a creation of God.

Nevertheless, as Browning ends his poem with the creation of an anti-Setebos in the Quiet, indicative of his own clear view of man's ultimate purpose, Lowell does not. Instead, his concluding picture of the boy hobbling "humpbacked through the grizzled grass" crystallizes failures both in the poem and in the volume to resolve finally the purposes morally and aesthetically to which the "Cal" masks are to be put. Lowell's own doubt about the validity of any answer to man's purpose results in a reluctance to create clearly distinct personal and non-personal actions. As a consequence, his historical perspective which normally measures his meaningful action comes crashing upon the world of personal experience and obscures both in an onrush of anguish. The meaning of the poem's action along with the means to weigh such meaning floods out like matchstick houses caught in a real overflow. Added to this is a corresponding failure on aesthetic grounds to resolve the nature of his artistic vision. Lowell does not know whether the vision is to be like "Life Studies," lyrical, direct, and personal, or like the earlier volumes, epical, complex, and didactic. Throughout the volume, as his helpless, hapless subject is acted upon by force after force, the anguish of the immediate experience prevents a quick and conclusive withdrawal into non-personal perspectives.

At the same time, in the lyrical poems like "Water" and "The Old Flame," he chooses to ignore the historical perspectives altogether and portrays in self-cancelling images the actions of life.

In the midst of Lowell's announced abandonment of contemplative poetry which appeared about the same time as the volume, both failures prove particularly unfortunate. Readers approached the book, despite the apparentness of its litany of doubt concerning man's purpose, and expected to find in it socio-political programs similar to, but more acceptable than those of Ezra Pound's active poetry. They were further encouraged in this by Lowell's real willingness to assume what Matthew Arnold called "the high destinies of poetry" and deal more and more with public issues in both his life and writing. This willingness, once backed by Christian conviction, prompted in the 1940's a refusal to be inducted into World War II because of America's policy of total bombing and the active poetry and socio-political attacks of *Land of Unlikeness* (1944). Now, backed by the possibility of similar convictions, it would lead eventually to his refusal in 1965 to take part in a White House Arts Festival because of America's involvement in Vietnam, to his newspaper protests against police brutality and his endorsements of artistic freedom, and possibly to a new active poetry based similarly on an Arnold belief that in the collapse of religion men must at least be true to one another. What readers found, however, was the delineation of man not as a doer but as some kind of elaborate receiver.

Robert Bly, for one, in his review of *For the Union Dead* in *The Sixties* (1966) reveals the results of such expectations. His review disregards almost entirely the integrity in Lowell's dealing with the teleological problems of his vision and launches an attack into his failure to form an acceptable, practicable socio-political program. Bly extends this failure generally to writers whom he groups about *The Partisan Review*: "The Partisan Review writers never broke through to any clear view of modern literature or politics. . . . Their insistence on the values of alienation, their academic notions of modernism, are dead, like fatigued metal. . . . Since the ideas behind the book are decrepit, Lowell has no choice but to glue the poems together with pointless excitement." The disappointment might have been less had Bly disregarded *The Partisan Review* altogether and proceeded along lines suggested by Ralph Waldo Emerson's "Self-Reliance" that the failure to believe in one's values makes for a literature and a life whose excitements can only be pointless. He might have then seen that Lowell's current message to a post-Christian world is precisely the portrayal of fatigue, decrepitude, and pointless excitement.

Despite the influence of Schopenhauer in the poetry which has appeared since *For the Union Dead,* Lowell has still not come to any firm convictions about man's ultimate purpose. Action is still minimal. It occurs mainly as ruminations on received stimuli. However, technical changes have occurred to suggest Lowell's ability in the intervening period to come to grips with the substance of his vision so that the anguish which disrupted his rhythms and lines has disappeared and the personal and non-personal elements of his juxtapositions which tended to merge now remain distinct and effective. First, suggestive of the new mastery over their content, the poems generally follow a plan of run-on, octosyllabic couplets. Enjambment occurs strategically to keep the content from the completely resolved sense of a closed epigram. Second, and paralleling this sense of mastery, the language is hard and clear and object, rather than emotion-oriented. There are no longer lines as in "Myopia: a Night," where the impression, nor the object takes precedence. Instead, there is a sense of detail which borders on what Mary McCarthy calls the woman writer's penchant for decor, but which here works well to evoke both the personal experience and its surroundings. In amassing this detail, balanced constructions are used, indicating again a sense of control. Finally, and perhaps most importantly, the tone managing the action is not involved, but detached. This permits for a better handling of the masks.

The means by which Lowell seems to come to grips with the substance of his vision and handle these tasks is twofold. First, having gained in the interval distance from his once Christian convictions, he is able now, for the purposes of his art, to sustain perspectives in which he does not necessarily believe. He is able to do so because in an age of overkill such perspectives evoke nightmare visions of a world either destroyed by continuing its wrong idea of a struggle for existence or else reduced to an equally destructive sado-masochism in the drive by its populations to prove their existences through their powers to inflict and endure pain. The real fears of both prospects in the absence of a constructive alternative contribute to Lowell's ability to make them visible, human alternatives rather than mental hypotheses. Moreover, he is able to strengthen his distance from them by adding to the outlines of the masks he formed elements which either so repulse his nature that they preclude his sympathy or so work to reinforce his initial antipathy that they provide complementary, supporting arguments.

For example, to the perspectives and theories of evolution which he develops in "The Neo-Classical Urn," he now adds the view of other evolutionists that not only man emerged from nature by chance, but also the earth emerged as well from some chance, cooled remnant of a cosmic explosion. In time, it, too, is threatened with extinction either by a second cosmic explosion or by the sun's burning itself out. In the prospect of such extinction, he complements the horror of a moral law based upon the fact of man's survival with allusions to the "survival of the fittest" notion of Herbert Spencer's *Principles of Biology* (1864), which rationalized most of England's will toward expansionism and America's turn-of-the-century cut-throat economic and social theories.

In support of his opposition to such brutal theories of man's origins and purposes, he turns to the work of Alfred Russel Wallace, who co-developed with Darwin the idea of evolution, but who later challenged the whole Darwinian position on man by insisting that artistic, mathematical, and musical abilities could not be explained on the basis of natural selection and the struggle for existence. Lowell seems also to gain support from the arguments of C. S. Lewis, who in *The Abolition of Man* (1947) propounds his objections to man's using his intelligence as a tool to turn everything into an extension of nature. Lewis sees in man's change from qualitative to quantitative values and in man's acknowledged ability to control quantity a will to extend control over more aspects of life much in the manner of the scientist's desire to control chance. He decries this drive to turn human engagement into disengaged problems.

Next, the effect in Lowell's poetry of this gained distance is a temporary acceptance of an ironic view of life similiar to that which began his career. Then, the intensity of a Christian vision in a world of perverted Christianity on the verge of the Last Judgment turned the irony into a source for invective and satire. Now, as his protagonists lack the grace for meaningful action, the irony results in a picture of the combined futility and absurdity of weighing the minimal actions which man can muster against an irresolvable purpose. Time and again these actions turn into a mockery of the protagonist as Lowell ends his poem by evoking a Schopenhauerian future. This future, if it will not solve the problems of meaning raised, will at least distance them into some perspective that perhaps may overcome their pain as time is reputed to heal all wounds. Thus, what begin as basically personal and ontological poems evolve into seemingly didactic, impersonal observations which record simply the biding of time.

The movement to these final observations with their releases from the bondage of the present by the acceptance of this Schopenhauerian will recalls structurally the release or escape to God in the contemplative poems of Lowell's initial volumes. A similar pattern of vividly constructed scenes which start off the contemplation which, in turn, proceeds to annihilate and escape the scenes is established. However, whereas the pattern of this annihilation in the contemplative poems followed a progression of humility (self-knowledge) to love (knowledge of others) to contemplation (knowledge of God), the pattern now seems to flow from egoism (the impulse toward one's own good) to malice (the impulse toward others' woe) to compassion (the impulse toward others' well-being). This last impulse, under the guise of Christian charity, is probably Lowell's strongest link with the past.

The poems which define most clearly how the acceptance of this ironic vision affects both the struggle for existence and the masks named in poems like "The Neo-Classical Urn," are "Central Park," "Fourth of July in Maine," and "Waking Early Sunday Morning." All picture modern man caught up as the protagonist in a world variously described in geological terms as "a dying crust" and a "volcanic cone." This predetermined world is warmed by the red coal of the sun "until it cinders like the soul," presumably the soul described by Jonathan Edwards in "The Future Punishment of the Wicked Unavoidable and Intolerable" and paraphrased by Lowell in "Mr. Edwards and the Spider." In such a world the Bible is "chopped and crucified," and religion in its truest sense is something far off somewhere when "the universe was young." It is past resurrecting.

The problem of this world is how to curb the brute natural force of the struggle for existence without some means of compassion. Unchecked, the force may otherwise destroy man altogether either in the "small war on the heels of small war" which Lowell envisions at the end of "Waking Early Sunday Morning" or in man's having been made victim of its brute force in "Central Park." Here he is imaged as having to beg "delinquents for his life" or else rely upon the clubs of equally brutal policemen behind "each flowering shrub." In a Heraclitean way, the brute force which society was created to control is triumphing over society as it gives way to an even greater brutality. This new brutality threatens in the conclusions of each poem to return man to a form of tribalism. The idea is similar to the second of three possibilities which Bertrand Russell draws in "The Future of Mankind" (1950). Russell feels that unless law governs the relations of nationals by the end of this century, "a reversion to barbarism after a catastrophic dimunition of the population of the globe" may well occur.

"Near the Ocean" concerns a second aspect of this post-Christian world. In it, Lowell enters the "New Carthage" of an absurd world similar to that which Edward Albee draws in *Who's Afraid of Virginia Woolf?* In its search for meaning, the poem outlines the marital "fun and games" of a husband who conceives of his wife as basically a monster whose love is at once both suffocating and devouring. Echoes of an archetypal pattern of thwarted male inconstancy emerge as the husband's fantasy dreams of direction (egoism) fail to coincide with his abilities to exercise this direction except by inflicting pain (malice). Thus, the poem projects a notion of love which insists that the psychological basis to most sex is not so much physical satisfaction as it is a will to power. What the protagonist sees is himself, first as an echo of Cellini's statue of Perseus in the Piazza della Signoria lifting the head of Medusa (his wife) to please the mob, and then, joined with her, as one of two children standing before a Terrible Mother, who on the basis of having given them succor makes her demands. In the continuation of such sado-masochistic dreams and actions, the husband concludes "nothing will age, nothing will last / or take corruption from the past."

The poem is, in fact, the latest variation on the continuing element of psychic individuation as a necessary adjunct to Lowell's preoccupation with teleology. His heroes, even in a post-Christian world, must encounter and subdue their imaginations' Terrible Mothers. Besides serving their reputed, necessary psychological need, these encounters work to provide the means by which the would-be hero may escape the lockstep of time. The pattern, established in *Land of Unlikeness,* first pitted the potential hero against the Biblical Whore of Babylon, whose subjection would give him knowledge so that he might in turn alter history's course which was then seen as "blood begetting blood." For her subjection, Lowell called upon Christian faith as both the weapon to slay the monster and the means of gaining the grace whereby history's lockstep would be broken. In *Lord Weary's Castle* (1946) and *The Mills of the Kavanaughs* (1951), the castrating Terrible Mother was variously portrayed as the constrictions of a perverse Christian tradition. Here Lowell called upon the founders of religious cultures, Noah and Aeneas, to act as liberators and to set into being the dialectic of liberation and constriction which characterizes this stage of Lowell's work. In *Life Studies* (1959), the evil mother became more identifiable with Lowell's own mother and the course of history from which man had to be set free, the destructive, terrible pipe dreams of the Winslow family. Here his failure to subconsciously subdue her led to the honoring of his first non-heroes and the despair which marked the volume's completion. Now the Terrible Mother has become his wife and their lies, the historical course which needs to be altered but which they cannot be freed from until "time, that buries us, lay bare." These lies which both tell each other and themselves prove their abilities to hurt and hence affect one another as well as provide the means to rationalize their basically irrational wills. Lowell would have done with such betrayals for their more charitable moments; but the failure to overcome these lies other than by the projection of a Schopenhauerian future leaves him egoless and committed even further to his continuing preoccupation with non-heroes.

"The Opposite House" speaks also of everything giving way to death. In this instance, Lowell traces the disappearance of a police station in a burst of flames. Before its destruction, like the empty churches of Philip Larkin's "Church Going," it had been abandoned to whatever sought to use it. Pigeons mainly fly in and out. With its destruction, the station, symbolic of social institutions which attempt to curb violence with violence, assumes the image of a catherine wheel lit at the end of a lawn party. The image is taken from T. S. Eliot's *Murder in the Cathedral* (1935), where it is among several proving man's passage "From unreality to unreality." Hopefully, here the station is to give way to a better world as the turtle-slow imagination of man churns onward more quickly than the moving squad-car to what must be new institutions and new unrealities. Out of the differing rates of the loss of these institutions and man's ability to construct others arises his sense of alienation. Eventually, as he loses touch with all social institutions, he feels imprisoned by them, and, since all people would soon find, by outdistancing the institutions proper to their development, a world filled with institutions they cannot relate to, anomie results. Thus arises man's need to strike through the social structures in Lowell's early poems or man's current need to accept not as a beneficial by-product of time's irresistible will. It is this second which Lowell

celebrates in the closing line of the poem, for out of this principle
of Death—the absolute of Existentialism—he is able to rationalize
his being.

In concert, the poems reveal that man is somehow at odds with the
structure of his world and ill-equipped to create permanent new
structures without some sort of absolute purpose. On the basis of the
purposes suggested by any of the perspectives left after Christianity,
Lowell advocates a preservation of Christian charity or Schopenhauerian compassion as basic to all social reform since it establishes the
spirit for law. On this spirit rather than on law or social institutions,
Lowell bases his socio-politics. Thus, the few specific references which
he makes to social and economic reform are principally to structures
which have been outdistanced rather than to structures which should
come into being. He does point out, for example, that somehow
inequities have to do with "poverty and fear" in "Central Park," that
the "poor" are still without rights in "Fourth of July in Maine," and
that the industrialist still "goes down to the sea in ships" in "Waking
Early Sunday Morning."

These references provide an additional, immediate, practicable, but
limited clue to why a poet whose system of history is consistently
cyclical may need to go into a negation of evolution and its basic
open-ended progress. They are the catch-phrases current in American
politics, which in the hands of President Lyndon B. Johnson does tend
to see itself capable of possibly evolving into a Great Society, and which
on that basis proposes a kind of cultural imperialism similar to that
rationalized in nineteenth-century England on the bases of Darwin
and Spencer. Peoples of primitive cultures, small societies lost on the
world's margins seem destined again to be absorbed, regardless of their
desires, into the benefits, gadgets, and politics of this Great Society by
virtue of the Darwinian law of America's superior technology and
consequently superior powers of survival.

The need to attack this political optimism has an equally important
corollary in two other current trends which Lowell may see as
contingent on the acceptance of an evolutionary ontology. He may well

be acting in opposition to the popularity of Pierre Teilhard de Chardin, who in books like *The Phenomenon of Man* (1959) proposes a kind of religious evolution that counteracts Lowell's picture of the demise of Christianity with an image of an evolving perfect Christianity. This concept is already under attack by theologians who question the concept of free will involved. There is likewise the popularity of literary figures such as Theodore Roethke and Dylan Thomas, who accept as good the single law of man and nature which is part of an evolutionary ontology and speak of a natural sympathy among all living things. The opening line of "Waking Early Sunday Morning" with its pun of "chinook-schnook" can easily be taken as an echo of Roethke's wish in "The Longing" to be "with the salmon," or the description of the salmon run in "First Meditation." In Lowell's vision, such sympathy is merely another sign of lost Christian purpose.

The main basis of Lowell's socio-political program, however, remains independent of these practical considerations. Ideally, it invests itself in a concept of politics which sees its end as identical with the end of man, now almost exclusively relegated to the problem of psychic individuation. As Lowell insists in his recurrent images of Terrible Mothers on the need for man individually to overcome restricting structures in order to provide the basis for his ego—however illusory, he manages to differ from most would-be social and religious reformers. The differences are pronounced. First, unlike most social reformers who see egoism as an end in itself, Lowell, like Schopenhauer, feels that this egoism must ultimately be surrendered for salvation. Second, he conceives of the clash then between man and social structures, much as the clash in the poem "Florence" between men and monsters, as a necessary part of the hero's development in that it provides the hero with a knowledge of the nature of evil. For this reason, he would have many structures remain. In this, he is probably closer to a tradition of writers which includes Herman Melville rather than one which includes Ralph Waldo Emerson, and closer still to a tradition of medieval carol writers who celebrated the Fall of man because it produced the glories of Christ's birth and death.

In an age when the unexamined life and the struggle for existence tend to threaten mankind with annihilation instead of survival and the controls which a Christian teleology once imposed upon brute force have disappeared, the importance of Lowell's continuing to probe man's purpose becomes clear. Regardless of their truths, upon the answers to such questions, the future pressing upon mankind will be rationalized and shaped. Thus, despite the paralysis of his characters who do little more than reminisce or indulge in self-pity, Lowell is able to continue according to the functions of the poet and of poetry outlined by Arnold in "The Study of Poetry" (1880), by not selecting any of the alternatives. Instead, he can be a moralist in a society where religion and science have been called into doubt by probing the ontological bases for law and order independent of any individual, prescribed purposes for man. Out of what he envisions as a basic human tendency toward self-awareness may come the awareness of others and the Schopenhauerian compassion for one's fellowman that will halt the mass destruction. Thus, although Lowell may no longer be able to see the true city of the religious mystic or even of the romantic, he can still tell the Vanity Fairs along the way. He may no longer be the conscientious objector crying out against the evils of war in *Land of Unlikeness* and *Lord Weary's Castle,* or the Arnoldian in "The Mills of the Kavanaughs" and *Life Studies* struggling with a belief in personal relationships which gives out in *For the Union Dead.* Nevertheless, he has still not lost faith with human concerns, nor with history, or rather faith with the inevitable will, which for him is now the reality of the future.

Richard Howard
Fuel on the Fire

Incandescence or ash, the igneous work of Robert Lowell—"energies
that never tire / of piling fuel on the fire"—has a way of joining, of
annealing itself to the canon of modern literature which readers, even
readers who do not care much for poetry, find to be an illumination of
their own experience as well as the truth, so painfully achieved, about
the poet's. Lowell has scaled that eminence from which, when he
speaks in certain accents, he wins not consensus but assent. We hear
these accents again—violent, vacillating, maimed—in *Waking Early
Sunday Morning**, the 112-line first section of the title poem in this odd
new clutch of texts (surely clutch *is* the proper noun for five poems
and nine so-called translations for whose collocation the poet himself
appears to be at a loss to account: "how one jumps from Rome, the
theme that connects my translations, to the America of my own poems
is something of a mystery to me"). Here in fourteen eight-line stanzas
of generally octosyllabic couplets, Lowell has produced one of those
devastating texts in which the torment of his private history and
the convulsive terror of our public one mirror and enact each other;
it is a poem in which

* The poem bears about the same allusive relation—one of longing and
revulsion both—to Stevens's *Sunday Morning* that *For the Union Dead* bears to
Tate's *Ode to the Confederate Dead*. Lowell can afford neither Tate's
plangency nor Stevens's pleasure.

By permission of Poetry, Vol. CX, No. 6 Sept '67. Copyright 1967 by Modern
Poetry Association.

> . . . the creatures of the night
> obsessive, casual, sure of foot,
> go on grinding, while the sun's
> daily remorseful blackout dawns. . . .

and its last two stanzas constitute the hugest statement Lowell has yet made about our situation, in the kind of excruciating, sybilline *song* that strikes the assaulted ear as at once authoritative and authentic:

> . . . fresh breakage, fresh promotions, chance
> assassinations, no advance.
>
> Only man thinning out his kind
> sounds through the Sabbath noon, the blind
> swipe of the pruner and his knife
> busy about the tree of life
>
> Pity the planet, all joy gone
> from this sweet volcanic cone;
> peace to our children when they fall
> in small war on the heels of small
> war—until the end of time
> to police the earth, a ghost
> orbiting forever lost
> in our monotonous sublime.

Waking Early Sunday Morning is a masterpiece of prosody, tone, and disastrous likelihood, and in organization of imagery, proportion of outward impulse to horrified withdrawal, control of scale, it stands with the poet's highest achievements. I cannot find, in the other poems of the title series, more than an effort to repeat this success, a mimetic undertaking far from worthless, but without the same note of equilibrium, of continuity. It is as if a very great opera singer had grown too conscious of her mastery of certain tones, and forced all her arias to supply those glorious occasions of combustion, every performance a matter of high notes and thrilling chest tones, but no *middle range*. The "translations" seem to me even less successful than the earlier imitations—wherever the poet departs from his text it is to screw the agony one thread higher, thereby losing the very sense of his original; where Góngora speaks of the hours that wear away the days and the days that are gnawing away the years, Lowell ups the ante and destroys the form:

> those brilliant hours that wore away our days,
> our days that ate into eternity.

It is "the years"—the middle range of experience—which this poet despises or despairs over, substituting the "monotonous sublime" of eternity or the convulsions of momentary violence. As for the Juvenal and Dante, the plunders and blunders seem to me to dissolve the poems' presence, though I am aware that scholars made fools of themselves for years over Pound's *Propertius;* I am not a scholar, and in the matter of translation may be a fool, but to me it seems that as Johnson said in *his* magnificent imitation of the Juvenal satire, Lowell's vandalism is merely more of his self-flagellation:

> . . . everlasting dictates crowd his tongue,
> Perversely grave, or positively wrong.

What we are given, then, or rather what we can buy for six dollars, is the great poem of the sixties, a smouldering heap of coals, often glowing with a terrible radiance:

> Sleep, sleep. The ocean, grinding stones,
> can only speak the present tense;
> nothing will age, nothing will last,
> or take corruption from the past . . .

or quenched by an equally terrible compassion, as in the dense little elegy for Roethke:

> Now, you honor the mother.
> Omnipresent,
> she made you nonexistent,
> the ocean's anchor, our high tide . . .

and for filler, some Presto-logs, quite calcified. But it is the great poem which counts, a poem written not only in the accents of conviction, but in the accents of sentencing and execution.

Michael London
Wading for Godot

Robert Lowell's prefatory note belies the design of his book. And by
design I don't mean his publisher's conspicuously padded product—its
clumsy size, dazzling white spaces, corrective type, artsy doodles and
six-dollar price tag. It's no mystery, as Lowell would have us believe,
how he jumps from his imitations (as defined in Cowley's preface
to his Pindar paraphrases, refined in Denham's preface to his Englished
Virgil, and legitimatized by Dryden) to the America of his own poems.
The greatness and horror of the Roman Empire is the connecting
theme of the imitations; the greatness and horror of the Roman and
American Empires the unifying design of the book.

In Lowell's End of the Road-Into the Ocean Sequence, Quevedo's
and Góngora's Spenserian Ruins of Time Sonnets of Rome, Juvenal's
Johnsonian Vanity of Human Wishes Tenth Satire and Horace's
Shakespearian Serving Under Brutus Odes, not to mention Dante's
George Santayana, that is, Brunetto Latini, there are recurrent images
and phrases, indicative of the deliberate design of the book. Rome's:
"... If you take a walk at night,/ carrying a little silver, be prepared/ to
think each shadow hides a knife or spear," becomes New York's: "We
beg delinquents for our life./ Behind each bush, perhaps a knife;/ each
landscaped crag, each flowering shrub,/ hides a policeman with a club."

No double-vision fogs the craggy landscape of *Near The Ocean*—
ancient Rome on the down-and-out and modern America are one and
the same. And Lowell has left no loopholes for the soul; he has

mapped-out what we've charted for ourselves: "I give you simply what you have already." We have "only restlessness,/ excess, the hunger for success," what Rome had, and we feel ourselves drifting toward that final Roman ruin: "O Rome! From all your palms, dominion, bronze/ and beauty, what was firm has fled. What once/ was fugitive maintains its permanence." The cartographer's vision is anachronistic, apocalyptic, sinister.

Lowell, like "some flower in which the fragile, sacred seed/ of ancient Roman virtue still survives," has risen above the swamp and mess, the dregs and dreck of American life, and written one of his country's greatest poems. "Waking Early Sunday Morning" is a great poem by virtue of its encompassing perspective, its passionate, impersonal poetry, grand and colloquial, which captures and conveys the tone and sense, the "fierce, fireless" temperament of an Empire in which "fresh breakage, fresh promotions, chance/ assassinations"— "business as usual"—are the order of the day.

Composed in the octosyllabic couplets of Marvell's "Garden" and echoing Donne's "First Anniversary" and Arnold's "Dover Beach," it is nonetheless deeply American. If the projective-proselytes, the starvelings weaned on Charles Olson, fail to respond to this poem, offer them milk for dehydrated lines and honey for hemorrhoidal words; then lead these crusading emasculators of the American idiom, manipulators of the low-moan, breathtaking asthmatics, chickenshit disclaimers, erudite dabblers, pipsqueak poetasters, from the page to the privy and let them be.

Far from assuming the false and comfortable stance of Accomplished Poet with Public Voice, as a number of waxy-eared critics have charged, Lowell has enlarged his range by moving from the compelling, yet limiting, confessional mode, into a realm neither private nor public, but which, for lack of a label, is prophetically Ours. Rather than living on the verge of the poet's psychic dislocations, in the midst of tensions that evoke our own *Walpurgisnacht,* "Waking Early Sunday Morning" transports us nowhere to where we are, here; no easy feat. The poet is with us and we're, alas, like the salmon journeying upstream, "nosing up to the impossible/ stone and bone-crushing waterful," with him. By poetically transforming our world, selectively reshaping it till we're wholly within a new conception of it, the poet provides a new occasion to perceive it, not the freedom to undo it. Like the salmon, we're "alive enough to spawn and die," no more. It is only fitting in a poem which predicts our children will "fall/ in small war on the heels of small war," that our response is acquiescence; fitting because it affirms at the same time our ability to create and recognize our Fate, making mere Gods and prophets of us all; no doubt a mark of our intelligence.

Our God, like the elusive divinity of Stevens' "Sunday Morning," is envisaged through a glass darkly. "His vanishing emblems" have become curio-pieces "like old white china doorknobs, sad,/ slight useless things to calm the mad." Waiting for Godot, the poet asks what we would ask: "When will we see Him face to face?" Our leaders, like the Romans who, "devoured by peace" sought "devouring war," are depicted as Philistines in full armor, anxious for the brassy phrase of triumph: our President, like the Roman orator "drowned by his torrential speech," swims ". . . nude, unbuttoned, sick/ of his ghost written rhetoric." And we, pitiful and joyless, are bound to the "monotonous sublime," what Lowell has proclaimed elsewhere as probably peculiar to America—that extreme condition wherein the "artist's existence becomes his art . . . he hardly exists without it . . . and almost sheds his other life."

"Literature" said Wallace Stevens, "is the better part of life. To this it seems inevitably necessary to add, provided life is the better part of Literature." On another page of his *Opus Posthumous* he says that "the relation of art to life is of the first importance especially in a skeptical age since, in the absence of a belief in God, the mind turns to its own creations and examines them, not alone from the aesthetic point of view, but for what they reveal, for what they validate and invalidate, for the support that they give." These adagia serve Lowell well, though not entirely. For Stevens, poetry was the supreme fiction among many fictions which he hoped in our time would replace the fiction of God; his exquisite truth was to believe willingly in a fiction he knew to be a fiction. His sublime was never monotonous, never could be, while reality and the imagination fed each other—that is, sustained the fiction. Whereas Lowell, for all his fictions, is skeptical of them, a condition which in the absence of a belief in God, can be disastrous. Worse than artistic self-consciousness, the bane of craft, is the self-consciousness of existence, with its resistance to the imaginative process, the creative act itself, or worse yet, with its final vision, which as Lowell indicates of Sylvia Plath's work, reveals "that life, even when disciplined, is simply not worth it."

The monotony of the sublime is also, as Lowell suggests, our impatient, implacable ambition to be major in whatever we attempt, to *be* sublime, and the strained and frequently violent means by which we pursue this ideal. Pound's "make it new," so natural a reaction to the Victorians, becomes for our time the Madison Avenue demand for novelty, while his "literature is news that STAYS news," becomes extended by, "for a moment or two." The Pop Artists, unable to sustain imaginative faith in their own novelties, or in Art and Tradition, ingeniously, and for the most part arbitrarily, duplicate the world in which they reside, thereby making their own, but necessarily less enduring, fictions. "Posterity" as Adrienne Rich recently wrote, "trembles like a leaf"; in more ways than one, I might add.

In the title poem, the ocean, the Earth's unfathomable burial ground, grinds the stones of posterity and "can only speak the present tense;/ nothing will age, nothing will last,/ or take corruption from the past." With fugitive Rome, America exists in the sheer here-and-now, free, confused and naked. All that remains "till time, that buries us, lay bare," is the groping of a hand for a hand in the hope that personal loyalty—which, if not always loyal, let alone everlasting, is at least binding—can surmount personal betrayal "Ah, love, let us be true/ to one another!"

Rome, "fallen in its grave," holds a sullied mirror up to an America "running downhill." The collective spirit of the cosmos, no longer gentle and innocent but polluted and corrupted by Time and Chance, is as harsh and "bloody" as the hands of God. We're hemmed-in, prowling our slummy cells, nearer to the ocean—"death's close clay"— than we'd like to believe. Even the sun, which "dives like a cooling meteorite to its fall" and "cinders like the soul" (Shelley's "fading coal"), and the earth, "this dying crust," are moribund: "We watch the logs fall. Fire once gone,/ we're done for . . ." Yet, ". . . blind,/ fratricidal, avaricious, proud," we silently and privately ". . . run/ through life to die . . .": we rush to beat Death's fixed dice, ". . . raise/ the ante, and stake our lives on every toss./ The hours will hardly pardon us their loss."

This book is no miscellany bridged by "brilliant" scribbling, but America's Last Stand against the bullets and bombs of outrageous fortune. It may be somewhat fanciful to consider these poems as the bastion of something or other, but can we consider them as anything other than a convincing testament to this strange time in the human universe when an obvious monument of the intellect can only dubiously be called "unageing"? Lowell has excavated our future from the past and provided a measure of our decline for which we must be terrified and grateful. *Near The Ocean* is a buoyant offering to a sinking Muse.

POET AS TRANSLATOR

Louis Simpson
Matters of Tact

As has been said before, Racine is nearly impossible to translate because he is perfect in his own language. The less style a man has, the easier it is to redo him. To put it another way, in certain writers subject and style may be separated; but Racine is his style. I would think that anyone who was curious about Racine would be able to read him in French. The next best thing would be to read Lowell's *Phaedra*. Lowell has done a good job of translation; if I am not wild about it, the reason is that, after all, it is a job, and I have been too well acquainted with *Phèdre* for too long a time to think that this is as good as *Phèdre*. But certainly, if Racine must be translated into English, this is as good a translation as we are likely to get.

What Lowell is up against, first of all, is the sound of the words. Racine's French is characteristically soft, feminine, serpentine—except where it rises in great tirades. English, on the other hand, strikes hard on the consonants, and Lowell's English is exceptionally rugged. So Racine, in Lowell's style, comes out a great deal harsher, more rugged, more rigid, then he really is. This is an interesting point—for in Wilbur's *Misanthrope,* Molière came out more polite and dandified than he is. Molière is more colloquial than Wilbur and not as witty. In translation we see the virtues and vices of our own poets magnified.

Another difficulty Lowell has had to contend with, is the rhymed couplet. Racine's habit is to pause at the end of a line, and to wind up the sentence in a couplet. Run-on's are comparatively rare. Now, if Lowell had tried to do this, he would have had to knot his lines like eels, twist the natural order of words, distort the meaning. On the other hand, if he had translated Racine into blank or free verse—well, anyone could have done that. . . . So he compromised, by writing in couplets but using run-on's lavishly and paraphrasing freely. Accustomed to the sound of Racine's couplets, my ear, to adopt a French way of describing things, found itself offended by Lowell's technique—but when I complained about it to a man of the theater, he said that, to the contrary, Lowell's run-on couplets are very pleasing. You hear the rhyme as an echo, a pleasant assonance—not falling with the regularity of a bell-clapper, as in the original. I sighed and withdrew my objection. To me, one of the sweetest sounds in the world is Racine's end-stopped couplets being inhaled by an audience of schoolgirls at the Comédie Française, and their punctual little gasps.

Allowing Lowell his version of the couplet—and there seems no alternative—I have only two faults to find with the job he has done. The first is the exceptional ruggedness of tone I have already mentioned. Lowell is a bit like Aeschylus. He may be the best poet we have, but I wish he sounded more tranquil in his poetry and less like the warrior of Marathon. The other fault is an occasional mistake in idiom. For example, to translate Phèdre's description of Theseus:

> Volage adorateur de mille objets divers

into this:

> lascivious eulogist of any belle

is a gross lapse of diction. The word "belle" conjures up Gibson Girls, *The Belle of New York,* etc. In such cases, a neutral word would be better. Unlike most translators, who err on the side of neutrality, Lowell errs through his energy and concreteness, his need to find striking phrases. Sometimes, as in:

> Your hesitation's killing me

colloquialism threatens to bring the rough edifice, the towering style, all tumbling down at once.

In general, Lowell is true to the original meaning, but on one
occasion at least he gives us a version of Racine that is more Lowell than
Racine. In Lowell, Phèdre's confession of her love for Hippolytus reads:

> See, Prince! Look, this monster, ravenous
> for her execution, will not flinch.
> I want your sword's spasmodic final inch.

Now, that third line is not Racine—it is pure Lowell, and a distortion.
Racine's Phèdre is not self-consciously making an up-to-date sexual
metaphor; to her, a sword is a sword. "A primrose by the river's
brim/ A simple primrose was to him." If Lowell frequently indulged
himself in this way, his translation would be spurious. Fortunately, he
does not.

It is easier to find fault with translation than to praise it. In
general, this version of *Phèdre* is a work of the intelligence, vigor and
imagination that we have a right to expect from Robert Lowell.

In the translations of French, German, Greek, Italian, and Russian
poems which he calls *Imitations,* Lowell is best when he is translating
passages that do not lend themselves to exaggeration or shock—that is,
passages that do not offer opportunities for the excesses which are a
defect of his own poetry. Thus, when he is confronted with Villon or
Baudelaire, he turns them into spooks to frighten himself and the
reader with, subtracting all that is euphonious, removing the beauty of
which the grotesque is a counterpart. We have a skeletal Villon, a
Leopold-Bloomish Baudelaire:

> Like the poor lush who cannot satisfy,
> we try to force our sex with counterfeits,
> die drooling on the deliquescent tits,
> mouthing the rotten orange we suck dry.

In Bauldelaire this is:

> Ainsi, qu'un débauché pauvre qui baise et mange
> Le sein martyrisé d'une antique catin,
> Nous volons au passage un plaisir clandestin
> Que nous pressons bien fort comme une vieille orange.

"Drooling on the deliquescent tits" is Lowell's invention, and it is not an improvement on "baise et mange/ Le sein martyrisé." Baudelaire's detachment from a spectacle that is appalling enough in itself, his generalized view, freezes the scene like a moment in Hell. Lowell, on the other hand, fastens the eye on physical details of the action. Is it worth throwing away poetry in order to spook the bourgeois?

On the other hand, when he is translating Leopardi, whose poetic temperament seems far from his own, Lowell is not tempted to exaggerate; instead he imagines himself into the poem:

> Once again the landscape is brown,
> the sky drains to a pale blue,
> shadows drop from mountain and thatch,
> the young moon whitens,
> as I catch
> the clatter of small bells,
> sounding in the holiday,
>
> I can almost say
> my heart takes comfort in the sound.
> Children place their pickets
> and sentinels,
> and splash round and round
> the village fountain.
> They jump like crickets,
> and make a happy sound.
> The field-hand,
> who lives on nothing
> marches home whistling,
> and gloats on the day of idleness at hand.
>
> Then all's at peace;
> the lights are out;
> I hear the rasp of shavings,
> and the rapping hammer
> of the carpenter, working all night

by lanternlight—
hurrying and straining himself
to increase his savings
before the whitening day . . .

(Il sabato del villaggio)

Perhaps this strikes me as better only because I prefer what Leopardi
is saying, because it is more useful than Baudelaire's masochism. Of
course, in talking about translation, in talking about poetry at all, we
are likely to fall into some psychological trap. But I do not think that
my preference is irrelevant to criticism of Lowell's skill as a translator.
Baudelaire, being so much in the vein of recent American poetry,
with its confessional air, its obsequiousness before prose—Baudelaire
encourages our faults. But to translate someone as far removed from
ourselves as is Leopardi, requires an effort of imagination.

Two of the poems by Rimbaud are splendidly joyous; Lowell's
handling of these shows his intelligence and sensitivity. The first is "At
the Green Cabaret"; the other, "A Malicious Girl":

In the cigar-brown dining room, perfumed
by a smell of shellac and cabbage soup,
I held my plate and raked together some
God-awful Belgian dish. I blew my soup,

and listened to the clock tick while I ate,
and then the kitchen opened with a blast;
a housemaid entered, God knows why—her blouse
half open, yellow hair in strings. She touched

a little finger trembling to her cheek
where the peach-velvet changed from white to red,
and made a schoolgirl grimace with her lips . . .

She swept away the plates to clear my mind,
then—just like that—quite sure of being kissed,
she whispered, "Look, my cheek has caught a cold."

A curious collection. . . . There are translations of Homer, Sappho, Rilke, Heine, Montale, and others, besides the poets I've already mentioned. I suppose that *Imitations* will interest some people as a mirror of Lowell's mind. However, I don't think that the mind of a poet is of much interest in itself; it is what he creates that matters. Thus, while Lowell's lines from the *Iliad* seem unimportant, for they are unimportant as poetry, whatever reason he may have had for doing them, his translations of Rimbaud or Rilke, for example, are interesting in poetic terms—that is, in every line difficulties of sound and meaning are resolved. To check his "imitations" against the originals is to learn something about the tact of poetry.

Ben Belitt

Imitations: Translation as Personal Mode

It would appear that the domain of Robert Lowell's *Imitations* is public rather than private in character: a "small anthology of European poetry" from Homer to Pasternak and Montale, drawing upon five languages, including the Russian; with the customary omission of the Spanish. To some extent the concessions to Homer and Sappho are perfunctory: lip-service to the museum of the Sixth Century B.C., except in some fragments from Sappho which engage Lowell's lifelong preoccupation with cosmic and personal deprival. As a "small anthology of European poetry," however, the collection is obviously sparse and crotchety: what is important is the poet's readiness to explore the European intonation, try the agonies and the vagaries of the European subject in a way that his American contemporaries have not, and prove them by translation on his pulses. The effect of his anthology in the long run is to draw the reader's attention constantly to the person of the translator, and away from the ambiance of "Europe." It would appear that Lowell, like Pound and Eliot, has employed a mode of translation to enact a repertory of "personae" native to his irascible and inquiring genius; that what we have is, in fact, not an anthology of European poetry, but a species of dramatism: an artist's mimicry of other artists.

It is Lowell's startling expectation that all—Homer and Sappho, Der Wilde Alexander and François Villon, Leopardi, Hebel, Heine, Hugo, Baudelaire, Rimbaud, Mallarmé, Valéry, Rilke, Saba, Ungaretti,

Montale, Annensky and Pasternak—"will be read as a sequence, one voice running through many personalities, contrasts, and repetitions." To this end, the mimetic brio of his assault upon the initiating voices is nothing short of ruthless. Sappho has been supplanted by "poems (which) are really new poems based on hers"; Villon has been "stripped"; Hebel has been "taken out of dialect"; Victor Hugo's "Gautier" has been "cut in half"; Mallarmé, Ungaretti, and Rimbaud have been "unclotted" at the translator's pleasure; a third of *Bateau Ivre* has been jettisoned; two stanzas have been added to Rilke's "Roman Sarcophagus": "And so forth! I have dropped lines, moved lines, moved stanzas, changed images, and altered meter and intent."

The scandalized purist need not search long for a vantage point from which to sink his knives where self-righteous pedantry has always found fair game: indeed, Mr. Lowell in his Introduction delivers himself up to would-be assassins with the resolute fatalism of Caesar in the Roman Senate. His admissions and omissions seem almost wilfully suicidal: in that European cemetery of noble utterances and awesome identities which he inhabits, his actions appear vandalous and his appetities necrophilous. The question of Conscience, so touchy to critical moralists, seems never to have occurred to him. What remains is only his need, which is apparently insatiable: to "find ways to make (my originals) ring right for me"; to make Montale "still stronger in free verse"; to "keep something equivalent to the fire and finish of my originals"; to be "reckless with literal meaning" and labor "hard to get the tone"; "to write alive English"; "to rashly try to improve on other translations"; and most significantly, to *keep writing* "from time to time when I was unable to do anything of my own."

Connoisseurs of the translated word have every reason to ask where such wilful gerrymandering may not lead the professed translator: or *why* it is that certain translators translate. Taking Lowell at his own word, one would have to say that the cause is everywhere personal and solipsistic, as well as feral. More than ennui, certainly, must be postulated in his candid admission that he turned to "imitation" when the real thing was for a time denied him and he faced the virility of the world's eloquence "unable to do anything of my own." In the hard school of *"Sauve Qui Peut"* the cannibalism of the large talent at bay must be applauded for finding other means of dining with Landor and with Donne; and I count translation among the most taxing counsels of expedience. It requires, in the first place, an expenditure of self equal to the banquet set forth on the rich man's table. It deploys every skill given the poet's hand in the service of identities and prodigies not his own. As such, it is a form of austerity which finds sufficient recompense in the hard morality of Blake: "All Act is Virtue." Incidentally, it also accomplishes a kind of homeopathic therapy for purging past excesses and preparing for exertions yet to come, as when Lowell informs us that his Baudelaire, for all its stunning accomplishment, was "begun as exercises in couplets and quatrains and to get away from the longer, less concentrated problems of translating Racine's *Phèdre."* At its worst, for which Lowell is also accountable, it "imitates" the bittersweet and the mistletoe in its search for symbiotic equivalences, attaching itself to a forest of host-plants to gratify its voracious determination to survive.

This is as much as to say that translation may serve the translator as a form of surrogate identity, as well as a labor of love. In the "parisitology" of translation, it is true, there are certain crustaceans which castrate their hosts, others which attach themselves to large aquatic mammals for the ride and prestige, others which strangle and infect: but the vitalism of Robert Lowell is another thing. I dwell upon it here precisely because his talent is massive enough to invite and master each of the dangers mentioned, in the service of a commanding identity, and survive. Modesty will get us nowhere in the attempt to arrive at any criteria of translation which may be said to underlie Lowell's accomplishment as intermediary for the European mind. The "one voice" "running through many personalities, contrasts, and repetitions" is unmistakably the voice of Robert Lowell—the most eventful and passionate voice of our epoch, whose voracity matters because it helps to give character to our century. Its impersonations, collapses, reassertions are never parasitical in the morbid sense of enacting flights from the poet's responsibility, or providing lines of least resistance in a peripheral struggle for existence.

On the other hand, little is to be gained from rushing to the defense of the *Imitations* with toplofty disclaimers which pay the poet the dubious compliment of removing him from the imputation of translation entirely. When Professor Alvarez informs prospective readers that the *Imitations* of Robert Lowell is *"Not* a book of translation"; that what we have is a "magnificent collection of new poems by Robert Lowell, based on the work of 18 European poets . . . in that constantly expanding imaginative universe in which Lowell orbits," no one is likely to benefit, least of all the translator. Robert Lowell cannot be dismissed as the space-man of recent American translation, circling the European scene in a rubbish of old sandwiches, astronautical weightlessness, and "expanding imagination." Doubtless, he winced, somewhere in the lower gasses, to find his "small anthology of European poetry" written off as "the most varied and moving book that this leader of mid-century poetry has yet produced" and "oddly, one of the most original." Edmund Wilson's equivocation is not much better: that the *Imitations* is probably "the only book of its kind in literature," whatever that happens to be. Nor can I, despite my mistrust of literalists dedicated to the subversion of inquiry and realism in translation, call the "complaint that Lowell has not followed Baudelaire literally" an "absurd" one, with Mr. Wilson. The gift of absurdity is precisely what the literalist has not got; and it is possible that absurdity may do more than sanctimony to justify the deeper claim on our imagination for the passionate integrity of utterance which characterizes the finest of Lowell's "imitations."

What must be asked in the long empirical run is another question: what are we to understand by "imitation"? Precisely what or who is being imitated in the *Imitations*—Robert Lowell? his great originals? or "due process of translation?" Is the essential premise of imitation: (1) "I will now proceed to English this poem *as though I were* translating it"; or (2) "I will now English this poem as though it were part of my own sensibility, moving from element to element inside my own identity rather than the translator's, assembling and disassembling all inside my own nervous system, committed at all points to my own language rather than the language of the original?" Does the "imitator" differ from the "translator" in that he performs as a kind of versifying dowser sensitive to the indicated pulls of a *terra incognita* and is capable of turning all into *faits accomplis* of prosody? Is he a virtuoso asked to re-invent at second or third or fourth-hand (at times he has no direct access to the language of the original) the occasion that was uniquely the poet's and the habits of mind and language that originally invested it? Are we concerned with fabrication rather than *mimesis?*

Current practise has no easy answers to these questions, and none is forthcoming in the term given the reader by Lowell. The word itself—imitation—has a notorious history of private and public misdemeanors from its awesome beginnings in Aristotle, up to the present. Life has been "imitated," Nature has been "imitated," Action has been "imitated," with nobody much the wiser. Indeed, the provenance of the "mimetic" factor is almost a certain guarantee of the surrender of the issue to polemical metaphysics and has helped to expose the bias of whole centuries. Thus, one generation talks of copies, phantoms, deceptions, in the name of imitation; another "holds the Mirror up to Nature"; another divinizes its literary models: "To copy Nature is to copy them"; another chooses "the mind's self-experience in the act of thinking" and re-invents Fancy and Imagination. Our own century has benefitted by the combined assaults of I. A. Richards, the debunkers of I. A. Richards, Butcher's preface to the *Poetics,* Francis Fergusson's bid for the "histrionic sensibility," and the long vista of verbal and compositional "dramatism" central to the poetics of Kenneth Burke.

None will serve to crystallize for us the intent of Robert Lowell in this volume. Among more recent symposia on the subject—notably, the barrage of 18 voices out of Harvard *On Translation**—Jackson

* *On Translation*, ed. Reuben A. Brower (Cambridge, Mass.: Harvard University Press, 1959).

Mathews' "Third Thoughts on Translating Poetry" comes closest to the issue at hand, in decidedly cautionary terms. "The temptation," he writes, "is much greater in poetry than in prose to fall under the spell of the model, to try to *imitate* its obvious features, even its syntax, or to *mimic* the voice of the other poet. The usual mistake is to believe that the form of the model must somehow be *copied*." The spectrum remains the same—*imitate, mimic, copy*—but the paradox accomplished here is to force Lowell's word to account for all that he has repudiated in the name of "imitation." For whatever its shortcomings, Lowell's *Imitations* is no mocking-bird in an aviary of European originals.

II

Where, then, are we to turn for clues to the criteria of license and translation in Robert Lowell's anthology? In the absence of a "philosophy of composition," I would like to propose a direct reading of the "imitations" into which all has been metamorphosed by the translator himself—a collation of *his* choices, without any hint of paradigms known or imaginable to me, to which they might conform. Among the eerie truths learned by practising translators is the fact that the One True Translation which all pedants seem to have to hand and consult at will, exists nowhere at all. The particulars of Lowell's originals and the particulars of his "imitations" do, however, and together they may help us to construe the personal venture he has undertaken in behalf of his great models. For this purpose I have chosen two poems of Eugenio Montale—"Dora Markus" and *"Piccolo Testamento"*—for reasons which seem serviceable enough to me, though I am aware that all acts of translation are unique to themselves, especially where the range of voices and epochs is as orchestral as in Lowell.

Lowell's special fascination in Montale is already apparent in his prefatory remarks on his distinguished contemporary. "I had long been amazed by Montale, but had no idea how he might be worked until I saw that unlike most good poets—Horace and Petrarch are extremes—he was strong in simple prose and could be made stronger in free verse." Here is both the admirer's profession of engrossment in an appealing and powerful talent, and the translator's discovery of a stance from which he might attempt an Archimedean moving of two worlds. Apart from such assurances—which are never idle in Lowell— there are a number of other considerations which confirm the appropriateness of such a choice. Despite Lowell's preference for Baudelaire as a *semblable* in spleen, guilt, and *"l'Inconnu,"* despite his taste for the nostalgias and demoniacal historicity of Rimbaud as an artist *"maudit,"* despite the neoclassical atavisms of Rilke and the delphic contemporaneity of Pasternak which he openly courts, the intonations and textures of Montale perhaps come closest to the temper of Robert Lowell himself. Like Montale, Lowell's prevailing cachet, after *Lord Weary's Castle,* is hard-bitten, melancholy, psychologically dense, with a subject that keeps curiously fluid despite the relentless pressure of despairing intentionality. Poem after poem in *For the Union Dead,* for example, eludes one in the midst of its restless thrust and circuition, as is also the case in Montale's *"Mottetti," "La Casa dei Dognani," "Iride," "La Primavera Hitleriana,"* and countless others. For all Montale's declared predilection for "occasions" (he is content to call a whole volume *Le Occasioni*) what puzzles the reader most in both Montale and Lowell is the nature of the poetic occasion itself: *where* the poem's center was supposed to fall in the midst of the seething interplay of scruples, particulars, recriminations, and insurmountable rejections.

The Italians, with their civilized tolerance of the ineffable, have an admiring word for this phenomenon which they apply like a water-mark to Montale: *hermetic.* The American reader has only the giddy afterthought: but what was it all about? Similarly, both Montale and Lowell carry a dense burden of personal and historical wretchedness, failed loves, psychological landscapes, existential incongruities inseparable from persons and places and electric with the pulsation of the moment. We have the unplumbed exacerbations of Montale's Bellosguardo, Eastbourne, Finistère, Proda di Versilia, to place alongside Lowell's Dunbarton, Nantucket Graveyard, Nautilus

Island, Rapallo, and Boston Commons as stations of a spiritual itinerary. Like Lowell, Montale has written a "Ballad in a Clinic," watched storms from "The Coastguard's House," untangled the oddities of a "gnomelike world" from a "Café at Rapallo," scouted the ironies of "A Metropolitan Christmas," turned mordantly upon his own failed purposes in city parks, orchards, on trains and on beaches, leaving an inconclusive savor that troubles the attention without wholly disclosing itself. As in Lowell's volume by that name, a whole genre of heraldic "life studies" is opened up in Montale's "Dora Markus," "To Liuba Leaving," "Arsenio," "Carnival for Gerti," and "Visit to Fadin"; and it is hardly necessary to point out the "confessional" bias of poems like "Little Testament," "Letter Not Written," "Two in Twilight," "To My Mother," and the whole sequence of "Motets." The uncanny impression remains, after many readings of Montale's "Eastbourne," that it is a poem which might well bear the signature of both poets.

As an instance of "life study" Montale's "Dora Markus" is especially noteworthy. Here we have not only "one of the most poignant love elegies of all time" (in the opinion of Glauco Cambon) but a counterplay of intimacy, psychological divination, and the displaced "oriental" mind moving between Porto Corsini and the Austrian Alps. As a study in exile it combines a rich texture of deprival and unrest (*"irrequietudine"*) in a shimmering context of suspended outcomes: the poet's implacable vision of a "voice, legend, destiny" already "exhausted" or manhandled; the *"antica vita"* of a Jewess miraculously surviving from one day to the next by talismanic powers whimsically attributed to an ivory mouse in her jumble of lipstick, powderpuff, nailfile; and an immediate scene—majolica interiors, seaside *pensiones,* complete to the bayleaf that "survives for the kitchen." The aim of the poet is, above all, to recover the peculiar *"ansietà d'Oriente"* (Oriental anxiety) at once so fascinating and appalling to the Italian's appetite for melodrama: the capacity of Dora Markus to drift without outcome in a Levantine haze, instead of opting for fatality like a heroine in an opera by Verdi or Puccini.

Formally, it is among the most expansive and readily accessible of

Montale's great set-pieces: open, conversational cadences undisturbed by the intrusion of eruptive afterthoughts—the *"dolce stil"* rather than the *"rime aspre"* of Montale's many voices, riding on its phrases, pauses, assonantal depths and graces with an unflinching objectivity. As such, it would not appear to offer the thorny talent of Robert Lowell an ideal vehicle of "imitation"; and it is hard to see how he was persuaded that Montale was either "strong in (the) simple prose of Kay's *Penguin Book of Italian Verse*" or "could be made stronger in free verse." The verse form chosen by Lowell is indeed free to the point of crudity: a prosody without pulse or that factor of inner rhyme which so often limbers the tensions and deepens the resonance of both Montale and Lowell. In comparison with the supple elegance of Montale, it is peculiarly shrill, prosy, angular, without reverberations. Its effect is that of an intermediate, rather than a final, draft, as though Lowell were still mired in the prose of *The Penguin Book of Italian Verse* or preliminary renderings of his own. The presence of Robert Lowell, sometimes playing at "imitation," sometimes pressing for the bare sound and the tough reduction of intricate matters which is his true signature, comes and goes; the equivalences of Montale do not.

Nevertheless, the fact remains that "Dora Markus," for all its ineptitude, is a *translated,* and not an "imitated" poem. Every sequence of Montale's thinking has been retained intact, every image has been confronted, for the most part, in its own context; every effort has been directed with scrupulous and laborious integrity on unfolding the progressions of the poem as they are given the reader by the poet himself—with one maddeningly tone-deaf exception. The last line of all, indispensable to both the pathos and symmetry of the poem— what Sergio Solmi calls "the special curvature of Montale"—weighted with the total charge of Montale's induction of a "voice, legend, destiny," is suppressed: "But it is late, it grows later and later." Characteristically, Lowell has preferred to bleed off into suspension points and ignore the Dantean return to inexorable judgment of the original.

The digressions of Lowell's Montale deserve close scrutiny because they encompass whatever remains of the purely "imitative." It would be pointless and tedious to attempt an exhaustive collation of the two texts, since this is not a study in detection but a glimpse at the propinquities and equivalences of translation. Turning to the most harmless deviations first—the permissible variants or extensions of meaning forced upon the poet by exigency or "inspiration"—one might note the following in the first section of "Dora Markus." A "wooden pier" (*ponte di legno*) becomes a "plank pier": all to the good. The "almost motionless" (*quasi immoti*) fishermen become "dull as blocks" —possibly as extensions of the same plank pier; a "sign of the hand" (*segno della mano*) becomes a Lowellesque "toss of your thumb"; a dockyard (*darsena*) becomes "outlying shipyards"—very Bostonian; what was "shiny" (*lucida*) in Montale becomes "silvered" in Lowell; an impassive spring (*primavera inerte*) is a "depressed spring," and a way of life called "dappled" (*si screzia*) by Montale is curiously "subtilized" in Lowell. In a key-phrase to the poem as a whole, the "soft Oriental anxiety" of Dora Markus is diagnosed by Lowell as "nervous, Levantine anxiety"—and surely "Levantine" is a triumph of the *mot juste*: one of those windfalls of which one says the translator has pinned down what the original could not. The "stormy evenings" (*sere tempestose*), on the other hand, are levelled into "ugly nights," the admittedly equivocal *"dolcezza"* (a word intransigently foreign to English) turns into "ennui" rather than "sweetness" or "blandness"; and the "lake of indifference" (*lago d'indifferenza*) invoked by Montale as the heart of Dora Markus, is modified somewhat myopically into a "puddle of diffidence," as though the word had been read wrongly by the translator.

In most cases, the changes noted are legitimate ventures in interpretation, in which, as Valéry has pointed out, the translator not only presses for language, but "reconstitutes as nearly as possible the *effect* of a certain *cause* (a text in Italian) by means of another *cause* (a text in English)." More arbitrary departures, however, follow fast. Lowell elects to turn the simple "lowlands" or "flatlands" (*bassura*) of Montale into a "patch of town-sick country"—his own invention—and renders "its calms are even rarer" (*i suoi riposi sono anche piu rari*) with the heavy-handed "the let-ups are nonexistent," preempting what the author has left suspended. Other modifications seem merely inept or gratuitous to the quizzical reader: why, for example, "full of amnesia" for *"senza memoria"* (without memory)? Why clutter the *"antica vita"* (old life) of Montale with the needlessly explanatory "old world's way of surviving"?

Similarly, there are some troublesome admixtures of interpretation and fabrication in Part II of "Dora Markus." It is of the essence of Lowell's temperament, and as such, allowable, that the "ragged peaks" or pinnacles (*gl'irti pinnacoli*) of a seascape should turn up as "frowsy shorefront" in Lowell, the geese's cry (*gemiti d'oche*) turn into "catcalls," the "throbbing of motors" (*palpito dei motori*) metamorphose into "the put-put-put of the outboards," American-style, and "the evening that stretches out / over the humid inlet" (*la sera che si protende / sull'umida conca*) contract into "night blanketing / the fogging lake coves." There are also less allowable thrusts, however, which represent not "due process" of interpretation, but random piracies on the part of an "imitator" writing as he pleases, precisely as Lowell declares he intended to. Carinthia "of flowering myrtles and ponds" (*tua Carinzia di mirti fioriti e di stagmi*) takes a curiously baroque turn of fancy: *"Your corsage is the crescent* of hedges of flowering myrtle." Where Dora Markus merely "stoops on the brink" (*china sul bordo*) Lowell's text explodes roguishly into "sashay on the curb of a stagnant pond"—certainly a strange outburst for the "exhausted" and "indifferent" Dora of Montale's legend. Similarly, there is a revving-up of the "big gold portraits" (*grandi ritratti d'oro*) which preside over her legend, into "ten-inch gold frames / of the grand hotels," as well as their subjects, whose "looks of men / with high(set) weak whiskers" (*quegli sguardi / di uomini che hanno fedine / altere e deboli*) shape up luridly as "the moist lips of sugar daddies / with weak masculine sideburns."

The passages cited, I repeat, constitute passing deflections, digressions, personal readings and renderings of detail; or incidental collapses and fumbled opportunities. Their telltale abundance in the case of "Dora Markus" constitutes a record of imprecision which forces one in the end to dismiss it as inept or provisional; the matrix of Lowell's English text itself, however, remains a *translated* rather than an "imitated" one. As such, "Dora Markus" presents a hard assay that need scandalize no one, however much it may disappoint the admirer of Robert Lowell who *asks* (as would I) for the sound of his voice and delights in following it as an attending presence through the translation it has chosen to inhabit. The failures of touch, the incidental occlusions of intent and tone, the occasional over-acting, over-posturing, over-reaching, the rare pratfalls into prosy approximations, are those of all poet-translators busy at their trade in the ordinary way, probing through that double identity which is the *néant* from which all true translation begins.

III

Precisely the same must be said for the modality and effect of Lowell's *"Piccolo Testamento"* (Little Testament). Here the translator's total encompassment of his original—his over-all felicity of touch, texture, compositional detail—is as impressive as the botched approximations of "Dora Markus." Perhaps one ought look no further for causes to such propitious effects, but merely acknowledge their existence as *faits accomplis* and pronounce the union of minds and languages fortunate. The nature of the original, in this case, however, in itself promises more compatible outcomes. In comparison with the pure line of "Dora Markus," the "Little Testament" is a poem more deeply scored with all the idiosyncratic merits of Montale—denser, stranger, nervier in its turns of rhythm and fancy, less immediate in its disclosure of the complex matters touched upon, more obdurate in its hermetic self-scrutiny, more oblique in its confidences. As such, it offers continuous resistance to all that is merely manipulative or "imitative" on the part of the translator and insists on its retention *intact*. At the same time, it is full of glancing turns of direction, texture, metaphorical and stylistic alignment, forging through its transpositions with a driving pulse, without the forfeit of a single misgiving or anxiety.

Presumably, this brings us closer to the vein of Lowell's "Skunk Hour," "Colloquy in Black Rock," "The Flaw," and "The Severed Head": there should be less need, under the circumstances, for the translator to punctuate, revise, delete, and transpose matters to his satisfaction. Deviations from Montale's original persist here as in "Dora Markus," and one might even wonder about the justice of passing incursions. When Lowell gives us a "pearl necklace's snail's trail" for Montale's "snail's trail of mother-of-pearl" (*traccia madreperlacea di lumaca*), the visceral exudation of the snail is falsely represented by a necklace which has nothing to do with the context and omits the special iridescence sought by the poet. Similarly, when Montale, in the "crepuscular" vein of Italian modernism, writes the powder and mirror (*la cipria nello specchietto*) of a lady's compact (probably) into his poem as another instance of talismanic delusion, the poignancy of the ordinary is lost in the *"spectrum* of a pocket-mirror." I see no good reason, moreover, for turning the "soft coal wings" (*l'ali di bitume*) of Montale's descending Lucifer into "hard coal wings," his shadowy Lucifer (*un umbroso Lucifero*) into a "torch-bearing Lucifer," his dance (the *"sardana"*) into an "orchestra," even if one grants that the Greek *orxestra* was actually a dancing-place. Lines 5-7, that universal stumbling-stone of translators of the "Little Testament"—and there are many—will of course please no one familiar with the elliptical fascinations of the original, and resists the best efforts of Lowell to improvise on his own. The "light of church or workshop / that neither the black nor the red cleric (acolyte?) / may nurture" (*lume di chiesa o d'officina / che alimenti / chierico rosso, o nero*), breathes heavily in Lowell's version: "The lamp in any church or office / tended by some adolescent altar boy / Communist or Papist, / in black or red." The question of which is the red and which the black, remains, as well as the pious orthodoxies of the adolescent Communist.

With every allowance made for near misses and far reaches such as these, I should still insist that the "Little Testament" of Lowell's Montale follows through from beginning to end as a *translated* venture of considerable beauty, intact in its own rhythms, illuminations, skills, and integrity: a meeting of minds and imaginations where they intersect in two artifacts—or Valéry's Italian "cause" wedded to his English "effect" which provides the reader, in turn, with a cause in itself. If this metaphysic is too hard or casuistical for the hasty to construe—and I suppose it is——the fault is not wholly Valéry's or Lowell's; or mine. It is part and parcel of a modern semantic bias which expects the croupier's handy transformation of blue chips into cash at the prevailing international exchange at each turn of the translator's wheel. For positivists such as these, the dropsical linguistics of Nabokov's "poetics" is a fitting crucifixion.

Debate on such matters is likely to be bottomless, discussion bad-tempered, and scholarship usurious. I prefer, instead, to dwell on the appropriateness of Lowell's continuing pursuit of translation as personal mode, in the years which have followed his initial *persona* as the castle-bound Lord Weary. Unlike the guerrilla nationalists. professional bridge-blowers, rooftop snipers, and nocturnal infiltrators and assassins of the translator's domain, he has steadily gone on learning his trade by open assault in a variety of skirmishes and full-dress battles, in full view of the enemy, cap-a-pie, in single combat. It is already a very far cry from the glowing fabrications "after Rimbaud," "after Valéry," "after Rilke," in *Lord Weary's Castle,* with their reticent preface: "When I use the word *after* below the title of a poem, what follows is not a translation but an imitation which should be read as though it were an original." The author of *Imitations* and the translator of *Phèdre* and the *Oresteia* need never apologize for poems which presumably "come after" his sumptuous models. His English now lives *simultaneously* with the tongues and talents to which he is beholden.

Similarly, it can be said of his "dramatism" that translation has made it increasingly possible for him to depersonalize his penchant for heroic and patrician *personae*: Jonathan Edwards of the spiders and the "surprising conversions," the memoirs of General Thiebault, the confessions after Sextus Propertius, Valéry, Rimbaud, Rilke, Cobbett—all out of Lord Weary's castle—and move on to the province of drama as such. Here, Lowell's activity has been dazzling in both the pomp and diversity of its passion for transformation. More and more his medium has become theatrical in the literal sense that Lowell has increasingly sought out the provence of the *played play,* rather than the pirated or inhabited identity of European masters. He has taken a craftsman's pains to "translate" Melville's Benito Cereno into objective theatrical artifacts, instead of appropriating the identity of Melville himself. He has translated the *theatre* of Racine, rather than turning Racine into an impersonation of himself. And lest *grandeur* remain "still unsatisfied" in Calvary's turbulence, he has most recently thrown his total force against the full weight of Aeschylus' *Oresteia* in a bid for total theater.

It is to be hoped that with the passing of time and the channelization of a sensibility which hindsight now shows to have been constantly "histrionic," Lowell will continue to leaven the integrity of his translation. Ultimately, there should be no need for him whatever to remove himself from the rank and file of translators as such, or work in a special aura of privilege, in the name of "imitation." I say this without much hope that translators are ever any the wiser for having translated for a decade or a lifetime, or that they can ever hope for Adam's dream, who "awoke and found it true." Indeed, Babel is always with us. The moralist will say, for example: Translation is a long discipline of self-denial, a matter of fidelity or betrayal: *traduttore, traditore.* The vitalist will say: Translation is a matter of life and death, merely: the life of the original or the death of it. The poet will say: Translation is either the composition of a new poem in the language of the translator, or the systematic liquidation of a masterpiece from the language of the original. The epistemologist will say: Translation is an illusion of the original forced upon the translator at every turn because he has begun by substituting his own language and occasion for that of the poet's and must fabricate his reality as he goes. The Sibyl sees all and says: Translation is the truth of the original in the only language capable of rendering it "in truth": the original language untouched by translation.

John Simon
Abuse of Privilege:
Lowell as Translator

Two concepts of translation have flourished in the western world. One, which we can call medieval (it earned Chaucer the title "great translatour"), consists of taking a story or poem by a "maker" in some foreign language and retelling it freely in your native tongue. The other, which we can call Renaissance, consists of transposing a piece of writing as faithfully as can be, word for word, into the other language. Except in the drama, it is the Renaissance mode of translating that has prevailed.* The explanation is not far to seek.

In the Middle Ages, for religious and political reasons, the concept of individualism was not highly developed. Writers were not particularly concerned with asserting their total originality. Culture was more truly international and there was a certain common stock of tales in prose and verse—the "matter" of Troy, for example—which poets considered their duty and privilege to pass on. With the rise in importance of the poet as individual, and with style becoming accordingly co-equal in status with content, respect for one's own individuality made one as different and original as possible in one's writing, whereas respect for another's individuality kept one as true as possible to his manner and matter in one's translating.

What Robert Lowell has done in his poetic translations, which he calls "imitations," is to return to the medieval mode: to retell a poem

---

* Renaissance translations were, to be sure, often very free by today's standards; nevertheless it is in them that respect for original authorship begins.

as though it came from some communal stock of plots or *topoi* in his own terms. One difficulty with this is immediately apparent. The medieval poet drew on stories that were vaguely but widely known, and his hearers or readers expected both a certain fidelity to and a certain variation on the themes. This poet-translator was dealing with stories in verse, and long story poems lend themselves to such "retelling": more or less following an outline while improving on some particular, embellishing a detail. But when poetry becomes predominantly lyrical and highly personalized, there is no story line to cleave to: everything is in the imagery, prosody, diction, sound. You render these—to the extent that you are able—or you render nothing.

Lowell's most important body of translations is the volume *Imitations;* let us begin by examining one of the pieces in it, a version of Rilke's famous "Orpheus. Eurydike. Hermes," whose title Lowell renders as "Orpheus, Eurydice and Hermes." Already by changing the quaint punctuation and adding the conjunction, Lowell loses the archaic, epigraphic quality Rilke is after. *"Das war der Seelen wunderliches Bergwerk,"* ("That was the wondrous mine of souls") Rilke begins; and Lowell: "That's the strange regalia of souls." Three things are clear at once. Lowell will not abide by the blank verse of the original, but will turn it into free verse; he will translate into a colloquial tone ("that's") antipodal to the austere elegance of the original; and he will change the imagery—*Bergwerk* ("mine") becomes, inexplicably, "regalia." The mineralogical image, souls in Hades that go like silver ores through the dark (and Rilke's line is all silvery i's and short e's—*"Wie stille Silbererze gingen sie"*), becomes sartorial: "regalia" made out of "platinum filaments." Poorer as this is in evoking the underground kingdom, it becomes confused as well: the filaments suddenly turn into what they are in the German, "arteries." But whereas metallic ores can be turned into arteries easily enough, especially in German where *Adern* means both veins and ores, the transition from garments to veins is unworkable. Rilke's image progresses from these veins to the underground blood that feeds the veins of living men. Lowell obtrudes with irrelevant references to powder beetles, otters, and an oak king, thus interrupting the flow of both the blood and Rilke's imagery.

Now Lowell inserts gratuitously, "The dark was heavier than Caesar's foot." What prompts him to stick Caesar's, not to mention his own, foot in it? Perhaps it is free association: *Porphryr* (which he doesn't translate) may suggest to him *porphyrogenetos,* and this, in turn, Caesar. But the result is as clumsy as it is irrelevant. Next, where Rilke is abstract as befits this lifeless realm, and speaks of *"wesenlose Wälder. Brücken über Leeres"* ("disembodied forests. Bridges over emptiness"), Lowell substitutes "distracted forests"—interesting, but what could it mean here?—and "bridges over air-pockets," which is too specific and more in keeping with the overworld of Pan-Am than with the underworld of Pluto. Where Rilke's lake hangs over its distant bottom like rainy skies over a landscape, Lowell's "moaned over the background canals,/ like a bag of winds over the Caucasus." It is hard to see how a lake could be suspended over canals, and background ones at that; moreover, by making the lake moan, Lowell dispels the ghostly silence that hovers over this landscape. Even more perplexing is the presence here of that "bag of winds over the Caucasus," which I can explain only as Lowell's proleptic or prophetic reference to his then unwritten adaptation of *Prometheus Bound.* Where Rilke has "meadows, mellow and full of forbearance (*Langmut*)," Lowell has "terraced highlands, stocked with cattle and patience," which, quite absurdly, implies husbandry in Hades. Again, where Rilke's road is "laid out like a long paleness," which is approximately mortuary, Lowell's is "unwinding like a bandage," which is merely out of the infirmary. Lowell is, apparently, mindful of the practical schoolboy precept that good writing is full of concrete, specific references and avoids abstractions (e.g., "paleness"); no less apparently, there are exceptions to this rule, exceptions that are called for here.

Rilke's Orpheus, *"der stumm und ungeduldig vor sich aussah"* ("who, silent and impatient, looked ahead"), undergoes a sad change: "he didn't say a thing. He counted his toes." Not only is this trivial and jocular without being original or funny, it is also preposterously inappropriate: why would—and how could—a man hurrying impatiently toward the world of the living and the return of his wife count his toes as he speeds ahead? The rest of the strophe is not without its minor inaccuracies, such as "His step ate up the road/ a yard at a time, without bruising a thistle," where Rilke has "Without chewing, his step devoured the path in great mouthfuls." Lowell's metaphor is mixed.

Then, however, Lowell mangles one of Rilke's finest images. Orpheus's senses are cleft in two: his gaze runs ahead like a dog, turns, comes back, and time and again stands waiting out there at the next turning (*"vorauslief/ umkehrte, kam und immer wieder weit/ und wartend an der nächsten Wendung stand"*—the rhythm, enjambment, and alliteration are noteworthy), while his hearing lingers on, like a scent, trailing backward toward her whom he must not look at. But Lowell has "cut in two" is the "intelligence," so that the conflict of riven senses gets lost. Next, "gaze" becomes "outlook"—too abstract; and, worst of all, this outlook "worried like a dog behind him." The point is now good and killed: the gaze must look forward by Pluto's stipulation, also it is eager to get home and, like an impatient dog that finds its master too slow, it keeps running ahead. But when you have this dog "worrying" something (a bone?) and getting "behind" Orpheus, the image is ruined: sight is now permitted to stay behind at times and thus is not fully cut off from hearing. And when this hearing "breathed myrrh behind him" instead of simply "staying behind" as in Rilke (who pushes the prefix graphically all the way back: *"blieb sein Gehör wie ein Geruch zurück"*), the confusion is compounded.

The rest of the strophe in translation continues the diminution of the original. Thus Lowell's Orpheus has behind him "the currents of air in his blue cloak," less effective than the terse *"seines Mantels Wind"* ("the wind of his cloak"). At the end of the strophe, Lowell seems plain ignorant of German. How else explain the reduction of "If he dared turn around once . . . he would have to see them, the two quiet ones who silently follow him" (the beauty of the German is chiefly in the assonance: *"die beiden Leisen, die ihm schweigend nachgehn"*) to this prosy bit of garbling: "And as a matter of fact,/ he knew he must now turn to them . . ." etc. On the contrary, Orpheus is trying very hard not to look back. Where I put an ellipsis Rilke has a parenthetic statement, characteristically displaced by Lowell, which drives home Orpheus's aching awareness of the terms of the bargain. If you translate *"müsste er sie sehen"* ("he would have to see them") as Lowell does, "he must now turn to them," the only charitable interpretation is that you do not distinguish this from the indicative *er musste sie sehen,* which would mean "he had to see them." Lowell makes Orpheus irresponsible and weak—especially with that casual "as a matter of fact" dragged in out of nowhere.

I have room here for only a few more of these egregious distortions. Take another Rilkean master-image: Orpheus's passionate lament for Eurydice has created "a world of grieving, in which everything is once again present: woods and valley, and path and borough, field and river and beast; and . . . around this grief-world there revolved, exactly as around the other earth, a sun and a starry, still sky, a grief-sky with disfigured stars . . ." Lowell imitates as follows: "out of this sorrow came/ the fountainhead of the world: valleys, fields,/ towns, roads . . . acropolis,/ marble quarries, goats, vineyards./ And his sorrow-world circled about her,/ just as the sun and stern stars/ circle the earth—/ a heaven of anxiety ringed by the determined stars . . ." Lowell muddies the clear correspondence of the world and the grief-world (or sorrow-world) created by the songs: "out of this sorrow came the fountainhead of the world" does not identify the replica as Orpheus's grief-stricken poetry. Then, all those specificities—marble quarries, goats, even an anachronistic acropolis—sound more like a tourist folder than Rilke's poem. But the main point here is that in the sorrow-world the phenomena, like the stars, are *entstellt* (disfigured, contorted with pain), something completely muffed by Lowell's epithet "determined." Previously, he gave us "stern stars," which is good fractured German from *Stern* ("star") but hardly conveys Rilke's beautiful *"gestirnter*

stiller Himmel," let alone the loveliness of the real world as opposed to
its distorted mirror image in Orpheus's dirges.*

Again, Rilke says that Eurydice is so fulfilled with death that she
has no desire to live again. In the text we get: "Like a fruit with
sweetness and dark, so was she filled with her great death, which was so
new that she fathomed nothing." In Lowell: "Like an apple full of
sugar and darkness/ she was full of her decisive death,/ so green she
couldn't bite into it." Plainly if death fills her with sugar like a ripe
apple, that death cannot also be green, unripe, and not to be bitten into.
Eurydice, next, is revealed in the "new maidenhood" of death, which
Lowell's "marble maidenhead," for all its alliteration and funerary
overtones, does not properly identify. Her sex 'was shut, like a young
flower toward evening," which Lowell mistranslates "Her sex had a
closed house/ like a young flower rebuking the night air." That "closed
house" is awkward enough, but "rebuking the night air" must be based
on sheer unawareness that *gegen* means "toward" as well as "against."
On the other hand, setting up an inapposite conflict between the
flower and the night air might also be a bit of that characteristic
Lowellian violence (as often the poet's downfall as his achievement)
intruding uninvited.

Lowell can as easily become overabstract as overspecific. Thus where
Rilke says, simply and concretely, that Eurydice was no longer "that
blonde woman who sometimes echoed in the poet's songs," Lowell
produces a bloodless abstraction: "that blond transcendence/ so often
ornamenting the singer's meters." Rilke continues: "No longer the
wide bed's fragrance and island, and that man's possession no longer."
Lowell has: "nor a hanging garden in his double bed./ She had wearied
of being the hero's one possession." This is a fiasco: who would want to
have a hanging garden in his bed, even if it's double? An island in
a wide bed is something else again: wide bed suggests ocean bed in
which an island is appropriate. Moreover, the beloved's body in a bed,

---

* Punning translations like this one probably derive from Ezra Pound, about
whose influence on Lowell see below.

which would otherwise be a place in which to toss shipwrecked, does become a life-saving island. Further, it is wrong to make Orpheus, especially in this context, "the hero," rather than just a man. And Eurydice has not wearied of him; it is just that the magnificence of death is beyond the humble competition of life.

And now consider the end of the poem. In the German, Hermes looks at the backward-glancing Orpheus sorrowfully, and escorts back a Eurydice just as entranced and unconcerned as before, walking "uncertainly, gently, and without impatience." In Lowell, the god looks at Orpheus reproachfully, and "His caduceus was like a shotgun on his shoulder"—a final piece of anachronistic violence that does violence also to the meaning of the poem: it implies the cruelty of the gods, whereas Rilke had in mind merely the incommensurability of life and death.

In his Introduction to *Imitations,* Lowell describes his aims as translator or adapter:

> I have tried to keep something equivalent to the fire and finish of my originals. This has forced me to do considerable rewriting. . . . I have been reckless with literal meaning, and labored hard to get the tone. Most often this has been *a* tone, for *the* tone is something that will always more or less escape transference . . . I have tried to write live English and to do what my authors might have done if they were writing their poems now and in America.

Except for making one wonder why "a tone" should have required such hard labor ("the tone," of course, would) this sounds very fine. But, I am afraid, what Lowell has done with Rilke's poem is neither a decent translation nor a good original work, merely a disaster. Lowell goes on to say, "I believe that poetic translation—I would call it an imitation—must be expert and inspired, and needs at least as much technique, luck and rightness of hand as an original poem." I am not sure I know the difference between technique and rightness of hand, but I can affirm that the foregoing translation is as devoid of them as it is of luck. I cannot escape the feeling that Lowell translates when he is unable to write anything of his own, not so much out of love for the poem translated as out of love for the sound of his own poetic vice. As a result, he rationalizes the admittedly difficult and essentially thankless art of the translator into something grander and even more difficult than it is. In actual fact, a version such as this of "Orpheus" is all the more shocking a failure since Lowell was neither faced with rhyme nor willing to be bound by meter. There are, to be sure, slightly better performances in *Imitations,* but there are also quite a few just as bad. This sort of thing should not be inflicted on great poetry; indeed, it shouldn't happen to doggerel.

For one thing, although Lowell translates from many languages, the only one he admits to not knowing at all is Russian. Yet one is compelled to question his competence in others as well. One would assume him to be most at ease with French, yet he is guilty of howlers even there. Valéry's Helen of Troy (in "Hélène") returns to the world of the living and exclaims, *"Azur! c'est moi . . ."* ("O azure, it is I!") Lowell, clearly mistaking this for *"L'azur, c'est moi,"* translates in his "Helen": "I am the blue!" Still, I suppose one can do good enough work from trots, if one will only abide by them. Yet questioned in connection with his Pasternak imitations whether he knew any Russian, Lowell told the *Paris Review* interviewer, "No, I have rewritten other English translations, and seldom even checked with Russian experts." This does not augur well.

Lest it be assumed that Lowell works better with strict, rhymed forms, let us look at his imitation of Baudelaire's famous sonnet *"Recueillement,"* which he calls "Meditation." Take the rhymes of the octave: care, here, atmosphere, care/ bare, back, bazaar, back. Not only are there no feminine rhymes to provide diversity as in Baudelaire, but also the similarity of all the vowel sounds is oppressive. Worse yet is the recurrent use of identities (care—care; back—back), which is aurally distressing. Baudelaire, to be sure, has *ville* and *vile* followed by *servile,* but these are homonyms, which, like *rime riche,* are perfectly in keeping with French prosody. The very first thing that strikes us in the French is the cadence, which sets the mood: *"Sois sage, ô ma Douleur, et tiens-toi plus tranquille./ Tu réclamais le Soir; il descend; le voici."* Lowell has "Calm down, my Sorrow, we must move with care./ You called for evening; it descends; it's here." In the first verse, Baudelaire makes the two main words the only polysyllables and places one at the end of each hemistich. Lowell has a disyllable in "Sorrow," but nothing to balance it. "Calm down," moreover, is much less affecting than *"Sois sage"* ("behave yourself," but with overtones of "get wise"), and "move with care" suggests some kind of stealthy maneuver, whereas Baudelaire is asking for dignified, stoical endurance. In the second verse, besides effects of vowel coloring that we can hardly expect the translator to get across, there is the dramatic progression from the long first hemistich to the quick staccato of the second; *"le voici,"* without a verb, being even more brusque than *"il descend."* The change from nominative to accusative is particularly effective. Lowell does what comes naturally in his English, which is fair enough, but here only some brilliant piece of strategy could have done the trick.

Baudelaire's crowd which, under the whip of pleasure, *"Va cueillir des remords dans la fête servile,"* becomes one that "fights off anguish at the great bazaar"—no equivalent for gathering remorse at the slavish feast: Baudelaire's crowd is more than a bunch of revelers trying to forget mortality; it is mankind so cursed with a subaltern mentality that its very exaltation is supine, its most longed-for fruit the bitter one of remorse. Now Lowell proceeds to exhibit that lack of a sense of place (or, sometimes, time) that is so frequent in these adaptations. Thus Lowell's regret emerges from the "sea," although the locale is Paris and the waters those of the Seine as the *arche* further implies. But it is the last two lines in which the translation truly comes to grief. The shroud of night is *traînant* ("dragging"), in motion, not "strung out," which is static. *"Entends, ma chère, entends la douce Nuit qui marche"* is not conveyed by "listen, my Dearest, hear the sweet night march!" What informs the original is the stately and inexorable forward movement, to whose ineluctability the repetition of *entends* contributes, even while suggesting also the intimate persuasion of a repeated pat on the head. Switching from "listen" to "hear" jettisons both effects. In the second hemistich the

sense of spacious progression is achieved by the rubato of *Nuit*
refusing reduction to monosyllabicity, and by the open feminine
ending of *marche* ("walks") continuing the disyllabic movement of
the line. Lowell's monosyllables ending with the incorrect "march"
(it should be something like "treading," "pacing" or "advancing"),
both too military and too short, suggest a night that arrives like a
platoon in close-order drill rather than a blessed solvent in which the
poet and his pain can dissolve and cease to be.

But perhaps we should pay special attention to Lowell's versions
from the Italian: in the *Paris Review* interview Lowell speaks of his
work with that language as something "which I have studied closely."
Let us look, then, at his rendition of Leopardi's *"L'infinito."* In the
case of such a particularly famous poem, the translator's responsibility
to the original is even greater than usual. Lowell ignores Leopardi's
hendecasyllabics and substitutes free verse, not the ideal vehicle for this
formally controlled, highly assonant, bittersweet reverie. Again
Lowell's sense of place is faulty and plays havoc with the topography:
"That hill pushed off by itself was always dear/ to me and the hedges
near/ it that cut away so much of the final horizon." But Leopardi
is himself on that lonely hill—"pushed off" implies that he is looking
toward it; the hedge, too, is *on* the hill—"near it" is utterly mystifying,
though "near" does, to be sure, rhyme with "dear." The poet on the
hill cannot see much of the farthest horizon because the hedge excludes
his gaze. This picture and its symbolic significance are neatly
obfuscated by Lowell's circumlocutions.

Lowell now gives us "I reasoned" for *"nel pensier mi fingo,"* which
is conjuring up before the mind's eye or imagining—anything but
reasoning. Thereupon we read, "I set about comparing my silence to
those voices" (of the winds); but that is not at all what Leopardi is
comparing: the silences of infinite space with the sound of the wind in
the trees. And where Leopardi cherishes "the living season and its
sounds," Lowell abstractively extols "things . . . and all their reasons
and choices." Leopardi's conclusion, "So amid this immensity my
thought is drowned; and shipwreck is sweet to me in this sea," turns

into "It's sweet to destroy my mind/ and go down/ and wreck in this sea where I drown." That mind-destruction is irrelevant Lowellian violence, and "go down ... wreck ... drown" is clumsy tautology.

But Lowell is supposed to have performed an outstanding service to Montale; what about his translations from that poet? The same problems obtain here. Take *"La casa dei doganieri,"* which Lowell translates as "The Coastguard House." Montale here recalls a visit to a shore-watchers' house (in no sense "a death-cell," as Lowell gratuitously suggests at the very outset) with a woman he loved and still loves. She, however, is not beside him now; she has forgotten that house. The poem is a night-piece; at a crucial point Montale observes "but you remain alone and do not breathe here in the dark." The dark, significantly, is here, not there; the poet is in it and vainly yearns to share its intimacy with the woman. Lowell translates: "but you house alone/ and hold your hollow breath there in the dark." To transpose the dark and the breath elsewhere, into a house of the woman's, is to miss the sad immediacy of the unshared *here*. The derogatory and uncalled-for "hollow" is likewise detrimental. But not content with missing the place, Lowell promptly misses the time as well. The last stanza continues the nocturnal meditation: "Oh, the receding horizon, where the light of the tanker rarely flares" is changed by Lowell into "Oh the derelict horizon,/ sunless except for the/ orange hull of a lonely, drudging tanker." Derelict horizon is nice, but now the time turns into day: "sunless" and "orange hull" perceptible only by daylight. By splitting the poem into night and day, the actual contrast between past and present, between this moment and the erosion of time, is forfeited.

Elsewhere, too, Lowell takes unwarrantable liberties with Montale. In *"L'anguilla,"* after evoking the life cycle of the eel, the poet asks the woman the climactic question, *"puoi tu/ non crederla sorella?"*—can you consider her (the eel) not your sister? Lowell stands this on its head: "can you call her *Sister?*" Nature, befriended by Montale (the woman cannot deny her kinship with the eel), is kept at arm's length by Lowell (the woman is suspected of inability to confess her closeness to the fish): Again, in *"La primavera hitleriana,"* Montale concludes, after conjuring up the horrors of the occupation, with a hopeful gaze into the future. Lowell, however, omits almost all of that long last strophe in order to be able to end his version, "Hitlerian Spring," on a note of despair, which he heightens by rendering "Oh, the wounded spring is still a feast if it freezes this death to death" as "April's reopened wound is raw!" Of course, in the Introduction of *Imitations* Lowell unabashedly proclaims that he has made all sorts of cuts, additions, transpositions, and seems to think it all quite justified. But does a translator—even if he calls himself by another name, such as "imitator," supposed to set him beyond the reach of criticism—have the right to change the entire mood, intention, import of a poem? Of a serious poem by a genuine poet? At what point does an act of "imitation" become an immoral act?

In the interview already quoted, Lowell speaks of the closeness and kinship he felt for the Rilke and Rimbaud poems he translated. We have already seen what he has done to his kinsman Rilke; how has he dealt with that other, no less major kinsman, Rimbaud? If, for instance, one reads Lowell's version of *"Les Chercheuses de poux,"* whose title becomes "The Lice-Hunters" (though it should, of course, be "The Louse-hunters"; thus one says "fox-hunters" in English, not "foxes-hunters"), one would never guess that Rimbaud wrote it in mingled gratitude and amusement for two maiden aunts of his friend Izembard. Upon emerging from a week's stay in jail, the young poet was deloused by these two good Samaritans. The poem, irrespective of its autobiographical basis, evokes the mixture of relief and awkwardness a boy feels while lice are being crushed to death in his hair. Lowell's version seems to be about two wicked fairies that descend on a child, perhaps in his fever dream, and somehow cruelly torment him by— of all things—delousing him. That makes no sense and no poetry. As for *"Bateau ivre,"* Lowell announces that he has cut out a third of it; he calls this procedure "unclotting," and the poem "some of the more obscure Rimbaud." What he does keep, however, does almost less justice to Rimbaud than what he omits. As if this were not enough,

Lowell takes a couple of poems by Rilke and adds to them stanzas of his own.

I could cite endlessly. What, for example, could be more distasteful than Lowell's taking three poems from Heine's final sequence, *Aus der Matratzengruft,* written with irony, tenderness, and no mawkish self-pity from the very deathbed, and turning these immensely simple yet trenchant poems into maundering, anachronistic, rhythmless lucubrations? One quatrain must illustrate the whole shameful procedure. Heine writes: "My day was merry, happy was my night./ My people cheered me on whenever I smote/ The lyre of poetry. My song was joy and fire,/ It kindled many a lovely blaze." No great poetry in this particular stanza, only the prideful invocation of past happiness, and, in the German, a graceful movement: *"Mein Tag war heiter, glücklich meine Nacht./ Mir jauchzte stets mein Volk, wenn ich die Leier/ Der Dichtkunst schlug. Mein Lied war Lust and Feuer,/ Hat manche schöne Gluten angefacht."* Lowell comes up with this: "My zenith was luckily happier than my night:/ whenever I touched the lyre of inspiration, I smote/ the Chosen People. Often—all sex and thunder—/ I pierced those overblown and summer clouds. . . ." This is a painful mixture of deliberate and inadvertent misreading. To translate *Lust* as "sex" ("lust") is to perpetuate a traditional freshman boner; the rest may be wilful distortion. Heine is happy that both his public life ("day") and his love life ("night") were fun; Lowell's pessimism has to change this to some kind of glum parabola (from zenith to night). Heine says that his poetry was beloved by his public; Lowell turns this into Heine's allegedly unrelenting attack on— whom? The Jews? The Germans? But Heine was never consistent in any of his likes or dislikes. He says his poetry was joyous and fierce (romance and satire), and that it stirred up some pretty passions (this could be taken literally and ironically). Lowell has Heine somehow deflating his readers with sex and anger. Lowell's image does not work: if the readers are pompous, overblown clouds, why bring in "summer" with its positive connotation?

An imitation such as "Heine Dying in Paris" is not only an act of poetic vandalism, it is also a falsification of Heine's life and of Heine's evaluation of his life. Ostensibly rendering Heine's spirit if not his letter, Lowell is actually lessening the man's human stature (ambiguous as it was) as well as his poetic gifts. This, perpetrated on a dead and defenseless poet, is an act of double indecency. And such cavalier insouciance is rampant in *Imitations*. For example, Rilke's poem that Lowell translates as "Pigeons," and whose original he identifies as *"Die Tauben,"* is not at all *"Die Tauben,"* written in Paris in 1913, but the last of a series of verse letters to Erika Mitterer entitled "For Erika, on the Feast of Praise," dated Ragaz 1926, only four months before the poet's death. But what are we to expect from Lowell who says in the interview I have been quoting from that these imitations "were both a continuation of my own bias and a release from myself." A curious contradiction that! And the Introduction to *Imitations* begins: "This book is partly self-sufficient and separate from its sources, and should be first read as a sequence, one voice running through many personalities, contrasts and repetitions." Not only is this megalomania, it is also, worse yet, nonsense. A book made up of so many diverse ingredients can neither be a sequence nor tell us much about the translator beyond something about his translatorial taste and competence. And if one voice really runs through the whole enterprise, the enterprise must be biased and sick to the core. Finally, I doubt that anyone who "first" reads this book "as a sequence" can be expected to come back for a second helping of any kind.

The begetter of Lowell's imitations is, without question, Pound, and particularly the Pound of the versions from Propertius. But though I am no great admirer of Pound's Propertius (and even less of such jesuitical champions of Pond's Propertius as Hugh Kenner), I cannot be wholly unmoved by Propertius's Pound, that is to say, by what Propertius brought out in Pound. But it is precisely because Pound was able to ignore his original so sublimely, and because Pound is a great enough poet in his own right, that the damage to Sextus Propertius becomes an homage to Ezra Pound and English free verse. Lowell, however, is not that free from his models, nor has his free verse the energy and variety of Pound's. It is the neither-fish-nor-fowlness of Lowell's imitations, plus all the red herring they contain, that makes them perverse as translation and unpalatable as poetry. And though there may be only a tenuous connection between literature and morality, there seems to me to be a more demonstrable one between this kind of translation and immorality.

Yet the fault is not entirely that of the poet-translator who, puffed up with a mixture of merited and unmerited praise, loses his sense of judgment. Almost as much to blame are the critics who well-nigh unanimously acclaimed *Imitations* at its publication in 1961, and the critics who in the years since then have not dared to raise a dissenting voice. Typical of the less than enthusiastic reviews was that by Louis Simpson in this journal, which, after some well-taken strictures, nevertheless concluded that Lowell's "translations of Rimbaud and Rilke, for example, are interesting in poetic terms—that is, in every line difficulties of sound and meaning are resolved. To check his 'imitations' against the originals is to learn something about the tact of poetry." That last sentence is not only a gem of overstatement, it is even an inadvertent truth—if one can learn to identify something elusive by its total absence. Hugh B. Staples, in his *Robert Lowell: The First Twenty Years,* considers these imitations "more than translations." As Mies van der Rohe propounded a kind of architecture in which "less is more," Lowell may have produced a type of translation in which more is less.*

---

* Lowell's *Phaedra* is a dramatic imitation: it does to Racine's play what *Imitations* does to the poems it attacks. Two examples will have to suffice. *"J'ai revu l'ennemi qui j'avais éloigné:/ Ma blessure trop vive aussitôt a saigné./ Ce n'est plus une ardeur dans mes veines cachée:/ C'est Vénus toute entière à sa proie attachée"* becomes ". . . I saw Hippolytus/ each day, and felt my ancient, venomous/ passion tear my body limb from limb;/ naked Venus was clawing down her victim." No comment could be as damning as mere juxtaposition, and I offer none. (I cannot, however, help wondering whether Venus became naked by way of fractured French: *"toute entière*—in the altogether.) And again: *"O toi, qui vois la honte où je suis descendue,/ Implacable Vénus, suis-je assez confondue?/ Tu ne saurais plus loin pousser ta*

To turn now to Lowell's most recent dramatic version, *Prometheus Bound*. He calls it "derived from Aeschylus," and I am forced to conclude that Lowell's derivations are no better than his imitations. Modern dramatists have frequently retold Greek myths or Greek dramas, even Greek dramas about Greek myths. The aim of these versions has always been to find a contemporary interpretation or application of the time-honored, timeless originals, so that what emerged was a new work by Molière or Giraudoux, by Kleist or Hebbel, that was an integral part of its author's *oeuvre*. Lowell's *Prometheus Bound* sets out, likewise, to be "an unbinding of Prometheus for us." In the same program note, Lowell asserts that though "nothing is modernised . . . my own concerns and worries and those of the times seep in." Lowell also affirms that there are no tanks or cigarette lighters in the play. True. There are, however, microbes, phalanxes, wastes of the moon, and various references and allusions to atomic cataclysm, to the Freudian son cutting off (in Lowell's flavorsomely idiomatic language) "his father's balls," to the war in Vietnam. But that kind of seepage is only natural.

What is unnatural about this play is that it is not as a whole about anything identifiable. Of drama as such there is not a great deal in Aeschylus, but at least we know what the issue is: power and intellect join hands to rule the world, power usurps the throne and casts down intellect, power finds (this is only hinted at in this first play of the trilogy) that it needs intellect to save it from self-destruction. In Lowell there is only generalized violence; expatiation on a variety of muddy issues (and mud, as Francis Fergusson has noted, is a dominant presence in the play); and indulgence in a thick, clotted prose full of

---

cruauté./ Ton triomphe est parfait; tous les traits ont porté" becomes "Implacable Aphrodite, now you see/ the depths to which your tireless cruelty/ has driven Phaedra—here is my bosom:/ every thrust and arrow has struck home." It will be noted that even where the meaning is more or less conveyed, the exquisite cadences of the original verge on, or indeed hurtle into, cacophony. What we are left with is (in a line of Hippolytus's perhaps significantly not translated by Lowell) *"Cette indigne moitié d'une si belle histoire!"*

headstrong, runaway images. The language is something of a cross between Abraham Cowley and André Breton, but with a typically Lowellian savagery informing most of it. The violence of the diction and the limpness of the "action" form about the only notable conflict in this work, which does, in a way, manage the impossible—to be more static than Aeschylus's drama.

If one looks very hard, one may catch references—besides those already mentioned to the Bomb and the Vietnam war—to the plight of the powerless intellectual in the Great Society; worthy themes all, but none is developed, nothing goes deeper than surface ripples. There are felicitous lines and occasional forceful tropes. Thus Prometheus says of men, "I gave them hope, blind hopes! When one blind hope lifts, another drifts down to replace it. Men see much less surely now, but they suffer less—they can hardly draw breath now without taking hope." Or this, from Io about her growing up, "I could speak to the cattle. Later, I could speak to the herdsmen. Later, I could speak to my father." But there is also an abundance of nonworking imagery, blindly drifting tropes: "When I close my eyes, I am able to think. I can almost move. In the darkness, the stars move down on us like burning metal." How do we get from closed eyes to stars? And if the stars shower us with sizzling metal, doesn't that interfere with our thinking? Again, Io says: "I seem to wade through my own heaviness, as if I were a pasture sinking back into a marsh." This conjures up a pasture wading through a marsh; moreover, wading through implies emergence, whereas sinking is submergence. But most typical is this from Prometheus to Io: "Water spiders will slow and clot on the thick syrup of your shadow." That is not metaphor, merely mucilage.

Whole paragraphs are murky. Thus Prometheus says, "I saw the head of Cronus was a slab of meat, and it seemed to me if I could cut through the slab of meat, I would find a silver ball. The ball was there, it cracked open, inside it another, and another and another, and then suddenly, the head of Cronus, my own head, and the heads of all the gods were broken spheres, all humming and vibrating with silver wires. The whole world was an infinite sphere of intelligence." This is an uneasy mixture of Andrew Marvell and René Magritte. But as for meaning: if Cronus is a fool, why are there all those silver balls of mind in him? Why should mind be a set of Chinese boxes, or balls? And what are silver wires doing *inside* those balls? And how do the spheres continue to hum and vibrate (i.e., function) when they are cracked open? Such imagery troubles one on the page; on the stage, it absolutely refuses to move forward.

One of the sources of confusion in the play is that it keeps contradicting itself. On the simplest level we get Ocean saying that one of his hands is paralyzed "from managing . . . this big bird" on which he rides. A few lines later he tells us "I guided him with my mind. No reins or bit." On a profounder level, Prometheus regrets: "I should have been more loyal to the idiocy of things," yet this is contradicted by what the *status quo* harbors: "The nothingness of our beginning is hard at work to bury us." These statements often sound wonderful until one starts to analyze them: "We have always wanted to escape with our lives from life"—upon scrutiny, this apparently penetrating paradox means either that we don't want to die or that we don't really want to live, probably true both ways but not very startling in either. Or again, "I know that I must suffer, because I suffer without grandeur or nobility"; this rings out like a giant aperçu, but proves to be only a medium-size non sequitur. Perhaps, however, we should examine a longer sample; here is a fragment of Prometheus's interminable prophecy to Io: "You will run faster than you ever ran before, but more peacefully now, as if you know [sic] the flies would never catch up, that now you had only to fight off the death-stings of your own body, that hound-pack of affliction, closing in to kill you, poor bleeding hound, your tongue dripping, your teeth snapping, the fur of some animal darting before you, grizzled white mixed with the red hairs, like the beard of Zeus, but no face there, no flesh, only a force dragging you forward to your death, a power so empty, so tireless and so cruel, it could only come from God." One gets a sense of meaningless, luxuriating brutality; of metaphors that clash and collide and cancel one another out—unless they don't make sense to begin with: what sort of an animal could Io, poor, persecuted cow, possibly be hounding? And why?

The one episode that seems to exercise Lowell's imagination is the story of Io. In seemingly endless speeches, Io and Prometheus rehearse her seduction by Zeus, her frantic, tortured wanderings, and her ghastly death to come. In fact, it is as if Lowell described at least three separate death scenes for her, each more agonizing than the previous, yet, for all that, not very different. The attitudes toward women and sex in the play are about as horrified as those toward despotism and death. Thus there is a gratuitous attack on Prometheus's wife, on the female Seabirds (Lowell's version of the chorus of Oceanids) who are made even less appealing than in Aeschylus, and, in a way, on Io, whose sufferings are dwelt on with monstrous relish. And what is one to make of Io's account of the first results of impregnation by Zeus: "two flies, as big as . . . thumbs . . . had crawled from my swollen stomach, half-dead, and already beginning to mate," an event on which Hera commented, "When women are warm enough to make love, the gods send them flies. The flies rise from your sticky flesh, are warmed by your heat, and kept alive by the blood from your thighs [!] or the milk from your breasts." We have come a long way from Aeschylus, but in what direction?

I find it impossible to say what the meaning or purpose of Lowell's play is. During certain scenes when Prometheus staunchly resists direct or indirect blandishments to play ball with Zeus, I almost wonder whether the whole thing is not an allegory of Lowell's famous refusal to appear at a garden party on Lyndon Johnson's lawn. If not that, it is just an all-around scattering of animosities, some justifiable, many not even fathomable. Structured hatred has produced, among others, some of the great plays of Ibsen and Strindberg; promiscuous hostility can at best, as here, yield a few good but disconnected moments.

Such as it is, Lowell's play did not deserve the treatment meted out to it by Jonathan Miller, who directed it for the Yale Drama School last May. In a program note characteristically five times longer than the author's, Miller explained his method. Prometheus figures in a myth that has "mysterious and erratic power." We learn next that "speaking with strict accuracy, plays of this sort [Greek drama? Plays based on myth? Plays whose protagonist is chained to a rock?] are located in something which for want of a better word we might call antiquity." Traditional productions of them, we learn, don't work, "But the point about these plays is that in some mysterious way their dramatic thrust seems to survive and transcend the time and space in which they were originally set." For want of a better word, we might call such utterances fatuity of the most advanced sort. Next we read that "contextual dislocation" is required for these myths to "become renewed and invigorated." In other words, we must update the play, see "round the edges of the text," but be careful to avoid changing dates only "to create a chic shock." The great difficulty with *Prometheus* is, it seems, that it "takes place in a primeval limbo," has characters "little more than talking vapors" and that any "antique" or "literal" rendition "would be almost ludicrous and even a bit pansy." Particularly to be dreaded are the "mechanical constraints indicated by the stage directions."

So Miller picked the early seventeenth century to set his play in, because it was a cultural watershed, because classical forms were then being reprocessed, and because the period was "full of peculiarly horrible politics . . . The Thirty Years War, Regicide . . . military theocracy." As a result, the setting (beautifully designed by Michael Annals) represents the outer walls of a "shattered castle keep" with strong overtones of the inside of Piranesi's dungeons. Thus the set suggests both that Prometheus is inside a dungeon and that he romps around outside it on a platform across a moat; and, to create total confusion, Lowell's text repeatedly locates him in "the thin, disabling air of this mountain top." Hephaestus and his crew seem, in the dark, to chain him to something as he utters piercing cries. When the lights go on, he is unchained and his trousers are bloodied, which, as Francis Fergusson has pointed out, may mean that he has been castrated. Thereafter, he moves about quite freely, despite frequent references to his immobilizing chains (presumably those "mechanical constraints

[of] the stage directions" by which no director worth his salt would be hamstrung or castrated). The costumes are shabby and seventeenth-century; Miller tells us they stem from engravings by Jacques Callot, and indeed the characters look like disbanded *lansquenets,* impoverished petty gentry, or, rather, like a bunch of impecunious strolling players impersonating them. Ocean, for example, appears in a battered admiral's hat and epaulets, and the Seabirds seem to be wearing the hand-me-downs of the lady of the manor. When the Seabirds harangue Prometheus, they often read from their schoolgirl slates; when Prometheus utters some of his homiletic tirades, they take these down as dictation on the slates. Sometimes he goes too fast for them and is obliged to slow down or repeat a word or two. When Prometheus tells Io she will bear a child to Zeus, the three virtuous ladies of the chorus avert their eyes and cover their ears in mock, or perhaps real, horror—who is to say what in this production is mock, and what real? When Io—desperate, tormented Io—asks Prometheus, "Tell me where I must go," she playfully slaps his arm and pettishly stamps her foot. When Prometheus tells her that he need not describe all the monsters she'll encounter—"When you have seen one, you have seen them all"—everything stops while the entire cast enjoys a hearty laugh. At the end of Act One, where Io is heartrendingly beseeching Prometheus to help her, all go off merrily for an intermission: the supposedly chained Prometheus offers his arm to the allegedly fly-haunted Io, and they walk off together across the fosse followed by the Seabirds animatedly chattering away among themselves. As Act Two begins, they all come out in the same informal way, plainly a troupe of down-at-heel actors in that most horrible age of regicide, military theocracy, and Puritan shut-down of the theatres.

It is clear that Miller does not believe in doing things by halves: why settle for being "almost ludicrous and a bit pansy" when you can be absolutely laughable and completely camp? On opening night, he also invoked Brechtian alienation, but that holds no water here, either: in Brecht there are full-bodied plots against which the alienation effect can pit itself; in Aeschylus the very remoteness, superhumanness, and elevated tone make alienation redundant. No, in reducing *Prometheus Bound* to the level of seeing "round the edge of the text," or, in other words, beyond the fringe, Jonathan Miller was simply using that directorial prerogative made famous in our time by Elia Kazan and especially Peter Brook, which consists of the director's virtually rewriting the play, and which corresponds on another plane to Lowell's imitations of Rilke, Rimbaud, and the rest.

There are two principles at work here. First, by adapting a celebrated poem or play, or by "dislocating" the play one is directing, one cashes in on the original's prestige while also exhibiting one's prowess in the alterations; at the same time, one can always blame the foreignness or intractability of the original for one's failures. Secondly, one uses this as a surrogate for whatever creativity one finds oneself lacking. A poet runs out of poetry of his own, so he makes it out of someone else's, rather like the fly that lays its eggs in the living body of a certain caterpillar for the larvae to feed on. A director wishes he were a playwright, and, by way of staging it, rewrites the play entrusted to him. It is all part of that most terrible contemporary phenomenon in the arts that mistakes for inspired innovation what is merely lack of respect.

APPRAISALS

Irvin Ehrenpreis
The Age of Lowell

For an age of world wars and prison states, when the Faustian myth
of science produces the grotesquerie of fall-out shelters, the decorous
emotion seems a fascinated disgust. After outrage has exhausted itself in
contempt, after the mind has got the habit of Dallas and South Africa,
the shudder of curiosity remains. Every morning we think, something
new and insufferable is about to happen: what is it? Among living
poets writing in English nobody has expressed this emotion with the
force and subtlety of Robert Lowell. In an undergraduate poem Lowell
described himself as longing for the life of straightforward beliefs
and deeds, of simple lust, conventional faith and boyish sports. But
'sirens sucked me in', he said; and painful, feverish contemplation
was his fate:

> On me harsh birches, nursing dew,
> Showered their warm humidity.
>
> ('The Dandelion Girls')

Like Baudelaire, he saw things so disturbing that they almost kept him
from making them into poetry.

Yet the confident life of public action might have seemed young
Lowell's certain destiny. For his family line ran about as high as an
American genealogy could go. His mother was descended from
Edward Winslow, a Pilgrim Father who came to America on the

From *Stratford upon Avon Studies* 7 ed. John Russell Brown and Bernard Harris.
By permission of Irvin Ehrenpreis and Edward Arnold (Publishers) Ltd.
Copyright © 1965 by Edward Arnold (Publishers) Ltd.

Mayflower. Edward's son was a mighty Indian killer and a governor of Plymouth Colony. Lowell's mother also traced herself to the New Hampshire frontiersman John Stark, who was made a colonel at Bunker Hill and a general in the Revolutionary War. Lowell's father, though trained as a naval officer, belonged to the intellectual family that produced teachers and clergymen as well as fighters. The original R. T. S. Lowell, five generations ago, was also a naval officer. Another namesake, Lowell's great-grandfather, 'delicate, sensitive, strangely rarefied', was a poet best known for a ballad on the relief of Lucknow, and spent four years as headmaster of St. Mark's, one of the most fashionable boys' schools in the United States. Lowell's great-great-uncle, James Russell Lowell, a Harvard professor and one of the famous poets of his era, became ambassador to the court of St. James's. For most of the memories on which Lowell was bred, Puritan New England, especially Boston, provided the setting; and in the history of the Massachusetts Bay Colony he could find his Tree of Jesse.

It was on these very elements that he was to turn his first great storm of poetic disgust. They supplied the object of a clamorous repudiation. The shape the outburst took, however, depended less on ancestry than on a set of experiences that seem to have determined Lowell's original literary colour: his meeting with the circle of John Crowe Ransom and Allen Tate, his conversion to Roman Catholicism and his dramatic response to the second world war.

At St. Mark's School, Lowell found his interest in poetry encouraged by the poet Richard Eberhart, one of the teachers. He began experimenting with free verse but soon switched to stanzaic forms. As an undergraduate at Harvard he went to see Robert Frost, bearing a 'huge epic' on the First Crusade. The great man perused a page, told the visitor that he lacked 'compression', and read him Collins's 'How Sleep the Brave' as an example of something 'not too long'. For a period Lowell tried to write simple, Imagistic poems like those of W. C. Williams; but the university around him seemed less than a nest of singing birds, and he heeded a recommendation that he should study under John Crowe Ransom. In the middle of his undergraduate career, after a summer spent with Allen Tate, he left Harvard altogether and went to Kenyon College, in rural Ohio, where Ransom was teaching.

For a while now, Lowell even lived in Ransom's house, and later shared lodgings with two other young writers, one of whom, Peter Taylor, has published a short story based on their college friendship ('1939'). During these years, the critic Randall Jarrell taught English at Kenyon, and he too lived a while with the Ransoms. It seems obvious that the network of literary affiliations gave the young student, who had been growing 'morose and solitary' at home, a welcome substitute for blood relations who felt small sympathy with his talent. Lowell often describes himself as belonging to the 'second generation' of the Fugitives; he spent long periods in a quasi-filial or fraternal connection with three or four of the authors he met in the years before the war, and he speaks of them with the sort of loyalty one extends to kin. The conservative politics, strong but orthodox religious faith and high literary standards to which these Southerners were attached must have seemed to him seductive alternatives to the commonplace Republicanism, mechanical church-going and materialist aspirations that characterised a 'Boston' formed (as he saw it) by successive lines of Puritans, Unitarians and low-church Episcopalians. To Lowell the home of his forebears stood for a rootless but immobile sterility.

In 1940, when he took a step towards establishing a family of his own, Lowell not surprisingly married another writer, the novelist Jean Stafford, whose 'flaming insight' he commemorates in a recent poem. He was also converted to Roman Catholicism, the church peculiarly associated in Boston with the large population descended from humble Irish immigrants, natural enemies, in politics and culture, of his own class. But the poet already felt committed to a kind of moral vitality that could for only a limited time be expressed in Roman terms. During the period when his new-found church was something defiant of the Boston he had repudiated, and so long as the language, symbols and ritual represented materials to be conquered and employed for explosive purposes, he could use Catholicism as an ingredient of poetry. But when it was only the faith he had to accept, the church came to seem as oppressive and self-contradictory as the code of his native class.

It was during the years of his first marriage and his adherence to the church that Lowell's earliest books of poetry appeared. Apart from what had come out in an undergraduate magazine, the first poems he published were a pair in the *Kenyon Review* 1939. But years went by before any successors could be seen in print, partly because the few he wrote were rejected when he sent them out. Then in 1943 about a dozen of his poems turned up in the literary quarterlies, to be followed the next year by a collection, *Land of Unlikeness*. This gathering, withholding and sudden releasing of his work is typical of the poet's method; for he labours over his poems continually and plans each collection as a sequence, the opening and closing poems in each making a distinct introduction and conclusion, and the movement between them tending from past to present, from question to resolution, from ambiguous negation to hesitant affirmative.

Above the influences of Ransom and Tate, or the steady use of Catholic religious imagery, or the many motifs drawn from Boston and New England, the most glaring feature of Lowell's two earliest volumes was a preoccupation with the second world war. Not long after the United States joined that war, he committed the most dramatic public act of his life. Characteristically, this act seemed at once violent and passive, and was calculated to make his parents very uncomfortable. In what turned out to be no more than preliminary steps, he twice tried to enlist in the navy but was rejected. Soon, however, the mass bombing of non-combatants shocked his moral principles; and when he was called up under the Selective Service Act, he declared himself a conscientious objector. Rather than simply appear before the responsible board and declare his convictions, he refused to report at all, and thus compelled the authorities to prosecute him.

In order to give his deed the widest possible significance, he released to the press a thousand-word open letter to President Roosevelt. Here Lowell drew repeated attention to the historic eminence of his ancestors. He described himself as belonging to a family that had 'served in all our wars, since the Declaration of Independence'; he told the President that the Lowell family traditions, 'like your own, have always found their fulfillment in maintaining, through responsible participation in both civil and military services, our country's freedom and honor'. He said that he had tried to enlist when the country was in danger of invasion but that this danger was past, and the intention of bombing Japan and Germany into submission went against the nation's established ideals. He could not participate in a war, Lowell said, that might leave Europe and China 'to the mercy of the U.S.S.R., a totalitarian tyranny committed to world revolution'.

Twenty years later he was still signing open letters of protest to newspapers; and although his opinions had altered, their direction had not shifted. 'No nation should possess, use, or retaliate with its bombs', he wrote in a 1962 symposium. 'I believe we should rather die than drop our own bombs.' It is suggestive of the poet's sensibility that he should link suicide with mass murder, as though the way to prevent the second might be to commit the first. The themes of self-destruction and assassination are often joined in his work, the one apparently redeeming or proving the altruism of the other. Yet parricide becomes a mythical, guilt-ridden route to justice and liberty; for by throwing over the traditional family pieties, the young Lowell seems to have felt he was destroying his begetters and oppressors.

II

The poems that appeared in *Land of Unlikeness* (1944) were mostly written during a year Lowell spent with the Tates after leaving Kenyon College. In them he devoted himself mainly to a pair of themes reflecting recent history. One was the unchristian character of the Allies' role in the second world war; the other was the causal connection between the doctrines of America's founders and the desolate condition, spiritual and material, of the country in the thirties. Looking back, Lowell saw in the ideals and motives of his ancestors the same contradictions, the same denial of a Christ they professed to worship, that made his own world a land of unlikeness, i.e. a place obliterating the image of divinity, a culture where the old metaphors that made created beings recall their creator, no longer operated. Those who had flown from persecution came here to persecute the red men; those who hated war made war on nature, plundering whales and neighbours for unspiritual profit.

In order to dramatise and generalise this view, he drew parallels between divine and human history: between the war and Doomsday, between the dust bowl sharecroppers and Cain. And he set up antitheses: between profits and mercy, between political slogans and charity. To the second world war he opposed Christ. In the social and political theories of the Fugitives, Lowell found support for his tendency to identify degeneracy with the city, the machine and Roosevelt's centralised democracy, even as he associated true civilisation with rural, aristocratic society. And since the South itself was yielding to the rapid movement from one set of conditions to the other, Lowell could apply his argument to humanity in general, through parallels drawn from *Genesis* and *Revelation,* from the myth of Troy, and from history. Thus the advent of cosmopolitan industrialism becomes a sign that we are all descended from Cain; the first Eden becomes a symbol of that ante-bellum, ostensibly Augustan society which the North supposedly destroyed; the fall of Troy becomes the analogue of the defeat of the South. Since the new war had the effect of speeding the hated process, it was easily drawn into this aspect of Lowell's rhetoric.

By the time he composed these poems, Lowell had given up free verse and was writing obscure poems in metre in a style of his own. Most of those in *Land of Unlikeness* are savagely ironical. Besides employing puns or conceits repeatedly and with great earnestness, he brought in hackneyed phrases and common tags of quotations, giving sarcastic new directions to their meaning. He invented grotesque metaphors, such as 'Christ kicks the womb's hearse'. Although the stanzas of most of the poems are elaborate, the rhythms are heavy, the sounds are cluttered, alliteration occurs often and unsubtly.

Into such verses he pressed enough violence of feeling to stun a sensitive ear. Certain dramatic monologues and visionary pieces on religious themes make the greatest uproar. The tighter the stanza forms, the wilder the bitterness: erratic rhythms, blasphemous images, deliberately hollow rhetoric erupt over the object of his onslaught. But instead of the tight form providing an ironic contrast or intensifying counterpoint to the violent tone, it seems arbitrary. The mind that follows the form seems cut off from the mouth that screams the sacrilege:

> In Greenwich Village, Christ the Drunkard brews
> Gall, or spiked bone-vat, siphons His bilged blood
> Into weak brain-pans and unseasons wood. . . .
>
> ('Christ for Sale')

In another poem the speaker is a slum mother apostrophising the corpse of her baby, who has died on Christmas Day, 1942 (soon after the sinking of the British aircraft carrier *Ark Royal*):

> So, child, unclasp your fists,
> And clap for Freedom and Democracy;
> No matter, child, if Ark Royal lists
> Into the sea;
> Soon the Leviathan
> Will spout American.
>
> ('The Boston Nativity')

In this kind of satire the irony sounds so wild that most readers ignore the poet's meaning while observing his frenzy. The caricature of the nativity scene does not succeed in mocking America's moral pretensions during the war. It only forces upon one's perceptions the distorted religiosity of the writer. After all, by Lowell's own argument, there could be no real heroes in history apart from Christ. As in Tate's 'Aeneas at Washington', the Southern gentleman comes finally to seem less like Hotspur than like Richard II, standing for ideals he did not die to defend.

Yet not every speech is a tantrum. In a few of the poems Lowell's detachment suggests that his churnings, in the others, are an effort to produce a heat wave in a naturally cold climate. Observation, dry and wry commentary, fascinated disgust—these are the marks of his subtler self, and these are what appear, for example, in 'The Park Street Cemetery'. This poem, a survey of the tombstones in a Boston graveyard, has less violence than distaste in its tone. Lowell treats the site as a repository of those Puritan colonists who bequeathed to the America they founded their own confusion of grace with fortune. The form is appropriately relaxed: three stanzas, each of seven unrhymed, irregular lines; and the poet ends not with a scream but a deadnote:

> The graveyard's face is painted with facts
> And filagreed swaths of forget-me-nots.

The positive doctrines of *Land of Unlikeness* seem less significant than the negative directions. Whether Lowell espouses Southern agrarianism or Roman Catholicism, his principles attract him less as ideals of aspiration than as possibilities disdained by his ancestors. Against early New England the real charge he makes is that it failed to meet its own ultimate standards; for Lowell is after all another sober moralist with a Puritan's severity. He scolds Boston as Blake scolded London: for the death of vision and the death of conscience. Nowhere does he imply that dogma bestows serenity, or that, as some Southerners would argue, the integrity of a ceremonious traditionalism outweighs the human misery on which it may rest.

For the poet, finally, the real problem remained unsolved. In most of this volume his best-integrated poems were his understatements; those that showed the highest technical ambition were bathetic. He had to find a style that would reconcile his interest in technique with his interest in justice, that would identify private with public disturbances. For such a style the elements lay not in the regularity of his stanzas, not in the depth of his piety, and not in his political judgments. It lay in Lowell's preoccupation with tone, in his humanitarian conscience, and in his sense of history. When he employed these to enlarge the meaning of an immediate personal experience, he produced the best poems in *Land of Unlikeness*: 'The Park Street Cemetery', 'In Memory of Arthur Winslow', 'Concord' and 'Salem'.

III

Not only the older writers belonging to the circle of Ransom and Tate but also several other critics gave unusual attention to *Land of Unlikeness*. It was praised briefly but intensely by F. W. Dupee and Arthur Mizener. There was a careful review by Blackmur and a eulogy by J. F. Nims. But when Lowell's next book *Lord Weary's Castle* appeared (1946), the critical reception became a thunder of welcome.

As usual, there is a link between the old work and the new. In the last poem of *Land of Unlikeness* the poet had mentioned the curse of 'exile' as the alternative to the blessing of Canaan: God offered Israel the choice, says the poet; and when Israel chose to turn away from God's 'wise fellowship', the outcome was Exile. The opening poem of *Lord Weary's Castle* is called 'The Exile's Return', suggesting a common theme for both books. But the theme has broadened. In the new collection the poet implies that nothing was or could be settled by the war. In rejecting divine leadership, it is moral justice, the creative principle bringing order out of chaos, that we have banished from its self-made home. Thus if the expatriate is taken to mean Christ, the lord still waits for the world he built to pay him his due homage. He still menaces us with the judgment that the war prefigured. As a creator, however, the Exile is also the poet or artist; and in this sense he wants to be paid for the truthful visions with which he has blessed an ungrateful world. For he holds out the threat of a poet's curse, and his isolation remains the mark of society's misdirection. In a private extension of this sense the Exile is Lowell himself, released from jail after serving about five months of the year and a day to which he had been sentenced. Coming back to ordinary routines, he meets in new forms the same moral issues he had wrestled with before his imprisonment.

All these implications are in 'The Exile's Return'. Here, an émigré comes back to his German home after the war, under the protection of American garrisons. But the shattered place looks the opposite of Eden; and if the first springtime brings lilies, it brings as well the agony of responsibility. To suggest the aspect of the neglected artist, Lowell crowds the poem with allusions to Mann's Tonio Kröger, who stood 'between two worlds' without feeling at home among either the bourgeoisie or the artists. To suggest the themes of heaven and hell, he has seasonal references to an infernal winter, a spring of rebirth, the 'fall' of autumn, and the entrance to Dante's hell. For the motifs of imprisonment and release he uses a jail-like hôtel-de-ville, a Yankee 'commandant' and a parcel of 'liberators' who are as yet innocent or 'unseasoned'.

In direct contrast, the closing poem of the book, 'Where the Rainbow Ends', deals with an American city, Boston, that has never been bombed but that faces the dissolution caused by decay of conscience. Not war but winter devastates this city. Not as a refugee but as a voluntary exile from worldliness, the poet-prophet offers his people the alternative to the Judgment prefigured by the cold season:

> What can the dove of Jesus give
> You now but wisdom, exile? Stand and live,
> The dove has brought an olive branch to eat.
>
> ('Where the Rainbow Ends')

Repeatedly in this book, Lowell shows an understanding of how his elemental powers might be fused, how his unnatural calmness of tone in dealing with horrifying material might be supported by an apparent casualness of style screening a meticulous exactness of underlying structure. His sense of the past justifies ironically the calmness of tone. For to the degree that one considers human misery and cruelty as the reflection of permanent instinct—rather than transient ignorance—one will view one's own corruption and one's neighbour's not with scandalised outbursts but with comprehending calm. Furthermore, through the distancing effect of history, as through the shaping effect of complex form, one can even achieve a coherent grasp of one's own deepest, most secret anguish. With these several powers Lowell also made good use of a set of influences that he had earlier felt only at some remove, as they were present in the work of Tate, Eliot and Ransom. These influences emanate from the great line of French Symbolists and post-Symbolists, to whom the 'modern' experimental movement in poetry owes its origin. When Lowell turned to Rimbaud, Valéry and Rilke for models, he was accepting the cosmopolitan conception of literature that American poets as diverse as Whitman and Pound have worked with.

The defect of *Lord Weary's Castle* is the same as that of *Land of Unlikeness*. In Whitman, Tate and Hart Crane, one cannot help noticing a habit of substituting rhetoric, in the form of self-conscious sublimity, for poetry. If Lowell, their heir, yields to this habit, it is because, like them, he has the highest conception of the poet's task. But the mere posture of soaring, the air of prophecy, does not make a speech either noble or prophetic. In Lowell's most commonly over-praised work, 'The Quaker Graveyard', the use of rhetoric joins with a denseness of symbolism to make a poem that seems more impressive for aspiration than for accomplishment.

Throughout this poem he contrasts two views of saving grace: the idea of a special gift to the elect, and the idea of something that infuses not merely all men but all creatures. The in-group's complacency Lowell attaches to the Protestant sects of colonial New England and to his patriotic cousin, who died at sea for a cause Lowell rejected. As a measure of the limitations of this ethic, which he associates with war-loving capitalism, Lowell invokes the great evolutionary chain of created beings. The world, he keeps saying, exists as a moral order in which separate men are not masters but participants: both the sea slime from which we rose and the whale that we plunder lie beneath the same law that subsumes humanity. To sectarian arrogance he opposes the innocence of the humbler orders of creation, for whom cruelty is an accident of their nature. As the solvent of arrogance he offers the Catholic compassion of Christ embodied in Mary his mother.

In Lowell's usual manner, the end of the poem recalls the beginning. We move back to the Quaker graveyard on Nantucket Island off the coast of Massachusetts. But where the initial scene was of violent death in a great war, the closing gives us the lifeless cemetery of wind and stone and tree. Now the poet glances back to the very start of the evolutionary process and contrasts that moment, when life and death were born together, with the present outlook of a corpse-littered sea. And suddenly the capacious cemetery of the Atlantic becomes a symbolic contrast to the filled graveyard of the Quakers: God has more room than this; the old covenant has given way to the new gospel.

In this fascinating work the failure of the rhetoric grows obvious if we notice the weakness of the poem's penultimate section. Here Lowell puts the snug, familiar salvation that his cousin might aspire to beside the Catholic vision of the universal but quite unknowable God reflected in the image of Our Lady of Walsingham. Though this passage is a deliberate understatement, the effect is not powerful by implication; rather, it sounds bathetic. Beyond human griefs or joys, says the poet, the Virgin

> knows what God knows,
> Not Calvary's Cross nor crib at Bethlehem
> Now, and the world shall come to Walsingham.

If we compare Lowell's two stanzas, in their attempt to express the inexpressible, with similar passages in Eliot's 'Dry Salvages' (which is, with *Lycidas,* one of the models for this poem), we must admit that there is a posed air, a willed simplicity, in Lowell's lines that never appears in, say, 'Lady, whose shrine stands on the promontory', etc. This forced tone seems the more regrettable because Lowell's passage is meant to deliver the positive alternative to the errors he denounces with such thoroughness. It is in the overcharged stretches of churning sounds, eruptive rhythm, and violent imagery that we seem to hear the authentic voice of the poet:

> In the great ash-pit of Jehoshaphat
> The bones cry for the blood of the white whale,
> The fat flukes arch and whack about its ears. . . .

We cannot help feeling that he enjoys his destructive vision in a way
not compatible with his role as prophet, moralist or recipient of wisdom.

In another long poem, 'At the Indian Killer's Grave', Lowell gives
a more appropriate display of his powers. The history of its composition
reminds us of his habitual alteration of his own work; for much of
the poem comes out of the 'Park Street Cemetery', and the closing lines
are a magnificent adaptation of verses from another early poem.
Moreover, as he transforms these materials, the poet enlarges their
meaning. Like the speaker in Tate's 'Ode to the Confederate Dead', the
poet here contemplates a graveyard where his direct or spiritual
ancestors are buried among their peers. Unlike Tate's speaker, however,
he searches for the meaning of their sins, not their virtues. Staring about
at the figures carved on the gravestones among the vegetation, he
contrasts the Puritan dead with the living Irish who now hold political
power in Boston. The sound of a train stopping underground makes
him think of time stopping and of the Judgment to come; and he
wonders about the fate of the Pilgrims' souls. He imagines the spirit
of the Red Indian chief, King Philip, addressing the Puritan Indian-
killers and reminding them that all their pretensions to being the
chosen of God have left them only the corrupted bodies that now serve
as carrion for sea-gulls. He looks at the toothed railing, thinks of
dragon's teeth, and ponders the double source, natural (i.e. Cadmean)
and spiritual (i.e. Adamic), of our instinct for evil. Then in a sudden,
astonishing close, the poet turns from the old law to the new, from
Adam to Christ; and he calls on the four evangelists to guide him
towards the inclusive faith of the Roman Catholic church, to a vision of
salvation that more than admits the Indian chief; for it promises
Philip that the blessed Virgin herself will deck out his head with
flowers:

> John, Matthew, Luke and Mark,
> Gospel me to the Garden, let me come
> Where Mary twists the warlock with her flowers—
> Her soul a bridal chamber fresh with flowers
> And her whole body an ecstatic womb,
> As through the trellis peers the sudden Bridegroom.

And there, in a fine identification of his private conversion with both the history of Massachusetts and the religious or mythical account of all human history, Lowell brings his poem to a close.

Generally, the poet sounds a tone of self-restraint, of calm but engrossed repugnance, that reminds one of Ransom's poems 'Necrological' and 'Armageddon'. This tone he drops appropriately in two counterbalanced passages: the outburst of Philip, who speaks with a savage violence of sound and image, and the lyric close and climax, when calm is replaced by rapture. The apparently loose-knit free associations rest on a carefully adjusted underpinning. Even the setting of the poet's meditation belongs to his subject, because the Puritan colonists brooded hourly upon death and the grave. They dressed in black and regarded the beauties of animate nature as bad diversions from the proper study of man, viz. death and judgment, heaven and hell. Nevertheless, they proudly gave themselves the title of the elect of God, promoting themselves to Paradise. It is a tremendous historical irony that their haughy Calvinism should have given way, in Boston, to the avowedly humble, Catholic faith of the Irish—to the church that in colonial times proselytised among the Indians instead of beheading them. In effect, the whore of Rome waltzes over the Puritan graves: 'the trollop dances on your skulls'.

A shimmering elaboration of imagery in the Symbolist manner connects the past and the present, the beginning of the poem with the end, the surface and the meaning. As the poet questions the spectacle before him, he wonders whether the fate of the dead is knowable or whether the pagan idea of vengeance may not be carried out, so that Philip may eternally scalp the self-styled righteous men (Blake's 'just man') who killed his people. This scalp-head-skull image appears again and again in the poem, reaching its most brilliant transformation at the end, when the Virgin is pictured as twisting Philip's 'warlock' or pigtail with flowers. Between these points the head becomes the English crown, responsible for building King's Chapel—a motif that opposes King Charles to King Philip. It then turns into the 'dome' of the Statehouse that replaced the royal authority. Next, Philip's head reappears on a 'platter' or gravestone. The phrasing recalls St. John and therefore the apostle or evangelist Philip. As a prophet now, the Indian can address his damned enemies and point out that the Catholics are raised over their heads. The dome becomes a globe that is the natural world, rejected (so says the poet) by the Puritans as they 'hurled/Anathemas at nature'. The head reappears in the headstones of the graves and finally in Mary's handling of Philip's head.

Parallel to these metamorphoses move the images of the garden. We start in the desolate garden of the cemetery, which the Puritans have reached in place of Paradise. Shrubs and sculpture remind one of similar scenes. So the view expands into both the Public Garden, where the Beacon Hill brahmins walked, and the Boston Common, which was more likely the playground of the Irish. Lowell toys with the ironies implicit in 'garden' and 'common', and with the further irony that though fashionable Beacon Hill is where his own class live, it is topped by the Statehouse that in effect belongs to the Irish. Under the Common, meanwhile, runs the subway, analogue of hell, with its serpentine green trains, symbolic of time. Easily enough, the Garden and the Common expand into the whole 'land' that the Puritans denounced and despoiled. This contracts at once into the mud that buries them now. The buildings around the Common are like palisades around the early settlements, intended, however, not to keep the wilderness from swallowing the villages but to keep, as it were, the remnant of natural ground from spreading. Finally, the motif reminds the poet of the ground in which Cadmus sowed the dragon's teeth, emblematic of original sin.

IV

It seems remarkable that while some of the best poems in *Lord Weary's Castle* were imitations, or free English versions, of works in other languages, some of the least effective were dramatic monologues. In a poem like 'The Ghost', based upon Sextus Propertius, Lowell performed a superb job of giving his own voice to another poet. But in the double-monologue 'The Death of the Sheriff', the structure of which depends upon changes of voice and shifts in point of view, the speaker's smothered, crowded, dull murmur hardly alters from beginning to end. It's as though Lowell had too much to say to be able to submerge himself in an imaginary personality, and for that very reason found it easy to submerge a sympathetic author's character in his own.

His next book, *Mills of the Kavanaughs* (1951), brought these complementary tendencies to a crisis. The unqualified successes in it are a dazzling pastiche of Virgil and an adaptation of Werfel. But the longest and most ambitious works are five attempts at narrative dramatised through monologue. In four of these one feels that the poet has contrived situations offering the greatest opportunities for allusiveness and symbolism, and has sacrificed to such opportunities the absolutely essential narrative line upon which any dramatic monologue depends. He had obviously worked with immense pains over the title poem, running to more than five hundred lines, many of them beautiful evocations of the Maine landscape that gives the piece its setting. Nevertheless, although the plot would sound irresistibly sensational in summary—dealing with the madness and suicide of a patrician Catholic who married his sister by adoption—the poem is so hemmed in by cross-references and correspondences as to be wholly static. At one point Lowell goes so far as to match the number of a figure on a bird guide, once memorised by the protagonist, to the number of the stanza in which the man tries to recall the bird's name. The same substitution of arbitrary parallelism for narrative drama almost makes an impasse out of the last poem in the book, 'Thanksgiving's Over'. Here Lowell sends his main characters to a church on Thirty-First Street in New York, and situates their home next to the Third Avenue elevated train ('El'), in order to supply allusions to the Trinity.

Yet 'Thanksgiving's Over' is one of the most revealing of Lowell's poems. Published two years after his divorce from Jean Stafford and the year after his marriage to the essayist Elizabeth Hardwick, it comes from a time when he no longer felt buoyed up by the church.

Louise Bogan called the book *Mills of the Kavanaughs* a 'dark midpoint' in his development, 'which must in some way be transcended'. In this closing poem Lowell shows that he was passing the midpoint and going on. All the ingredients of his false rhetorical style are here: the monologue, the nightmare, madness, murder, suicide and blasphemy. But the implications are not the old ones.

To the speaker of the poem Lowell gives the voice of a man who has lost the struggle to maintain his Christian faith and now ponders the events that culminated in his failure. He is a Roman Catholic, a New Yorker and a widower, whose young, demented wife had believed herself impregnated by the Holy Ghost. After she tried to kill herself by jumping from a window, he sent her to a sanatorium in the mountains of Vermont, where she died. It is now Thanksgiving Day, 1942, and Michael the widower half remembers, half dreams of his dead wife. As he tries to make sense out of the monstrous experiences, he thinks he hears her talking.

The themes of the wife's increasingly disconnected chatter are love and peace, her assumption being that these are united in the church. But as her incoherence deepens, it becomes clear that the serenity she offers is available only to those who are as credulous as children. Within the wife's character, therefore, the themes are split so as to suggest the opposition between religious doctrines and human nature. She would like to feel love as spiritual charity, and therefore denies her passionate impulses. She would like morality to issue from the passive acceptance of authority, and so she denies the need for a struggle between the good and evil in our constitution. Through suppression, her hidden passions become adulterous lusts projected on other persons. Towards Michael her affection turns to jealousy, and she feels like killing him. When this wish is thwarted, the hate turns inward, and she tries to kill herself.

The poet implies that by giving up religion one might resolve some of these conflicts, but one would then have to face the pain of a life without ultimate meaning. Michael must choose between abandoning God and abandoning his rational conscience. As the peculiarly shocking symbol of his dilemma the poet focuses on the doctrine of the Trinity. Thus the action of the poem is set at the very end of the Trinity season, the week before Advent Sunday. Since the third person of the Trinity appears iconographically as a dove, there is a profusion of sacrilegious bird imagery. In order to involve other aspects of doctrine of ritual, the poet complicates the central theme with allusions to the Eucharist (etymologically 'thanksgiving'), the Incarnation (as enacted in the Annunciation), and so forth. As a kind of parody of each, he produces natural analogues. Within the fantasy of the girl's unconscious the Trinity takes the form of a love triangle. She confuses the Dove with a celluloid parrot and imagines herself pregnant with birds. Since the conventional dish at an American Thanksgiving dinner is a turkey, the poet can introduce grotesque ambiguities signifying the sterility of the Holy Ghost or the end of Michael's belief: 'My fowl was soupbones.'

In flying from adultery to death, the girl was impelled by a guilt due to religion. So against the ideal of sexless conception displayed in paintings of the Annunciation, the poet sets the pagan fertility of 'St. Venus' in Botticelli's *Primavera*. Against the child's sexless world of faith (evoked by allusions to Mother Goose rhymes, nursery tales and Peter Pan) he sets the world of parenthood. In a distortion of phrases from the *Messiah* we hear the solution that Michael cannot yet accept: birds singing, 'Come unto us, our burden's light'—not the Dove but the birds of nature, of light and Lucifer and reason.

Over such themes the poet builds his characteristic sort of towering edifice; for the poem stands on an amazing reticulation of allusions. *Paradise Lost,* for obvious reasons, is continually evoked. The wretched couple are identified with Faust and Gretchen or with Hamlet and Ophelia. From her asylum window the wife sees the harpies of Baudelaire's 'Cythere'. Yet the essential image and meaning of the poem do not hinge on such clues. Michael sits and listens at the end of the poem, but he does not pray or receive a sign. It seems certain that when he boards a train, it will take him away from 'this deaf and dumb/ Breadline for children'—as the wife unintentionally describes Roman Catholicism for the poet.

In Michael we confront again those linked themes of passive observation and wild impulse to travel that underlie so much of the nightmare violence in Lowell's poems. The wife's confinement in a cell reflects Michael's emotional seclusion. For the faithful Christian, life is a cage from which he escapes to Life; for the fallen Christian the limits of mere life make another kind of cage. Afraid to stir, for fear of wrecking the object of his stirring, the poet repeatedly speaks as a walled-off voyeur frantically watching the lives of others. Like a traveller in a sealed railway car, he passes over the earth, looking but never doing, always on the move and never in motion: he has replaced action by vision.

V

Lowell has said it was hard for him to find a subject and a language of his own. He can describe himself as writing a rather formal style coming out of Tate, Hart Crane, Ransom and Eliot. But when he composed the brilliant, influential poems that were collected in *Life Studies* (1959), he took a line less reminiscent of those masters than of Pound. At last he had discovered his language and subject.

By the time this book appeared, Lowell had received enough prizes and awards to ease most men's desire for public recognition. He was the father of an infant daughter (born January, 1957); he was a member of the Boston University Department of English; and he held the honorary degree of Doctor of Letters. Yet he had suffered a deeply disturbing experience when his mother died (February, 1954); and the emotional pressures evident in his poetry had undermined his health until he was forced to turn for aid to hospital treatments.

The continuance of the emotional strains, tempered by domestic amenities and balanced by extraordinary marks of success in his career, seem to have enabled Lowell to discover the best uses for his talent. Superficially the transformation appeared in the lightening of his style. Lowell has said that soon after the *Mills of the Kavanaughs* came out, the pace of his writing slowed almost to a halt, and his allusive, rhetorical manner came to seem 'distant, symbol-ridden and wilfully difficult'. He felt that his old poems too often hid what they were about, presenting a 'stiff, humourless and even impenetrable surface'. So he began paraphrasing Latin quotations when he used them, and adding extra syllables to lines in order to make them clearer or more colloquial. With such a poem as the short, perfect 'In the Cage' (1946)—a tetrameter sonnet recapturing the grimness of the months he spent in jail—he had already shown the strength of a comparatively unadorned language, free from obscurities but suffused with irony. This manner now became not the exception but the rule. Line after line, in poem after poem, reads like a well-turned but easily spoken remark made by a fastidious, self-critical speaker who is at home with slang.

But the ease of language was only the outer sign of Lowell's new attitude towards his own nature. Without losing the tone of fascinated disgust, he now found it possible not only to treat himself as part of history but to treat history as part of himself. The course of his life became the analogue of the life of his era; the sufferings of the poet became a mirror of the sufferings of whole classes and nations. It was not as a judge that he now claimed his authority: it was as the heroic artist, the man capable of turning vision into act. Through the title of his book Lowell gave himself the status of a craftsman who reveals life in general by the rendering of his own life.

Appropriately enough, *Life Studies* opens with a train journey from the city of priests to the city of artists, Rome to Paris. But the speaker is neither a character in a dramatic monologue nor an impersonal commentator. He is the poet talking about his own experiences. Here as generally in the book, Lowell has of course invented facts and altered truths. Yet the reader feels himself in touch with the real author and not with a mask. Similarly, the entrance into the poem is deliberately casual, with what look like random associations suggesting the real flow of a unique consciousness.

If the formal frame is thus a common earthly journey, the object presented is a miraculous one: the bodily assumption of the Virgin, proclaimed as dogma in the jubilee year 1950. So the title 'Beyond the

Alps' means not only a trip towards France but also its opposite, 'ultra-montane', or the old epithet for supporters of papal infallibility. Lowell is using that doctrine, which the proclamation of the new dogma pressed to a record-breaking extreme, as the emblem of vulgar human credulity—the decay of imagination into superstition—a principle embodied in the pope. To escape from such tempting corruptions, the poet struggles within himself, during the night of his train journey, emerging at dawn into a sense of rebirth, a commitment to the creative imagination. Turning towards the intellect and the arts —towards Athene and Apollo—he rejects Mary and Pius. The pope is depicted, with grotesque irony, between a purring electric razor in one hand (the cat of rational science) and a canary in the other (the dove of faith).

In keeping with the opposition between religion and art, Lowell treats the mountains that appear in his poem as versions of Parnassus. So the journey recalls the celebrated simile, in Pope's *Essay on Criticism,* comparing the Alps to the challenge that art sets before the ambition of genius: 'Hills peep o'er hills, and Alps on Alps arise.' It is thus appropriate that at the time the poem opens, the inartistic Swiss should just have failed to climb Everest.

Violence, as usual in Lowell's work, accompanies the polarity of stillness and movement. By mentioning the Swiss (historic mercenary soldiers), the poet hints at the third principle of human nature which the poem deals with, i.e. destructive violence, personified by the warrior-king. The success of Caesarean terror in chaining the mind differs only in mode from the success of the magician-priest: Mussolini is as Roman as Pius. For an ideal culture, that could make violence, magic, and reason work together, Lowell offers not Rome but inimitable Hellas; and while the morning sun, like the imagination, transforms the bleak moonlit peaks into dazzling Parthenons, the reborn poet thinks of another traveller, Odysseus, escaping symbolically from the dark cave of Polyphemus by blinding the cyclops with a dazzling firebrand. Athene, the guide of Odysseus, easily united in herself all the roles to which popes and dictators aspire; the reader recalls that she was also *parthenos* or virgin, born miraculously without a mother, inspirer of a temple outshining St. Peter's; and Lowell reminds us that she sprang not from the flesh but from the intellect of Jove. To this white height the poet dare not attempt to climb. Only Paris is left, the 'black classic' city of our own disintegrating culture; for our age seems unable to give direction and purpose to the primeval, irrational violence of human nature.

The intellectual design of this exhilarating poem has little system about it. Yet the texture, phrasing and versification offer immediate pleasures to the ear. It consists of three sonnets with slightly irregular rhyme schemes, the last of the three ending in a couplet that also serves as epigrammatic close to the whole work.* This pattern is enriched by a fullness of alliteration, assonance and internal rhyme that, so far from obtruding upon the offhand casualness of phrasing, only seems to deliver an ironical counter-thrust to it. Puns and other witticisms supply an elegant distance from which the poet can regard his own discomfort:

> I envy the conspicuous
> waste of our grandparents on their grand tours—
> long-haired Victorian sages accepted the universe,
> while breezing on their trust funds through the world.

The imagery has the same sort of forceful inconsequence: mountains and birds, tyrants and feet reappear in startling transformations as the wonderfully managed tone deepens from humour to bitterness to sublimity. The elaborate manipulations of height and depth, white and black, the four elements, are old habits of the poet. But the similar treatment of tiny details turns accidents into beauties. Thus the train stewards' tiptoe walk (while they ritually bang on their dinner gongs in a startling allusion to the Mass) becomes, in the second stanza, the toe of St. Peter, superstitiously kissed by pilgrims; and then, in the third, the splendour of the dawn of our culture as the poet sees

---

* When Lowell revised this poem for *For the Union Dead,* he also restored a fourth stanza which was judiciously omitted from the text in *Life Studies.*

> Apollo plant his heels
> on terra firma through the morning's thigh.

It is not easy to overpraise *Life Studies*. I suppose the most startling ingredient in the book was the new direction taken by the poet's conscience. In place of either direct protest or the fusion of his own morality with that of a Christian community, Lowell attached himself to several classes of heroic victims: children, artists, imprisoned criminals, and the mentally ill. Though these have always been linked in the Romantic tradition, most poets dealing with them risk the dangers of posturing and sentimentality. Precisely through making his own case the central case, Lowell avoids either fault. Instead of merely seeing him, we see his view of his peers.

Thus by reviewing his early memories not as they point inward but as they revolve about this or that pathetic adult, he gives a toughening perspective to the sufferings of the child; for these are balanced by the sufferings the child either causes or ironically ignores in the adult. Dealing with poets, he secures a similar distance by balancing the ignominies of the external life against the victories of the imagination. When he handles his most recalcitrant material, the humiliating lives of psychotics, he can allow himself a comical irony that would sound intolerable coming from anyone but the inmate of an institution:

> There are no Mayflower
> screwballs in the Catholic Church.
>
> ('Waking in the Blue')

Of course, each of these figures also stands as a measure of the disorder in society: the unrewarded artist, the corrupted child, the madhouse that mirrors the world. Each further becomes an extension of the past: thanks in part to the mere movement of decades, Lowell can bestow on personal recollections the dignity of history:

> These are the tranquillized *Fifties,*
> and I am forty.
>
> ('Memories of West Street')

Not through the public aspect of his ancestry but through the independent private experiences of the struggling poet, he can serve as the record of his age, and connect that age with the sweep of earlier epochs.

In all these accomplishments the controlling factor is a matter of tone. If Lowell had not managed to infuse the despair of his disgust with the humour of his irony, he could not have established the framework that screens the reader from the simple pathos of most confessional verse. In the production of this tone, the use of slang, re-sharpened cliches and witticisms is crucial: instead of straining, as in Lowell's earlier work, to give the banalities of life a moral urgency (often without succeeding), they now suggest the speaker's mastery of his experience. It is this saving irony, energised by disgust, that carries him across his most difficult, self-destructive nights. When he emerges from the darkness of 'Skunk Hour', the penultimate (originally the last) and almost the finest poem in this almost uniformly splendid book, what supports him and us is surely the power of his tolerance and humour, shoved smack up against a hideous crisis.

VI

In tracing Lowell's career up to 1960, one may describe it as following two successive motions. When he wrote his earlier works, the poet tried to give them importance by starting from the great moral issues or crises of history and then matching those with themes derived from his private ordeals. After *Mills of the Kavanaughs,* however, he was willing to start from his private experiences and project these upon history and public life. Since the effect of the change was a fresh and distinctive kind of poetry, Lowell seems to have felt impelled to push his explorations further. Preoccupied as he was with the continuity of his own work, and educated as he was in Eliot's idea of literature as a body of classics that the innovator alters and enlarges, Lowell naturally looked around among established masters to find either foreshadowings of his discoveries or parallels to his themes and tone.

From the very beginning he had in a sense been doing this. When he incorporated other men's lines into his own verses, when he made a Latin, French or German author's words the basis for a new poem in American English, he was suggesting that at least in certain corners of their *oeuvre* the strangers shared his moods. As if to show there were no limits to his ambition, Lowell now set about discovering his own qualities in the whole range of European literature. Having projected his experiences as a human being upon the history of the twentieth century, he now projected his identity as an artist upon the meaning of 'poetry'; for he began producing free adaptations or 'imitations' of the work of a dozen and a half poets from Homer to Montale. Even before they were reprinted in the collection entitled *Imitations* (1961), these poems were received with a surprising degree of incomprehension, which was aggravated rather than lightened when the whole book came out. Only the rare reader either observed that the arrangement of the book was not chronological, or accepted the author's statement that the contents were a sequence rather than a miscellaneous collection.

In fact, of course, *Imitations* is Lowell's attempt to find his voice in the high places of literature, to fashion retrospectively a tradition for his accomplishment. He is legitimising his progeny, replacing the Lowells and Winslows by Baudelaire, Rimbaud and Rilke. In drawing up such a genealogical tree, Lowell again implies that he has found his essential identity not in a social class or in a religious communion but in his character as a writer. So it seems appropriate that the bulk of the models belong to the Symbolist tradition. For Symbolism is the movement that defined the creative mind as the supreme object of poetic contemplation.

Once again, the opening and closing poems have special significance. Lowell begins with a startling extract from the *Iliad,* which picks up the motif of his 'For the Union Dead'—the last poem (under a different title) in the revised edition of *Life Studies.* 'For the Union Dead' had dealt with the mystery of heroism, in which a human life reaches nobility by the manner of death: 'man's lovely/peculiar power to choose life and die'. To open *Imitations,* Lowell gives us 'The Killing of Lykaon'. Suddenly Homer is not the Olympian whose view shifts

with dignified ease from Greek side to Trojan, or from man to God;
but he is the singer of the 'mania' of Achilles. 'Mania' rather than
the conventional 'wrath', says Lowell in his version of the epic
invocation. No doubt he is punning on *ménin,* the first word in the
first of all our poems. However, he is also, and quite fairly, discovering
in the ancient poet his own tendency to regard any irresistible passion
as a sort of madness. The extract that follows the bit from the
invocation comes from Book XXI of the *Iliad,* and contrasts heroic
murder with ignominious death: Achilles insists on despatching the
vanquished Lykaon and spurns his victim with a tirade on the killing
of Trojans. The hero, foreseeing the dissolution of his enemies' corpses,
suggests that the reduction to nothingness eliminates their value as
persons. Lowell makes the speech his own by infusing it with a
love-hate hysteria that sounds feverish and self-conscious but possesses a
marvellously nervous vitality:

> You too must die, my dear. Why do you care?
> the dark shadows of the fish will shiver,
> lunging to snap Lykaon's silver fat.

The answer to Achilles' debasement of the human spirit is the final
work in *Imitations,* 'The Pigeons', from Rilke. In the middle of this
poem we meet a band of Greek warriors about to die. But here they
personify the poet's army of creative impulses, destroyed through being
realised. The word 'mania' appears too, in the last line of the poem
and the book. Yet it is no longer Achilles' rage to annihilate; it is now
the resistance of reality to the artist's drive towards perfection; for
the imagination of course opposes itself to nothingness and aspires to
eternity. So the metaphor changes, and a poem becomes a ball flung
from 'all-being' towards eternity, 'almost out of bounds', but gaining a
tragic intensity, or 'body and gravity', from the pull that draws it back
towards non-existence. In the exquisitely phrased first half of this fine
work, Lowell-Rilke employs not a ball or any army but the flight and
return of pigeons as a metaphor for the artist's impulses. Each bird is
like a creative vision seeking independent life. So the most beautiful

pigeon is always the one that has never left the coop, the pure
conception not yet embodied; for to be fixed is to be finished.
Nevertheless, says Lowell,

> only by suffering the rat-race in the arena
> can the heart learn to beat.

The soaring unity, in such lines, of slang, passion and insight reveals
the strength of Lowell's talent.

The progress from the death-bounded battles of Achilles to the tragic
campaigns of the artist reaches its peripety in the poems from
Baudelaire, placed ironically after Hugo's tributes to the defeated
warrior Napoleon and the dead artist Gautier. In Baudelaire the great
themes of *Imitations* surge together: death, love and art. Lowell has
selected poems that carry us from the revulsion of the artist against
passion to the welcome the artist gives death. If his style sounds drier
than Baudelaire's and less felicitous in rhythm than Pound's, it has a
decorous violence of language and imagery that no other American
poet can produce. Yet not intensity of expression alone but strength of
intellect, the consciousness enveloping the intensity, draws the
disruptive forces together. Lowell's confident metres, the bold, catchy
phrases, express not simply what Baudelaire felt but what we still
want: a power to transcend lust and decay by the imagination that
digests them:

> reptilian Circe with her junk and wand....
> Desire, that great elm fertilized by lust....
> It's time. Old Captain, Death, lift anchor, sink!

If in artistic sensibility Lowell seems peculiarly at home with
Baudelaire, he seems as a person still more at ease with Rimbaud, whose
work is placed at the exact centre of the book. With both poets he
finds continual opportunities for employing his own tone and his
imagery of passivity eager for motion. But Rimbaud brings our
attitudes towards childhood and corrupted innocence that remind us at

once of *Life Studies*. Mme. Rimbaud as 'Mother' inexorably recalls Mrs. Lowell:

> she thought they were losing caste. This was good—
> she had the true blue look that lied.

So also the isolated 'poète de sept ans' brings back the 'last afternoon with Uncle Devereux Winslow'. Yet in revealing what he shares with Rimbaud, Lowell also reveals what the rest of us share with them both. The double image here has the distancing but clarifying effect that irony produces in *Life Studies*. When he gives us his amazingly fresh, rich version of 'The Lice-Hunters'—with its symmetry of disgusting perceptions, its complexity of assonance or rhyme, and its steadiness of rhythm—Lowell evokes the whole tendency of our nagging generation to inspect, regret, and enjoy emotional crises:

> He heard their eyebrows beating in the dark
> whenever an electric finger struck to crush
> a bloated louse, and blood would pop and mark
> the indolence of their disdainful touch.

VII

From a glance at Lowell's most recent work, coming out in periodicals, one can prophesy that his next book will establish his name as that normally thought of for 'the' American poet. It will be a wide shift from the frame of Robert Frost, whom so many non-readers of poetry were able to admire along with the literary audience. Frost did many things that Lowell does not. Though unsuccessful as a farmer, he could celebrate aspects of rural life that Lowell never touches. He knew how to tell a story. He was the last important American poet to use the old forms and the old language convincingly. If Frost endured, in the fate of his family, more frightful disasters than Lowell, he was blessed with the power of maintaining his ego against them. Yet he stood for few extraordinary or wayward ideas. His connection with literature outside the conventional English and American models was slight. It is remarkable how often his early poems are indistinguishable from the early poems of Graves or Ransom. He opened few roads that other writers could travel. No one could call Frost a poet's poet.

Lowell, on the contrary, seems determined to maintain his intellectual distinction, his subtlety, his rigorous complexity of form. What appears most astonishing about the recent work is the way old motifs persist in new transformations with deepening significance. There are the city garden, the parallels of beast with man, the bitter pathos of memory working on the fixed character. But in the new poems of private recollection Lowell inclines to emphasise the hold that history has on the present, the powerlessness of the self to resist the determination of open or hidden memories. The insatiable consciousness of the poet comments sardonically on the very self-censuring auto-analysis that produced *Life Studies*.

At the opposite extreme from the private self the poet can now draw human as well as Symbolist analogies between the terrible numbers of suffering people and his own unique experiences. 'Buenos Aires', one of his finest new 'public' poems, has the wit and clever phrasing that make lines attractive on a first reading: 'old men denied apotheosis' (i.e. equestrian statues of defunct dictators); 'Peron,/the nymphets' Don Giovanni'. The poet's games with expressive sound have unusual vigour—for example, a crescendo of echoes of 'air' towards the end, preparing for the name of the city that is the subject of the poem. This 'air' becomes a sarcastic pun; for foul air, miasma, 'hot air', cold fog, emptiness, seem what the place betokens. In the final line the last word, 'crowds', echoes the last word of the first stanza, 'herds', and reminds one of the likeness drawn throughout the poem between cattle and people; for it is the suffering and passivity of the humblest class that connect them with the author.

As usual, the images are what make the poem work. This time they depend on the old partners, love and war, Venus and Mars, united here by means of Peron's name *Juan,* which suggests the Don Juan legend. Lowell, disgusted by the official facade of the city, treats it as a depopulated, over-furnished opera set, which he contrasts with the off-stage crowds of the real Argentina. The opera is of course *Don Giovanni;* and the centre of the poem recapitulates history with dead generals in white marble recalling Mozart's Commendatore. Instead of the file of Don Juan's abandoned mistresses, we meet marble goddesses mourning deceased heroes; or sex and death joined in a skull-like obelisk. Instead of the great lover in hell, we hear Peron bellowing from exile, the seducer of his people.

Among these scenes the poet moves on foot in a circular path, as spectator or sufferer. He starts from and returns to his hotel, caressing inanimate statues (his muses) en route but speaking to nobody. Instead of virile love, he encounters homosexuals in a park; but like Donna Anna, though unlike Argentina, he fights off seduction. Fascinated as so often by what repels him, he sees the truth behind the scrim and delivers it to us by way of his conscience.

A similar solidity of structure and depth of implication pervade the best of the new poems of introspection, 'Eye and Tooth' and the superb tribute to his wife, 'Night Sweat'. 'Eye and Tooth', a skilful extraction of humour from despair, illustrates a truism about middle age: viz. that so far from bringing us serenity, the years leave us naked; only we learn, not without some disgust, that the self can survive even the shabbiest humiliation. The poem depends on a brilliant use of the *eye-I* pun. Treating vision as memory or id, Lowell presents the voyeur poet's eye as an unwreckable showcase of displeasing memories that both shape and torment the person. The dominating metaphor is, so to speak, 'I've got something in my I and can't get it out.' Towards the end Lowell neatly ties the public to the domestic by implying that just as his readers observe his gestures with the unease provoked by their own recollections, so his familiars must in the routines of living find his condition hardly more bearable than he does:

> Nothing! No oil
> for the eye, nothing to pour
> on those waters or flames.
> I am tired. Everyone's tired of my turmoil.

Ransom once played with the idea of Lowell's becoming the Ovid or Virgil of America. But if Lowell feels drawn to themes of epic scope, his mode is neither narrative nor celebratory. For a closer parallel we must look at another epoch in another nation, at the difficult life and disquieting art of Baudelaire. Besides the fundamental similarities of their childhoods, Baudelaire during adolescence inclined like Lowell to a lonely, morose disposition; and it was in the community of artists that he found a lasting family. He was attracted to painting but not to music. As an adult he responded more intensely to city scenes than to country landscapes. In his personality he combined deep passivity with an eagerness to keep working and moving. Though he had begun writing poetry while at school, he always procrastinated about publication, working over his poems with perfectionist ardour. When he produced a book, it was no miscellaneous gathering but an organisation of separate poems into a general scheme reflecting his peculiar outlook.

Still more persuasive are the similarities in the works. Both men have the posture of a fallen Christian. Both deal rather with the horrors of passion than the pleasures of love, and treat death as more seductive than frightening. For both of them, art emerges from profound intellection, from labour, suffering, self-disgust. They build their best poems around complex images linked by connotation, and not around arguments or events. They introduce coarse, distasteful words into a style that is rich and serious. Their poems follow circular movements, with the end touching the beginning.

Their differences are obvious. Lowell's use of history is deliberate; Baudelaire clings to immediate reality. The development of Lowell's characteristic successes depends on an impression of haphazardness at the start turning into a highly wrought climax, whereas Baudelaire's surface has elegance of workmanship throughout. Lowell relies overwhelmingly on visual imagery, whereas Baudelaire appeals elaborately to sounds, and is remarkable for a synaesthetic use of smells. Rhythmically, Lowell sounds less interesting than Baudelaire.

Yet if we search still further, if we place 'Le Cygne' beside 'For the

Union Dead', the two sensibilities reveal still more intimate kinship. There is the same sympathy with the wretched, the same disgust with the life that imposes wretchedness upon them, the same transformation of the city-pent poet into an emblem of the human spirit exiled from its original home. Finally, it seems important that Lowell and Baudelaire take so much of the matter of their poems from the most secret rooms of their private lives; for the true biography of them both emerges not from a tale of their friendships or families or external careers but from their works alone. The real Lowell, like the real Baudelaire, is met with in the poetry to which he has given himself altogether.

John Bayley
Robert Lowell:
The Poetry of Cancellation

> All that grave weight of America
> Cancelled! Like Greece and Rome.
> The future in ruins!
>   Louis Simpson

In attempting the appraisal of a modern poet the critic does well to
remember Auden's reminder to his tribe—'X's work is more important
than anything I can say about it'—but such a proviso leaves one still
free to ask just how and why Robert Lowell's poetry is important. For
where a living poet's status is concerned, the word is apt to be little
more than the hand-out of a public relations man, retained by a society
which supposes it must have 'important' poetry as it must have
important breakthroughs in space travel and cybernetics.

And much of Lowell's early poetry lends itself to this public notion
of importance, on the score of which Hugh Staples, who wrote the
first critical study of Lowell, called *The Quaker Graveyard in
Nantucket* 'a major poem of sustained brilliance, which challenges
comparison with the great elegies of the language'. Of this judgment
one can only say, and with confidence, that it is not true. The critic
has assumed a pretension and mistaken it for an achievement. Another
book on Lowell,* which has just appeared, also assumes a real size
and importance in the inflated verse of the early collections, and

* *The Poetic Themes of Robert Lowell,* by Jerome Mazzaro.

By permission of *London Magazine,* Vol. VI, No. 3 (June, 1966). Copyright
© 1966 by The Shenval Press.

reverently sorts through the frenetically but meaninglessly cunning entanglements of its religious imagery. This is importance as the D. Phils have it. What in fact is extraordinary is that the poet who wrote so much resounding stuff could also have written the remarkable poems of the later volumes, which neither critic sees as contributing much to this phantasmal 'importance' of Lowell. It is on this point that criticism should concentrate.

The early poetry is a signal instance of what T. S. Eliot called 'a poetry that is purely verbal, in that the whole poem will give us more of the same thing, an accumulation rather than a real development of thought and feeling'. It creates no world into which we can move, explore, discover. And the creation of such a world can be a real criterion of an important poetry, a world like that of Eliot himself— or Auden—a world which our own consciousness can inhabit and find out more about each time the poetry is re-read. But such a poet's world is necessarily a retrospective thing. When it has become fully visible to us, and livable in, it has already receded a little into the comfort of history. The poet himself may not have left it yet, but in a sense he is already in the past when we see how to live with him. It *may* be only a question of time before we see how to live with Lowell, but I doubt it. I think the real and radical importance of his best poems is of a different kind—a kind we can diagnose historically in *The Phoenix and The Turtle,* in a sonnet of Wyatt or a lyric of Blake, no less than in such a poet as Baudelaire—the importance of a poetry which does not create a world of its own in its age, but looks out.

Lowell's poetry looks out in an unexpected direction. It yearns towards non-existence. If a poetry can be said to have the death-wish, it has it. As his poetry has transformed itself it has perfected a capacity for self-extinction. The words of the early poems lie about helplessly, turgid and swollen: the words of the later ones achieve a crispness of cancellation, leaving behind them only a kind of acrid exhaust smell. A lot of *poets,* no doubt, have had a death-wish, but none have entailed it by method on their poetry—their poetry is on the contrary an insurance against the extinction they may personally seem to crave.

The contingency, tedium, disgust enshrined in much modern poetry—
Auden's suburb 'where helpless babies and telephones gabble untidy
cries'; Eliot's 'their only monument the asphalt road and a thousand
lost golf-balls'—these become in fact a monument, before which the
poet's audience can stand in satisfaction and intimacy.

The cancellation, or alienation, so marked in Lowell's best poems
severs this bond of intimacy, and in so doing emphasises how much we
have come to expect it in modern writing. The writer alienated from
society, the creator of madness, meaninglessness, the extreme situation
—he is indeed a commonplace today, but the greater the alienation he
describes the more uncomfortably close he comes to *us,* the reader,
the more he depends on a personal relation with us. Like a drunk in a
bar this author needs his finger in our buttonhole—the further off he
is from the social and moral world the more urgent is his need to
share his alienation with the reader. It is Lowell's achievement to
have successfully alienated *the poem itself,* to have made it as unaware
of us as the suicide caught by the camera flash. And this seems to me
the real thing. It gives *Life Studies* and many of the later poems their
quality of nicking the advanced edge of time, the moment that burns
us before the unmeaning future and the numbed unordered past.

Professor Fiedler, in *Partisan Review,* has associated Lowell with
Messrs Burroughs, Ginsberg, McClure, etc., because, as he said, the
young respond to the madness in him and associate it with the same
drugged or alienated mental states celebrated by their other favourites.
If indeed the young do so they are missing the point, which here means
missing the style. The camaraderie of alienation is not essentially
different from the camaraderie of surfing or stock-car racing; it has the
same cosy clubbable quality; it is the fashion in common. For all that
their subject is alienation and the states induced by drugs, the writings
of Burroughs and the rest share the artless and rather pathetic cosiness
of the campus magazine. And this togetherness is not really very far
from more conventional kinds of togetherness in American writing,
that of the 'poetry workshop', of the neat, delicate, civilised shoal
poetry in which recent American schools have excelled, and which we

find in collections like the Faber *Five American Poets* and the Penguin *Contemporary American Poetry*.

Like the Tribe of Ben, or certain Japanese schools, these poets are not so much individuals as a way of life, and their poems a way of writing poetry is perfectly self-satisfied, which does not mean complacent. It creates a moment of being which is designed to last, and which appeals, in that ambition, to what we cherish as durable moments in our own mode of being. A poem by William Stafford, for instance, *Travelling Through The Dark,* admirably creates such a weighty moment. The poet driving on a mountain road sees a dead deer, and alights to remove it in case it causes an accident. Finding it had been a female about to give birth, and that the foetus is still alive, he stands in indecision—a moment solicitously registered:

> I thought hard for us all—my only swerving—
> Then pushed her over the edge into the river.

It is the claim of this well-written poetry that it thinks hard for us all, —the phrase well suggests its outlook and method—but it does so with extreme self-consciousness. Though the poetry is in a sense so homogeneous, its method means that each poet attempts, almost embarrassingly, to establish his own individuality with the reader.*

And it is just this self-consciousness which is lacking in Lowell. Though his best poems seem constructed from the same sorts of material as theirs—moments in a considered life, life studies in fact— nothing in them is making this appeal to us. When Lowell says in *Skunk Hour*:

> I myself am hell
> Nobody's there . . .

we believe him, not because he is asserting it to us, but because this moment when we read does indeed seem the last moment before there is nobody there, not even the poem:

* The doyen of this sort of forthcomingness was probably William Carlos Williams.

> One dark night,
> My Tudor Ford climbed the hill's skull,
> I watched for love cars. Lights turned down,
> they lay together, hull to hull,
> where the graveyard shelves on the town . . .
> My mind's not right.

The bald assertion, 'my mind's not right', seems neither less nor more than the fact. 'What use is my sense of humour?' asks Lowell in another of these poems. What indeed? But he is not asking us. Reliable old concepts like irony—bonds between poet and reader which sustain the poem on its journey into the reader's mind—fall flat on their faces here. So does the shared and knowing allusion. *One dark night . . .* yes, Lowell is no doubt recalling the first line of a famous poem by St John of the Cross, but the connection gives us none of the usual pleasure to make, since it seems to have given him none to select it. And for all that the lovers are subsumed into their cars, the human into the mechanical, there is no insistent and reassuring note of misanthropy. These are life studies in the sense that life is the thing that happens before death, no more than that. They could only have been written in America today, because they afford a peculiarly American style of cancellation, a refusal of all that America has stipulated, stood for, taken for granted. And stylistically the impressive thing is that this refusal, this cancellation, is not said by the poem but *is* the poem.

It is all the more singular because these poems appear, on the face of it, to build up a whole world of intimacy with Lowell and with his family and provenance, his father and mother, grandfather and grandmother, their incomes, estates, and social standing. We hear of the poet's own wife and child, job and friends. The ease with which these facts are related is itself remarkable, and indeed probably unique in American literature—it reminds us of the aristocratic simplicity of an earlier class of English memoirists, and of Tolstoy and Aksakov in Russia. It beguiled the first reviewers into enthusing over the poem's 'touching' and 'human' quality. But this was surely to miss the point. The point is that these simple intimate things—all involuntary, as it might be, with the common good of life—come before us here in a context of total alienation. Commander Lowell, like his son, is caught by the camera just before hitting the ground. And the facts of his life—how at the age of nineteen he was 'old man' of a gunboat on the Yangtse, and left Lafcadio Hearn's 'Glimpses of Unfamiliar Japan', a present from his mother, 'under an open porthole in a storm'—these facts do not come before us redolent with the Betjemanish charm and queer pathos of a family past; they are nothing but the facts. When Lowell tells us:

> Father's death was abrupt and unprotesting.
> His vision was still twenty-twenty.
> After a morning of anxious, repetitive smiling,
> his last words to mother were:
> 'I feel awful.'

he is not being smart. Smartness, like irony and humour, depends upon an eye kept on the reader that is here kept staringly on the object. It is almost frightening when Lowell makes a claim which in another poet would sound coy:

> 'My Grandfather found
> his grandchild's fogbound solitudes
> sweeter than human society.'

No doubt it was so. The word 'human' ambushes us with a glassy stare, seemingly unaware of its own charge of meaning. If it is loaded and pointed it contrives utterly to conceal the fact, and that is what one means by style in Lowell. If there *is* a moving quality in these poems—and in a muffled way there can be—it is that of a drama without an audience, even that of the poet himself. We have the intimation of a human life in a state of shock, remembering, like Wordsworth's Old Man, 'the importance of his theme'—or at least its human potentiality—'but feeling it no longer'.

Lowell has managed to freeze into the style of these poems the utter detachment of the mad, and he may be the first poet to have done this systematically. It might itself appear a characteristically modern achievement—certainly Clare, writing in the Northamptonshire County Asylum, was as aware as any other poet of the normal 'I and my audience' relation. But so, in many poems, is Lowell; and his sanity then makes one wonder about the rumour that American alienists sometimes actually *help* their patients to go mad, by way of therapy, as the LSD and morphia popularizers proclaim that we should. Perhaps alienation is the logical and coming response to the madness of modern society? For when Lowell is writing *about* himself and his state of mind, instead of compelling the poem to *be* it, he is not only a less good poet but—which makes the transition more painful— inferior in an area in which other modern poets have shown their most specific superiority. Yeats, for instance, can not only be openly rhetorical about himself but can combine, as Lowell cannot, the tone of open rhetoric with the confidence of intimacy. Lowell tries it in a poem which has often been admired, *Night Sweat*:

> My life's fever is soaking in night sweat—
> one life, one writing! But the downward glide
> and bias of existing wrings us dry—
> always inside me is the child who died,
> always inside me is his will to die—

That 'always inside me' couplet is strangely unconvincing, which does not of course mean that Lowell is not telling us the truth as he sees it, but that he cannot tell it in this way. It is mere bow-wow, mere gloss. Instead of extinguishing itself in one of Lowell's multiple acts of poetic suicide the poem lingers limply in the area of mere explanation.

For The Union Dead is an ambiguous poem, nearly very fine, but significantly not quite able to carry off the contrast between Lowell himself and the high title's imputation. Yet to take the intention of this title as just a smack at Allen Tate's *Ode to the Confederate Dead* does not help at all, for satire—even oblique satire—is as little Lowell's *forte* as humour or ironic and Empsonian cosiness. 'What was said by Lincoln, boys, what did he perpend?'.... no, such a suggestion

won't do. Cancellation cannot be imputed: American history cannot
be alienated like the poet's own world. Which amounts to saying that
Lowell cannot speak on behalf of other people. He himself is as
alienated from the dead, and from their hero Colonel Shaw, whom he
attempts to celebrate in Whitmanesque lines:

> He rejoices in man's lovely,
> peculiar power to choose life and die

as he is from the 'giant finned cars' of modern America, its 'savage
servility'. The tone of denunciation and nostalgia in the poem is not
quite real, because these impulses claim an open relation to the
traditional human world of value which Lowell's most effective poetry
does not and cannot have. Lowell himself, one receives the impression,
is a good man, who has the right views on Vietnam and the race
problem, who is against sin. But about these things he can only
be poetical.

II

'The man really sounds like a prophet!' exclaimed John Berryman of
Lowell's early poetry, apparently without irony. It was just the trouble.
Lowell did, and on occasion still does, *sound* like a prophet. The
thunderous title of his second volume, *Lord Weary's Castle,* aided the
effect. It recalls the Scottish ballad of *Lamkin*:

> O Lamkin was a mason good
> As ever built wi' stane.
> He has built Lord Weary's castle
> But payment got he nane.

'America', suggested Berryman, 'is Lord Weary's Castle, the rich house
we use without paying for, which the defrauded one will enter
suddenly.' It may well be so. But all the gravely incongruous weight of
conscience implied—the puritan family's and the Catholic convert's—
is mere water under the bridge. Lowell's most ambitious attempt to
create a prophetic myth of the American past and present—*The Mills*

of the Kavanaughs—is a complete and incoherent failure. He has written no open public prophecies, no *Waste Land* or *Second Coming*. And one must emphasise again that the notion of him as 'important' in that way is quite misleading. He is not a prophet, but his best poems are in themselves prophetic indications of a state which may be becoming increasingly common in Anglo-American society, the state in which traditional 'feelings' are ceasing to exist, or to have their traditional status assumed—the state in which more and more people come to have knowledge of, even to desire, the symptoms of clinical alienation.

It is this state which Lowell catches, in himself and others. But the 'others' are in fact usually himself, for, as I have suggested, one cannot project madness. Lowell's attempts at a Browning-like seizure of Men and Women (something of a confidence trick in Browning himself) do not come off as creations of outside people but as images of states within the poet. The best are the shortest: *Katherine's Dream* and the Jonathan Edwards poems extend the thing too far and risk the reader's disbelief in the actuality of the portrait. One of the most superlative is *'To speak of the Woe that is in Marriage'*:

> . . . My hopped-up husband drops his home disputes
> and hits the street to cruise for prostitutes,
> free-lancing out along the razor's edge.
> This screwball might kill his wife, then take the pledge.
> Oh the monotonous meanness of his lust . . .
> It's the injustice . . . he is so unjust—
> whiskey-blind, swaggering home at five.
> My only thought is how to keep alive.
> What makes him tick? Each night now I tie
> ten dollars and his car-key to my thigh . . .
> Gored by the climacteric of his want
> He stalls above me like an elephant

This is Lowell's style at his most brilliant: style and matter, as in the studies of his own life, are fused into one, wholly effective for the given fact, wholly extinguished where the fact ends. The lightning coherence and bite of the words cannot be and are not intended to be followed into the world of relation and probability (in the marital predicament she claims the lady would scarcely have chosen her thigh as a hiding-place?) but each word makes its precise electrical contact—*lance* and *razor* with *kill,* the seductive *thigh* with the desolating and comic sexual image of the last couplet—and then goes off with an almost audible click. This way of using words in poetry reminds us of Dryden, who never looks towards us, whose vocabulary is always perfect for its context and yet never goes on to create a livable world. That last couplet, with its powerfully Augustan image of the husband *stalling* like a car (we remember the amorous cars of *Skunk Hour*) at the beginning of the end of sexual desire, and *stalled* above his wife like an animal presence—one can almost imagine Dryden flourishing it off as a sample for his bookseller! The alienated aspect of Lowell's genius fits in oddly well with its professional side: in both there is no lingering, no hopeful glance in our direction, only the cancellation of the account when the job is done.

III

The *Imitations* and the translation of *Phèdre* are done in this spirit, and Dryden would have approved Lowell's words in the preface to *Imitations*. 'I have tried to write live English and to do what my authors would have done if they were writing their poems now and in America.' The older poet who rewrote Virgil and Chaucer would also have been robustly different to the implications of the poems' *not* having been written now and in America. Lowell's success comes from the same assured and business-like confidence: he does not agonize, like most translators, over whether he is getting the precise *nuance*—he rewrites the thing in his own way. None the less, the impulse involved is a destructive one. By the time that Dryden, in *All For Love,* has finished with Cleopatra's barge there is nothing left of Shakespeare's creation. And Lowell exaggerates the mordant brutality of Baudelaire's *Voyage à Cythère,* and the brooding sleep march of Rilke's *Orpheus,* until there is nothing left but a number of insistent words and striking phrases. The implicit has become all too explicit. The destructive process, it is interesting to note, works best with Rimbaud, for it brings out that poet's odd and rather disconcerting extensibility and open-endedness. You *can* tack more of the same on to Rimbaud—it merely deepens and emphasizes the *dérèglement* which led logically to silence and self-extinction, and which seems in accord with Lowell's own poetic temper.

But with Racine it is a different matter. Lowell tells us himself that he took the English restoration dramatists as his model here, and that he has tried to give Racine's lines 'speed and flare'. In this he has succeeded admirably. But again one cannot but feel the unspoken wish to pulverize the original, to convert it into mere energy as an engine converts its fuel. I take it that the triumph of Racine is somehow to have admitted the predestinate obsessions of lust, and the misery of monstrous longings, within the strict limits of a classic poetry; and that the miracle of the thing is its exhibited control. Venus is suggested in all the grossness of her power, but she is never allowed to disturb the Apollonian clarity of speech. In destroying this balance Lowell destroys dignity. 'Frothing with desire', his Phèdre is almost as energetically ludicrous a figure as the poisoned Nourmahal in Dryden's *Aurungzebe*. She calls on Hippolytus—in a phrase which mocks the simmering coolness of the Racinian confrontation,—for his 'sword's spasmodic final inch'; and converts the unearthly sorrow of Phèdre's statement about the youthful pair:

'Tous les jours se levaient clairs et sereins pour eux!'

into a chatty banality,

'For them each natural impulse was allowed
Each day was summer and without a cloud.'

Does it matter? Not really, for the adaptation is a success in its own right. But it makes one wonder what is Lowell's motive in this way of writing. The tormented confusion of his early poetry, which seemed bent on burying itself and everything else in 'the dark downward and vegetating kingdom', is still strangely apparent in the urge to obliterate 'all that grave weight', the poetic selfhood of the past. One might even suspect an unconscious irony in his statement that he is trying to rewrite these poems now and in America, where the latest film version of some classic reduces the celluloid of its predecessor to literal nothingness. As long ago as *The Quaker Graveyard* Lowell treated *Moby Dick* in this way, thrashing Melville to pieces in his own frenzy; and *For The Union Dead* makes a not dissimilar use of the moving recollections of Colonel Shaw and his regiment by William and Henry James. Lowell's most recent enterprise, three lengthy playscripts based on three short American tales, belabours their slight, strange point until it has yielded up its last drop into obviousness. This is not imitation but execution. One might remember, too, that for all their occasional absurdities and mistranslations the 'imitations' of Pound had none of the destructive background of Lowell's. They carried on, as Eliot did in his poems, the American tradition of cherishing the European past, as fragments to shore against our ruins. Lowell seems to want to add its ruins to our own.

It is all the odder because his poems, at their best, understand so well how to be; and these Imitations are usually saying, and at some length, what their originals are. In them Lowell still seems to be attempting by other means the rhetorical and explanatory side of his poetry which is also its weakest side. However much he is expected to be in America he simply is not a poet of the 'big bow-wow'—he is a big poet who cannot write 'big' poems. Unquestionably his best poems to date are the most seemingly trivial ones, poems which find their precision and their weight in the slightest context; and when he moves us, as in such a poem as *Man and Wife,* he does so unexpectedly and as it were unmeaningfully, as Dryden does in his *Epistle to Congreve.* In an age when destruction and madness oppress the poet, like every other citizen, Lowell has learnt not to write about these things but to take them on; and he has taken them on with brilliant success and logic in terms of a style which can perfectly *be* its own alienation, if it can be little else.

Herbert Leibowitz
Robert Lowell: Ancestral Voices

From the start of his career, Robert Lowell has possessed a sense of the
past that has forced its way into his verse, dominating both subject
matter and style. His poetic voice emerged from a talking contest
with his ancestral voices: literary, familial, historical[1]; the qualities of
his rhetoric, modified from volume to volume, are frequently the
qualities of American rhetoric, just as the private experiences he
transcribes are the salient features of American experience. The
Puritans' fanatical certainty of Doom, their Draconian paradise; the
arch-Calvinism of Jonathan Edwards; the grim pessimism of
Hawthorne and Melville who, considering America's violent search
for Absolutes, punched through the pasteboard mask of appearances
and discovered the reality of evil; and the history of Lowell's family,
respected and respectable, its roots deep in the stony soil of New
England and the parlors of Back Bay—all these were the shapers of
this uneasy democrat.

If he seems to have lived and suffered in the margins of his time,
this is a false impression, for in his imagination past and present work

[1] Except for the sake of an occasional comparison, I shall not discuss the
modern representatives of the American heritage who influenced Lowell: Eliot,
Pound, Ransom, Hart Crane. This reluctant decision is due to the limits of space.
It is interesting to note that Eliot and Lowell traveled opposite routes to and
from some version of Catholicism, and that the others represent values and a
life-style different from those of the world Lowell was brought up in.

By permission of Salmagundi I, IV Fall-Winter (1966-1967). Copyright by
Asyla Corp.

simultaneously. History is Janus-faced. Thus the stereotype of Lowell as the confessional poet struggling for identity is only half true. The forces of darkness that swell in his mind and those that aggrandize the world are often the same: the history of his personal salvation cannot be separated from the social and political destinies of his countrymen.

Land of Unlikeness, Lowell's first volume, was an odd debut. It announced the arrival of a "genius of misfortune," a mercurial performer who could orchestrate his poems with a coloration that promised even greater achievements later on. The importance of this volume is that it established Lowell's poetic mannerisms—a mastery of intricate stanzas and complicated lines, a nervous rhythm, a kind of religious ranting—mannerisms that were refined and scrubbed of obscurity in successive volumes, but which remained steady until the rather late change of manner in *Life Studies.* What impressed readers in the desperate rush of images, so often vividly grotesque like gargoyles, was the rage in the act of self-definition.

The land of unlikeness of the title is partly America but mostly some country of the mind whose topography cannot be mapped with precision. It is only outwardly a Catholic duchy. True, the poems abound with references to Jesus' crucifixion, the Holy Ghost, and the Virgin Mary, anathema to the Puritans. True, the poet rails against the aridity of the Puritans. But, a Catholic convert descended from a distinguished New England family, he addresses Mary and Christ in the raw, driven idiom of Cotton Mather. Charon, the ferryman who figures so largely in the volume's imagery, is a Puritan helmsman, his raft a Mayflower, and Lowell, his passenger, a wandering soul ferried across the gulf of doubt and unknowing to a New Land that might or might not be hell.

The Puritans, who came to the New World armed with their ardor and their doctrines of the Fall, proceeded to impose on the wilderness their harsh belief that most men faced arbitrary damnation and that only an elect few would be saved. This created strains of discord in the self—and created drama. In the Puritans' perpetual warfare of the spirit Lowell found a handy verification. For him, too, the Fall is the imperial event that brings not the calm of answered questions but the persistence of lived agonies. Resurrection, a central tenet of the Catholicism he has adopted, is a vague symbol of his will to transcend chaos—but he mistrusts it as dogma. The title is accurate: he abides in a land of unlikeness.

The effect of this volume therefore is one of willfulness, of a gesture toward belief, a set of elaborate misfitting metaphors for the poet's real concerns: an exploration of vexing personal experience; a gauging of the power of Satan (evil), the smallness of the self, and the elusiveness of grace. His darkened imagination violently confronts the violence in history and nature—and is battered into submission to God. The poems are quick with a gauche, hysterical spirituality that is closer to Puritanism than to Roman Catholicism. There is, despite the profuse religious nomenclature, little of Hopkins' awe of Jesus and tenderness toward Mary; there is none of the grave sweetness and piety of Herbert; there is not even the humbleness and reticence of an Edward Taylor. Instead we have a series of willed literary effects, Crashavian in their intensity and playfulness: Lowell calls Mary "Celestia Hoyden," for example, or writes, "They shall find you are their belle / And belly too."

Lowell's ambivalent attitude to the Puritans is central to an understanding of his poetry. Although he repudiates them intellectually, he is at home with their buffetings and morbidity. From them he takes or rather corroborates the habit of self-examination and the strenuous burden of their, at times inexplicable, guilt. They are the injectors of a foul self-righteousness into the national life; they are carved in the heroic mold but are mean-spirited (the poet, self-castigating, sees himself as the inheritor of a "poor bred-out stock"); they are visionaries but theirs is a carrion vision. In "The Park Street Cemetery," Lowell mocks at the Puritan dream of a theocracy, unfulfilled, which drenched the continent in blood, mocks at their barbarous creed and severe eschatology. The irony deepens in "The Boston Nativity," as the poet taunts:

The Mathers, Eliots, and Endicots
Brew their own gall,
Here Concord's shot that rang
Becomes a boomerang.

. . .

Soon the Leviathan
Will spout American.

In "Salem," he associates the greatness of these New Englanders with Leviathan, with power misused; they are spiritual buccaneers, driven by a sense of mission, "Who quartered the Leviathan's fat flanks / And fought the British lion to his knees." If this adventure is exhilarating, its dark side is sickening: a blind violence that exults in killing. This later becomes a major theme of "The Quaker Graveyard in Nantucket."

The Puritans wrestled with the devil, with the powers of blackness, and this drama, spelled out in their theology and acted out in the colonial experience, intrigues Lowell. The serpent is an omnipresent figure in the gardens of his America. Evil is double-dealing, vital, corporeal; it inflicts a lasting isolation. It is precisely because he denies the crucifixion, "washes out the blood-clots on my Master's robe," that Emerson is rebuked in "Concord." Unlike the Puritans, Emerson lacks a tragic sense; he fails to account for human conflict, war, evil, "the Hanging Jesus." As a rival system to Puritanism, in the "lurch / For forms to harness Heraclitus' stream!" (the flux), Transcendentalism comes off second-best. "Concord," Lowell chides, "you loved the heart / Without a body."

Lowell excels at funerary art, at epitaph-making, and in the elegaic sequence "In Memory of Arthur Winslow," the finest poems in *Land of Unlikeness,* he mingles his Gothic religiosity with ambiguous pride in his birthright and discomfiture at the Puritan heritage—even if his ancestors had not burned any Salem witches like Hawthorne's. The weight of his ancestors is heavy; they speak to him from the grave of loss: loss of power, loss of a secure selfhood, loss of grace.

"The faith / That made the Pilgrim Makers take a lathe / To point their wooden steeples lest the Word be dumb" is indeed cleft. Because he reluctantly sees the devil's dominion extended to his family's homestead, his problem is to avoid their spiritual errors so that he will hear clearly "The *resurrexit Dominus* of all the bells." For although "the Ghost / Of risen Jesus walks the waves to run / Arthur upon a trumpeting black swan / Beyond Charles River to the Acheron / Where the wide waters and their voyager are one," the poet frets that he will strike out for shore and find himself embarked in Charon's raft, and that he will be stranded in an estuary of hell.

Where his grandfather and the Puritans went wrong was in the spiritual fraudulence of their speculations. "All our fathers won / When Cotton Mather wrestled with the fiends from Hell" is an ironically futile victory: an artificial system of rewards and punishments, a complacency that justified their reckless and man-demeaning power as a longing for God. But neither their mercantile vigor nor their quest for a sure witness to their Election won them a spiritual haven: grace is inaccessible to them. Similarly, his grandfather, fearful of history passing him by and eager to recover not only the family's wealth but its vanished eminence, imperils his soul by acceding to the "devil's notions" that gold could revive life. Curtly, Lowell rejects their doctrines and appeals to Mary for aid, but the fourth and final poem ends on an unresolved note because, hell burned out and "heaven's harp-strings" slack, Lowell identifies two Lazaruses, only one of whom was resurrected; it is not clear whether Mary actually pours "Buckets of blessings on his burning head."

Notwithstanding his God-intoxication, his Edwardsean belief that God is glorified by Man's dependence, Lowell cannot shake free of his confusions and overwrought crises to write simply about the things that matter to him: his boyhood, family, and Americanness; his sense of engulfing chaos. It is not a matter of insincerity—Lowell believes that he believes and that he is unworthy of grace—but poetically his Catholicism is probably responsible for the Baroque embellishments of his language, for a feigned knowledge and contrived emotionalism, whereas his Puritanism, as in "Children of Light," calls forth a spare, stark language and a relative fidelity to his emotions.

The virtues of *Land of Unlikeness* are considerable: a wittiness, a range of materials, and a sonority that give the volume its literary precocity. The parodic elements and declamatory style, the jeremiads, mirror Lowell's unquiet, diffuse sensibility. Even while aspiring to largeness of statement he fails to achieve it because of bathos, bookishness, and intellectual inchoateness, and even more because he could not yet, or did not think to, sort out his feelings about his ancestors and marry his rhetoric to those feelings: the strain is excessive. Nevertheless, to a remarkable degree, the outlines of his sensibility and his historical imagination, ununified as they might be, took shape in this volume.

II

While Lowell rejected many of the poems from *Land of Unlikeness,* and rewrote many others, for his second volume, *Lord Weary's Castle,* the rhetorical surge continues. But an important change takes place. Technically, the heavily stressed lines are given more breathing space, and the hyperbole that produced the clotted rhetoric is pared down. In his best poems, Lowell is now not so much at the mercy of his monotonous brilliance, but can convert what was merely histrionic into tense paradoxes and what were mere religious ventriloquism into an authentic poetic voice. A credible "I" breaks through the recurring crises. The poems, one feels, are the works of a secular Manichee unable to endure the almost unbearable pressure of living in a world of contingent freedom that requires recreating the self every moment.

Lowell's predicament is well described by Wallace Stevens in "Esthétique du Mal." There are two categories of world,

> The peopled and the unpeopled. In both, he is
> Alone. But in the peopled world, there is
> Besides the people, his knowledge of them. In

> The unpeopled, there is his knowledge of himself.
> Which is more desperate in the moments when
> The will demands that what he thinks be true?

What Stevens could face with meditated calm, with the Imagination's "miraculous thrift," Lowell had to overwhelm with "rugged gesture" and prodigality. It is not just that Stevens possessed a philosophic temperament of imperturbable ripeness and that Lowell seemed to write out of an exacerbated will and an overheated nervous system. Rather, it points to the different ways the contemplative and the dramatic poet go about solving the problem of evil and representing their salvational ordeal on this "imperfect globe." Willing to struggle along unaided by tradition, never losing his essential poise, an unsentimental "connoisseur of chaos," Stevens patiently sets about constructing a central man. His is a heroic mind that fashions order out of the pluralist things of this world and places them in the lucid argument of a poem. By contrast, Lowell's schemes seem hasty and quickly discarded. He besieges reality and hammers at the gates for an otherworldly revelation. Armaggedon is always near. "Time, the Turk, its sickle on its paunch," and its infidel cohort Death are arrayed against his Christian faith. Lowell wishes, to invert Melville's phrase, to speak "Yes! in Thunder," but he is forced to pull up short against the strength of his negations. His is a heroic anxiety. The verb "lurch" appears frequently, reflecting the uncontrollable gait of a mind that condemns itself to watching the spectacle of its own damnation. Lowell's imagery, as Randall Jarrell has noted,[2] is predominantly kinetic and tactile, as though he were trying to hold himself together by clenching his will and the world's body. The poems are jagged, shrill, muscular, energetic; their aesthetic weakness is that their abundant miscellany of details blots out the whole. Finding little pleasure in the sensuous things of this world, Lowell

[2] Randall Jarrell, "From the Kingdom of Necessity," *Poetry and the Age* (New York, 1953), p. 196. This essay and Jarrell's review of *The Mills of the Kavanaughs* are still the finest statement of the strengths and weaknesses of Lowell's first three volumes.

pushes past them—and confirms his sense of essential disorder and his status as a fractional man.

In this early stage of his spiritual growth, his soul in revolt, Lowell turns less to the history of his family than to episodes in American history and to American writers for evidence that man is a poor, guilty internal migrant who deserves to be mercilessly judged and whose only hope for redemption lies in throwing himself before the throne of Jesus or Mary. Yet Lowell's poetic imagination is empirical, concrete, not transcendental; the pain rather than the resolution convinces the reader. The hands are the hands of Jesus but the voice is the voice of John Calvin. The narrowness and iron of the Puritans seep into his heart's blood. He writhes in the shadow of war and death. America is indicted in the brief poem "Children of Light":

> Our fathers wrung their bread from stocks and stones
> And fenced their gardens with the Redman's bones;
> Embarking from the Nether Land of Holland,
> Pilgrims unhouseled by Geneva's night,
> They planted here the Serpent's seeds of light;
> And here the pivoting searchlights probe to shock
> The riotous glass houses built on rock,
> And candles gutter by an empty altar,
> And light is where the landless blood of Cain
> Is burning, burning the unburied grain.

At once heroic and petty, destroyers and creators in the Eden of the New World, the pilgrims are doing Satan's work, sowing dissension and a malign knowledge, not salvation. "Unhouseled," a word used of Hamlet's father, they are denied holy communion, because they have tamed the wilderness and created an enclosed garden (order) by murdering the Indian. They are unhinged, like Cain, an outcast and fratricide whose offering to God is spurned. There is something niggardly in the Puritans' schemes: the plenty of America and her ideals are unharvested, devoured by the flames of hate.

Lowell has always been exceptionally sensitive to the hypocrisy in

American democratic institutions, to the gap between the pious preachings of equality and freedom, couched in evangelical terms, and the abuses of power in practice. The Puritans' fanatic will to master the New World, which they assured themselves was in keeping with God's bidding or Providential design, is, to Lowell, the disease in American character. This heritage disquiets and outrages Lowell: the tendency to carry individuality to the extremes of unreason so arrogantly that it seems to war, like Ahab, against Being itself.[3]

The paradoxes of "The Quaker Graveyard in Nantucket" are instructive on this point. The Quakers, pacifists turned expert whale-killers, have misinterpreted God's ordinance giving man dominion over the fishes of the sea and all creation. Religious zeal is matched by commercial zeal, and the vast resources of American power, including the spiritual "funds" of idealism, are marshaled ruthlessly to destroy the whale for profit. As for Ahab, the assertion of the self's infinite freedom turns into a religious vendetta. "The Quaker Graveyard in Nantucket" is a dirge in the grand manner, like *Moby Dick,*[4] which examines with a mixture of fascination and horror the self breaking down in violence—and seizing death. Section V, a half-mocking, half-worshipful apocalypse describes vividly how the grim American reapers "hack the coiling life out" of the whale—and out of their demented selves.

There is nothing honorific or derived in Lowell's use of Melville. He grasps intuitively Melville's feeling that the sea is filled with sharks, that the evil in the self daringly quests to crush and challenge creation and the creator. Lowell's mind is not as metaphysical or profound as Melville's, but it is similar in seeing a hideous (cosmic)

[3] On June 3, 1965, Lowell turned down an invitation to the White House Festival of the Arts in protest against the Vietnam war. In his eloquent statement, one can hear his pained conscience: "We are in danger of imperceptibly becoming an explosive and suddenly chauvinistic nation, and we may even be drifting on our way to the last nuclear ruin."

[4] The poem is, of course, an elegy for his cousin, Warren Winslow, a Destroyer captain in World War II whose ship hit a mine and sank without trace of survivors.

allegory in the American exercise of power, wracked as it is by paroxysms of violence. Both have an edgy intelligence. Both use rhetoric to appease their demons—the awful Father, Authority, pain, death. Both are twisted, in Hart Crane's phrase, by a "love of things irreconcilable."

As the quiet prayer to "Our Lady of Walsingham" shows, Lowell can propose a faith in which man can find peace: if he shakes off the "dragging pain" of his willful interrogations and comes as a pilgrim to this rustic shrine. This requires not so much a belief in the efficacy of the Virgin's intervention[5]—her face "Expressionless, expresses God," and the expressionless demeanor is the key—as a humility that enables a man to stand apart from the fury of the world and contemplate the plain truth, a truth that surpasses even "castled Sion," the promised land of the church and other illusory havens. Mary teaches that there is a knowledge beyond the strife to know.

But this interlude of safety amid the frenzied pitch and roll of the verse, and the intensely dramatic posing of the questions of active evil, punishment, and atonement, is no remedy. The sea boils with the wrath of Jehovah. The covenant has been violated, and the American commonwealth, like the Pequod, packs off to hell, after trying in vain to harpoon "IS, the whited monster." The Atlantic is not their artery of commerce, or lifeline, but their undertaker. Dying "When time was open-eyed, / Wooden and childish," deluded that the "mad scramble of their lives" is in accord with God's commands, that His will is revealed to them,[6] the Quakers "are powerless / To sand-bag this Atlantic bulwark." Their enterprise was heroic but ignoble, desperate, ignorant, prideful. And Ahab, "The

---

[5] The imagery is not exclusively Christian, even in this section. There are references to the Druid tree, to Poseidon, Jehoshaphat's ash-pit, Shiloah's whirlpools, and so forth. They give the poem a broader scope.

[6] Section III ends with these ironic lines, parodying a Quaker hymn: "In the spermwhale's slick/I see the Quakers drown and hear their cry:/'If God himself had not been on our side,/When the Atlantic rose against us, why,/Then it had swallowed us up quick.'"

mast-lashed master of Leviathans," the American Odysseus, does not survive his voyage to oust his enemies; he is lashed to the back of Moby Dick, his adversary, and returned to the "sea's slime." He is too vengeful—for all his guile, too blinded by solipsism.

The slashing rhetoric of "The Quaker Graveyard in Nantucket" has been both highly praised and derided.[7] Its language, modeled on that of *Moby Dick*,[8] makes no concessions, except in section VI, to a serene alternative to the malevolent sea, its dissonances and its "hell-bent deity." Unlike Hart Crane, Lowell does not trust much in Orpheus' power to pluck life back from the underworld. No Romantic proclamation that poetry consoles man for the pains and setbacks of experience is heard. The bones that "Cry out in the long night for the hurt beast / Bobbing by Ahab's whaleboats in the East" pierce the mind: the world is filled with a cacophony that art cannot harmonize. We are left with a view of men as sailors, doomed voyagers, "seamonsters, upward angel, downward fish," who dance upon the void. The sovereignty of the Lord God hovering over the face of a universe in which "blue-lung'd combers lumber to the kill" is a permanent warning of cataclysm. That it shares in such ominous power and tremendous presence signals the near-greatness of Lowell's poem.[9]

"At the Indian Killer's Grave," the companion poem to "Quaker

[7] Hugh Staples, in his slim useful volume *Robert Lowell* (New York, 1962), devotes an entire chapter to the poem, pp. 45–52, comparing it favorably with "Lycidas" and "Adonais" as an elegy. But compare John Bayley's judgment in a recent issue of *London Magazine* (June, 1966), p. 78: "The early poetry is a signal instance of what T. S. Eliot called 'a poetry that is purely verbal, in that the poem will give us more of the same thing, an accumulation rather than a real development of thought and feeling.' It creates no world into which we can move, explore, discover." English critics are perhaps too glib about, and frightened by, American rhetoric.

[8] Staples points out in an appendix, *op. cit.,* p. 101, that much of the imagery of section I comes from Thoreau's *Cape Cod*.

[9] Most of the poems in *Lord Weary's Castle* were written during World War II; the historical context helps explain why the dark moments of the American past cast a long shadow over Lowell's mind.

Graveyard," brings together a more ruminative style with another investigation of the themes of corrupt spirituality and Judgment. The Puritans are again the culprits. The quotation from Hawthorne's "The Gray Champion" that stands as the headnote to the poem states the ugly paradox: "Here, also, are the veterans of King Philip's war, who burned villages and slaughtered young and old, with pious fierceness, while the godly souls throughout the land were helping them with prayer." The poet, standing in the graveyard of King's Chapel where the Puritans are buried, and where, incidentally, Lowell's ancestors, John and Mary Winslow lie, is genuinely shocked and baffled by the presumption of these Indian-killers. That their theology could countenance such "holy" wars so repels him that he consents to their punishment. They have made the garden rotten. The "laugh of Death" mocks their dust, their memory; their contentions have come to naught. King Philip is made to say, interrupting the poet's dream vision:

> "The Judgment is at hand;
> Only the dead are poorer in this world
> Where State and elders thundered *raca,* hurled
> Anathemas at nature and the land
> That fed the hunter's gashed and green perfection—
> Its settled mass concedes no outlets for your puns
> And verbal Paradises. Your election,
> Hawking above this slime
> For souls as single as their skeletons,
> Flutters and claws in the dead hand of time."

There can be no atonement, and their judgment is as terrible as their Calvinist creed. In the words of the Gospel (*Matthew* 5:22): "But I say unto you, That whosoever is angry with his brother without a cause shall be in danger of the judgment: but whosoever shall say, Thou fool, shall be in danger of hell fire." Man is apart from Nature: the inanimate world and his own. Putrefaction spreading throughout the poem, the poet turns at the end of his pristine vision of the Virgin

Mary's conception of Jesus, where "Grace-with-wings" vanquishes "Time-on-wings," as the only exit from his impasse:

> Her soul a bridal chamber fresh with flowers
> And her whole body an ecstatic womb,
> As through the trellis peers the sudden Bridegroom.

This outburst of religious cantillation closed a long tortuous chapter in Lowell's life—and in his art.

III

The Mills of the Kavanaughs is a transitional volume, the bulk of which is given over to the title poem, an extended monologue that moves in the realm of revery, dislocated by occasional nervous shudders. With the exception of "Mother Maria Theresa" and "Falling Asleep over the Aeneid," I do not think that the poems succeed, mainly because Lowell cannot disguise his voice (or construct a *persona*), but they mark a decisive shift away from the historical to the domestic, a gradual secularizing and relaxing of his imagination, an increase in self-understanding. The passionate earnestness, the startling prophetic images of *Lord Weary's Castle* remain, and a new stillness is added, as though the lives of these ordinary Maine people he records reminded him that his own memory contained a rich gallery of human portraits usable in poetry: his family universe. In the sketches of *The Mills of the Kavanaughs,* the style of *Life Studies* struggles to emerge. Like Yeats, Lowell learned that he could revisit his ancestral houses, and by capturing the fugitive voices of their inhabitants in his verse, open a new world of meaning, plant the self in an agreeable tradition—all the while keeping a valuable quarrel with that past alive.

IV

In *Life Studies,* a poetry of the nerves and the mind turns slowly into a poetry of the heart. The strands of family heirlooms, so tangled with historical personages and religious gropings in the earlier poems, now earn prominence. The stridencies are gone, subdued, not by an act of will, but an act of imaginative empathy. It is not that Lowell attains, at one stroke, a harmonious attachment to the world, that he becomes a healed or whole man. That would be inaccurate. One still hears the anguished music of a man rent by a sense of inadequacy, sometimes situated in dour isolation, sometimes, as in "To Speak of the Woe That is in Marriage," prowling the streets to satisfy the hunger of his spirit for splendors dreamed of. He is still the tainted wether of the Lowell flock, incomplete, desiring a more spontaneous, easygoing self. For that reason, he is not a great love poet. His erotic life, as presented in the verse, is too embattled, just as his poetic line remains too taut. He lives in a purgatory of spasmodic fulfillments and penitence: the Puritans' unhappiness with the body obtrudes, as does a suppressed sexuality that alarms and delights him. Beyond Lowell are Auden's air of convivial domesticity, his ironic tenderness, mirrored in the silken civility of his line, and his worldly grasp of love's manners.

Nevertheless, there is, without any loss of his usual linguistic spiritedness, a distinct loosening up in *Life Studies*. Lowell discovers his remarkable gifts as a memorialist. He stops painting proto-religious allegories or wild huddled landscapes of his mind and American history. Where previously he walked through the brambles of America, like a hermit, thorns cutting his flesh, he now seeks community. He is captivated by his boyhood, by his origins, by the people and places that sheltered or astonished him with their eccentricities. It is as if coming upon a family album, he suddenly realized that these personal icons and pieces of statuary breathed, and held the secret of a more genial self; whereupon he set out to reconstruct that past in reminiscent poetry and in the superb autobiographical fragment *91 Revere Street*. As he remarks, "There, the vast number of remembered *things* remain rocklike. There, all is preserved by that motherly care that one either ignored or resented in his youth. The things and their owners come back urgent with life and meaning—because finished, they are endurable and perfect."

With characteristically painful candor, he chronicles the decline of

his family from its position as "The Hub of the Hub of the Universe."
Through a tinted glass he views them and a Boston living on the
accumulated capital of its favored past, a Boston of Public Gardens,
swan boats, St. Marks, Harvard, Symphony Hall, its tumble-down
religious and social life, its crotchets and class biases. Lowell can be as
satirical as T. S. Eliot toward the proprieties and anemic intellectual
life of Boston, and the high-minded maunderings of its religious life.
(He can also appreciate its reverence for and pursuit of civilized
order.) His characters, we imagine, take in The Boston *Evening
Transcript,* too. Unsparingly, and with deprecating humor, poise, and
affection, Lowell delineates the environment of his rearing, which
means, particularly, his parents. These portraits help explain certain
qualities and themes of Lowell's verse: why, for example, he feels so
often an outcast from his body, why he anatomizes failure, why
his inner life is divided.

His father was a Naval officer turned business-man, considerate,
feckless, discontent, a "matter-of-fact man of science" who withdrew
from responsibilities and settled into a round of ritualized habits.
Militantly respectable and acerbic, his mother, on the other hand,
was apparently the decisive influence on his character; from her he
seems to have assimilated elements that are "chic, romantic, impulsive."
As inheritors and haphazard guardians of a once illustrious past,
they passed on to him his high sense of his calling as a poet. He is
alert to but alienated from the heft and expansive vulgarity of
democratic America. Lowell's place in the social hierarchy, from
which he fled—his plight, one might say—was like Henry Adams':
uncomfortable with the robust pragmatism and technological spirit of
industrial America, and suspicious of the freedom the Whitmans and
Emersons conferred upon the self as natural law. Lowell's observations
of his family, like his earlier scrutiny of the Puritans and American
writers, make him doubt that power can be humanely and wisely
used, and even skeptical of camaraderie, though the poem "To
Delmore Schwartz" celebrates a rare carefree spirit. Above all, his
mind is purged of a need for doctrine and ideology.

If *91 Revere Street* towers over the entire volume, the fourth and last section, which at first reading seems merely a poetic gloss on the autobiographical text, is a brilliant recapitulation of his relation to his ancestors. It is a *bildungsroman* in verse, an American *Prelude,* told with more relish and charm than Wordsworth could muster, detailing the growth of a poet's mind and sensibility through select encounters with generations of Lowells and in a social milieu bounded by Beacon Hill and Dunbarton, New Hampshire. The poems take Lowell from boyhood to the birth of his own child, the cycle continued yet altered. Rich documentaries teeming with life and death, with daft people and curious artifacts grown musty with age, they disclose an unexpectedly precious heritage.

His verse forms grow freer and more casual than in his earlier poems, and his wit is released from bondage to rhetoric and rhyme, just as his will is unclenched. In "My Last Afternoon with Uncle Devereux Winslow," the adult retracing the pathways of his childhood, without fussing to extract a pattern, leafs through the family annals and finds in its oddities of dress and personality, its bibelots and events, not just the paraphernalia of family legends, but the texture of life itself. Section III illustrates Lowell's method and vision:

> Up in the air
> by the lakeview window in the billiards-room,
> lurid in the doldrums of the sunset hour,
> my Great Aunt Sarah
> was learning *Samson and Delilah.*
> She thundered on the keyboard of her dummy piano,
> with gauze curtains like a boudoir table,
> accordionlike yet soundless.
> It had been bought to spare the nerves
> of my Grandmother,
> tone-deaf, quick as a cricket,
> now needing a fourth for "Auction,"
> and casting a thirsty eye

on Aunt Sarah, risen like the phoenix
from her bed of troublesome snacks and Tauchnitz classics.
Forty years earlier,
twenty, auburn headed,
grasshopper notes of genius!
Family gossip says Aunt Sarah
tilted her archaic Athenian nose
and jilted an Astor.
Each morning she practiced
on the grand piano at Symphony Hall,
deathlike in the off-season summer—
its naked Greek statues draped with purple
like the saints in Holy Week . . .
On the recital day, she failed to appear.

The passage is redolent with the flavor of a bygone age, but there is
nothing merely picturesque. The household setting is composed like
a Bonnard interior. It is a novelistic scene of extraordinary
compression, which yet gives one the feeling of the slow passage of
forty years in which to measure the tragicomic spinsterhood of
Aunt Sarah. Just cataloguing the "dummy piano," "Tauchnitz
classics," the canny tone-deaf Grandmother, the notorious jilt, and
above all, the poignant figure of Sarah enthralls the poet. But he
preserves his distance. He reserves moral comment. A master of pace,
he weaves the lines from long to short and back again, shrewdly
guiding the reader to the climactic revelation of Sarah's failure to
appear at her recital. The reader discovers afterwards that a civilization
has been rendered and judged. The conversational style has an
infectious authority; even the faint rhymes and the punctuation, as in
the penultimate line, contribute to the drama. And one must look
twice to notice that the tumble of similitudes is a low-keyed, cadenced
version of the clangorous plenty of *Lord Weary's Castle*.

"Dunbarton" is Lowell's generous tribute to his grandfather, the
patriarch who made a community of two with the child and who
presided over stout delights and the first hesitant steps to try out

various roles and experiences. By the poet's own testimony "He was my Father. I was his son." The two like boon companions rake leaves from the family graveplot, drive the New Hampshire roads, "pumpship" together. Lowell juxtaposes racy local facts, like old Mr. Burroughs, who "had stood with Sherman at Shiloh," with the larger uncertainties of life and death. His grandfather Winslow represents the stability and security which reassured the young boy as he suffered his sense of the miniscule, passive, defenseless nature of man, embodied in his fantasy of the newt:

> In a tobacco tin after capture, the umber yellow mature newts
> lost their leopard spots,
> lay grounded as numb
> as scrolls of candied grapefruit peel.
> I saw myself as young newt,
> neurasthenic, scarlet
> and wild in the wild coffee-colored water.

Lowell's art is primarily elegaic, and "Grandparents," the next poem in the sequence, shows the persistent and nostalgic clutch of memory. He mourns the death not only of his grandparents, but of a slower age that has passed into history like "the last Russian Czar" on whose picture he doodles "handlebar mustaches." The poem, and his remembrances (he is now in the period of his adolescence), are shot through with a bitter sense of unalterable alienation; the tone, one of contained heartbreak, is almost frigidly objective until the poet bursts out emotionally in the liturgy of the marriage ceremony: "Grandpa! Have me, hold me, cherish me!" His grandparents had provided the compensatory love and protection against the hurtful bickerings of his parents' fragmented married life. Filtering through his consciousness are images of failure, or morbid self-disparagement. The farm now his own, bereft of the warm presence of the family, he tries to recapture their sentience and clarity but feels ruefully estranged.

The next four poems of the sequence—"Commander Lowell,"

"Terminal Days at Beverly Farms," "Father's Bedroom," and "For Sale"—record his father's decline and death, and the aftermath: the breaking up of the family's home. The emotions are reticent, as if Lowell felt a perturbed forgiveness and stern love for his father, difficult to express. The lines have the factual crispness of reportage but underneath they are charged with complicated feelings:

> Smiling on all,
> Father was once successful enough to be lost
> in the mob of ruling-class Bostonians.
> As early as 1928,
> he owned a house converted to oil,
> and redecorated by the architect
> of St. Mark's School. . . . Its main effect
> was a drawing room, "longitudinal as Versailles,"
> its ceiling, roughened with oatmeal, was blue as the sea.
> And once
> nineteen, the youngest ensign in his class
> he was "the old man" of a gunboat on the Yangtze.

Reviewing the highspots of his father's career——his tour of duty as a Naval officer in China, his pride in his up-to-dateness (owning "a house converted to oil")—and his life as a kindly misfit among "the mob of ruling-class Bostonians," Lowell displays a caustic allegiance to him. "Sailing from Rapallo," a threnody for his mother, ironically contrasts the warmth of life on board the ship taking her body back from Italy and the cold finality of death, imaged in the wintry graveyard in New Hampshire where she is to be buried. "During Fever" speaks the final judgment on his mother:

> Terrible that old life of decency
> without unseemly intimacy
> or quarrels, when the unemancipated woman
> still had her Freudian papá and maids!

All this effort at becoming re-acquainted with his past taxes Lowell, and does not set him free. The rest of the poems deal with marital discord, and Lowell's two incarcerations: in McLean's Hospital for mental illness and in the West Street jail for being a conscientious objector to World War II. His mood as he approaches middle age is contradictory, sometimes torpid ("Cured, I am frizzled, stale and small"), and sometimes one of jocular pain. "I myself am hell," he cries out in "Skunk Hour,"[10] echoing Satan's self-consciousness in *Paradise Lost* ("who sees undelighted all delight"), and we are aware that for the poet the universe is still as inhospitable as in his earlier days, only now he can accept the fact with mature equanimity. "Skunk Hour" depicts a dark night of the soul ("My mind's not right") whose terror is more intense because the tone is full of an autumnal dejection and a troubled, restrained tenderness.[11]

In the final poem of the volume, "Colonel Shaw and the Massachusetts' 54th," later retitled "For the Union Dead," Lowell almost consciously tries to leave behind the private world and write a public elegy about a heroic incident during the Civil War. But something recessive still holds him: "I often sigh still / for the dark downward and vegetating kingdom / of the fish and reptile." He has journeyed far from the brackish truths of "The Quaker Graveyard in Nantucket," yet returned unwittingly to them. The difference is that he now lives courageously without the aid of Christianity or myth.

V

There are roughly four basic kinds of poems in *For the Union Dead,* only a few of which are concerned directly with Lowell's ancestors and the American heritage. One set of poems, about middle age, is often set in Maine or New York, and has a flat uninflected twang;

[10] There is an interesting discussion of "Skunk Hour" by Richard Wilbur, John Frederick Nims, and John Berryman, with a rejoinder by Lowell, in *The Contemporary Poet as Artist and Critic,* ed. Anthony Ostroff (Boston, 1964), pp. 82–110.

[11] The genre of this and other poems in *Life Studies* is related, I think, to the conversational poems of Coleridge, especially "This Lime Tree Bower" and "Frost at Midnight," though of course Lowell's idiom is contemporary American.

it is a poetry of statement calling forth from memory once again a shared experience: "Old Flame," which attempts to recover the excitement and insight of an earlier intimacy, or "The Scream," which quarrels with the very ability and value of the mind's remembering something for a long while. Not surprisingly, a second category consists of topical poems, like "July in Washington," "Buenos Aires," and "Fall 1961," which mix political commentary with the poet's taking of his emotional pulse. The latter poem discusses the possibility of nuclear extinction with impatient resignation, or even worse, an immobility filled with mirthless laughter and gabble, not panic; as time ticks off the moments to Armageddon, we are as helpless and puny as minnows to prevent it.

The third group of poems, by far the largest, are direct confessions of his fatigue, querulous announcements of his myopic vision. Feeling is distraught. "I am tired. Everyone's tired of my turmoil," he complains in "Eye and Tooth." His body aches ("Child's Song"); *angst* increases. His despair and vulnerability are out on the surface, but they are so rationally presented, without hysteria, that one scarcely notices them go by ("Lady Ralegh's Lament" and "Going to and fro"). In short, Satan is back in the garden, challenging and triumphant, though this time the Fall is mainly re-enacted in personal and social rather than religious and historical terms. And the voice of the gangling, embarrassed self is that familiar one of the Puritans. Like them, the more Lowell tries to achieve freedom, the more he ties himself up in knots; but he does not, as Robert Bly wrongly remarks,[12] apotheosize this alienation. He is sickened by his own hectic fever, by his shrieks of pain, by the struggle not to run himself down. Sloth, or its modern form, extreme self-consciousness, not lust as in *Life Studies,* is his besetting sin. The Muse visits like death. And while the verse is as technically proficient as ever, the line being chopped up into small bits, the stanzas lightly brushed with rhyme, and the tempo marked *largo,* a prosiness takes over at times.

[12] Robert Bly, "The Dead World and the Live World," *The Sixties* (Spring, 1966), pp. 2–7.

In the poems about Hawthorne and Jonathan Edwards, the fourth and smallest group in the volume, Lowell finds two kindred souls or fellow sufferers. The Hawthorne poem, the simpler of the two, pays homage to the novelist who survived the boredom and drabness of the Custom House in Salem and who, unlike the bland and bearded Unitarian patriarchs, the Longfellows and Holmeses, brooded on "the commonest thing, / as if it were the clue. / The disturbed eyes rise, / furtive, foiled, dissatisfied / from meditation on the true / and insignificant." We are meant to identify Lowell with the older man's "shy distrustful ego" which "felt those flashes / that char the discharged cells of the brain." The irritability is Lowell's.

It is logical that, given his inward-turning mind and his long feud with the Puritans, Lowell should twice write about Jonathan Edwards, the archetypal Puritan. But it is a mistake, I think, to interpret the two poems, "Jonathan Edwards and the Spider" from *Lord Weary's Castle* and "Jonathan Edwards in Western Massachusetts," simply as indictments of Edwards and rebellion against the falsity of the New England Calvinist tradition. Especially in the second poem, derision yields to respect, to a recognition of what Perry Miller called Edwards' "aboriginal and monolithic power." "Ah paradise!" Lowell addresses Edwards, "I would be afraid / to meet you there as a shade. / We move in different circles." But do they? Edwards is a mirror refracting Lowell's image. Both are mild men "under a sentence of condemnation to hell," solitaries doubting the adequacy of their salvational schemes, knowing that "Hope lives in doubt. / Faith is trying to do without / faith." The fires of the Calvinist hell may be banked for Lowell, but he allows the possibility of a far worse self-generated hell where numbness, terror, and a sense of imperfection prevail, where love is absent. "Edwards," says Perry Miller, "was a Puritan who would not permit mankind to evade the unending ordeal and the continuing agony of liberty."[13] So is Lowell. And if Edwards could believe that "people are spiders" in spite of the glories of God's world, so does Lowell. Not intellectually, perhaps, but emotionally.

[13] Perry Miller, *Jonathan Edwards* (New York, 1949), p. xiv.

Edwards' spider recurs obsessively in the imagery of *For the Union Dead*: "Your lightness alters everything / And tears the black web from the spider's sack," he says to his wife in "Night Sweat," and we share in the muted pain, in the awful truth that the will to die is locked in the breast of all men, and self-belittlement is often its name. Like Edwards, Lowell says numerous times "I am contemptible, / stiff and dull." "White wig and black coat, / all cut from one cloth, and designed / like your mind!" Lowell exclaims. Largeness of spirit and flexibility save Lowell from Edwards' antinomian rigor, but even as late as this poem he is compelled to concede Edwards' argument that "All rising is by a winding stair." Lowell's development has been to venture that arduous climb.

The world of Lowell's poems is a world of wonderful particulars. The qualities most conspicuously missing in his verse are not hard to locate: joy and jubilation certainly, in Stevens' phrase, "the rotund emotions"; a sort of Keatsean indolence that takes a pleasure in the sensuous creation this is unaccountable—and need be so. This sometimes shuts out a sense of inevitability as well as lyrical repose. But Lowell has what no other American poet writing today has: scale, featly energy, inventiveness. His singular achievement does honor to his ancestors and to his predecessors in the American tradition: it illuminates the moral history of our time.

Hayden Carruth
A Meaning of Robert Lowell

A book reviewer looking at Robert Lowell's new book, *Near the Ocean* for the first time would find good reasons to be annoyed with it and to say so forcibly. The book itself, for one. It is a pretentious volume; printed on expensive paper, bound in heavy cloth and stamped in three colors, decorated with twenty-one drawings by Sidney Nolan, designed lavishly and wastefully in an outsize format, jacketed in varnished sixty-pound stock—in short, a very self-conscious-looking collector's item, which might easily provoke a reviewer into making a little investigation. He could learn without difficulty, for instance, that publication of the book had been postponed several times, and that the price had been announced progressively at $4.95, $5.50, and $6.00. Why? Our reviewer would soon discover that the longest piece in the book, a translation of Juvenal's Tenth Satire, had appeared in a magazine version, in *Encounter,* only a few weeks before the book came out, and he would see significant differences between the two texts. He would surmise that last-minute revisions had been made in the poem—hence, very likely, the delays in publication—and he would wonder if other equally impetuous revisions had been made in other poems, especially the personal ones whose texts are spattered with ellipses. He would wonder also if the resetting of so much type had required the increases in price. He would read the note at the front of the book, in which Lowell, speaking of Nolan's drawings, says: "May my lines throw some light

By permission of *The Hudson Review,* Vol. XX, No. 3 (Autumn, 1967).
Copyright © 1967 by The Hudson Review, Inc.

on his!"—apparently meaning that the poet hopes a certain reciprocity of example will ensue between texts and illustrations. But what a curious way to say it, what a slip of the two-edged pen. As for the drawings themselves; would indeed, our reviewer might exclaim, that the poems could illuminate them, they need it! Next he might look at the table of contents, where he would count the titles, seven poems and six translations, and wonder if readers should be asked to pony up six dollars for so small an offering of untried work. Finally our reviewer would turn to the texts themselves, where he would find, first, an ill-assorted group of translations from classical and Renaissance poems, not Lowell's best, and second, among the original pieces—the slight heart of this slight book—one conventional tribute to Theodore Roethke and six personal poems: strange poems, not poorly written in the usual sense, on the contrary fairly glittering with the acuity and verbal shrewdness we expect from Lowell, and yet so awkward nevertheless, so fragmentary, devious, elliptical, and even stilted that they seem—well, to make the best of it, bewildering.

How could our reviewer fail to give the book an angry notice? Hifalutin ostentation: nobody likes it. All the less do we like it in contrast to Lowell's other books, which, in their quiet formats and with their modest crosshatch illustrations by Francis Parker on the title pages, make an attractive and more reasonable appearance. *Near the Ocean* looks unmistakably like a "big production" that was supposed—if not by Lowell, by someone—to catapult the poet into the cushiest seat in stardom; as if he weren't sitting there already. But by its own overreaching, it has failed.

Our reviewer, if he had an enquiring mind, would not be satisfied simply to blast the book's appearance, however. He would wish to find out why Lowell wrote these strange new poems, and what purpose their new style is intended to serve. In short, he would change himself, if he were able, from a reviewer into a literary critic. He would study all Lowell's work, he would divide, classify, elucidate, analyze, and compare, and he would give us a schematic judgment which might or might not be useful to us, and which might or might not have something to do with the poems.

Incidentally, if he were a proper scholar, he would begin his essay with a review of previous critical opinions, which in the case of Lowell's poetry comprise a truly splendid range: from servile adulation to contumelious rejection. Obviously this hodgepodge offers a great opportunity to a critic who fancies his own rhetorical prowess.

For my part, I am no critic. More's the pity perhaps, because I do find, like our hypothetical reviewer, that I am unwilling to rest on the simple distaste aroused in me by Lowell's new work, a distaste which is uncertain, at that, inconsistent and unformed. I would like to know more. In consequence I must attack the poems in the only way I can, namely, as a fellow poet, someone who has worked the same side of the street for roughly the same period, and who presumably knows something about the difficulties of the job. This is what I propose to do, i.e., to look at the poems less as finished works than as objects coming into being. Indeed, for reasons I shall elaborate, I think this is the only way one can look at Lowell's work of the past fifteen years.

The risks in my method are great, of course. One is that I shall stray from my literary topic into what is normally considered personal or biographical. To those who may charge me with this, I give two answers. First, I shall not stray far because I do not know Lowell personally, having met him only twice, for a few minutes each time and at an interval of more than a decade. My knowledge of the man comes either directly or by inference from his own writing, and from what I have heard during twenty years on the edge of the literary world. Secondly, in dealing with poetry as personal as Lowell's, or as personal as most poetry written nowadays in America, the risk of infringing upon the poet's privacy is properly speaking no risk at all. An invitation has been extended to us: why shouldn't we accept it?

II

The place to begin then, I think, is with a biographical datum. Robert Lowell is, and for some years has been, the most envied poet in the country. The consequences of this are many, but for the moment I wish simply to enforce the fact. I envy Lowell. Everywhere I go among literary people I meet only others who envy Lowell. The reasons for it are obvious enough: his great advantages. First, the advantage of his birth in a distinguished family. One does not wish to insist on this, but at the same time it is not negligible. No doubt being born with a ready-made cultural and social status is sometimes a hindrance, but often it is a help too, and in our hearts most of us would be glad to put up with the one if we could thereby attain the other. Secondly, the advantage of talent and intelligence. I am not speaking of the particular concrete expressions of these properties, but of the properties themselves. From the first Lowell's poetry has had an inner force bespeaking his great native gifts. It has put him in the class of wonder boys, along with poets like the early Auden and Dylan Thomas who, however idiotic they may sometimes look in other respects, were simply unable to write a trite or flaccid line. Most of us must cultivate poorer gardens. If we console ourselves with the idea that the best crop sometimes comes from meager soil, nevertheless we yearn often enough, in our adverse labor, for the facility of mere brilliance. Thirdly, the advantage of success. Let anyone say what he will, Lowell is our leading poet. It is a fact. He has power, influence, and an enormous reputation. His books, for example, are kept in print and they sell steadily—what a joy that must be! We all, I know, are reasonable creatures, and we realize that success is more often a nuisance than a blessing. But are we so inhuman that we deny our envy of those who have it? I hope not.

Envy is a tricky thing, of course. It takes many directions. At bottom it accounts, I believe, for ninety per cent of the critical response to Lowell's work, the wide range of opinions, and it accounts too for the concentration of responses at the extremes of the scale: adulators at one end, detractors at the other. As for the adulators . . . but why not call them by their right name, the flatterers? In their multitude we dismiss them; and we need add only that although their opinion in the long run may turn out to be right, and Lowell's poetry may be seen to be precisely as great as they say it is, if this happens it will be not because of, but in spite of, what they themselves are saying and doing now. The detractors, whose motives may be equally disreputable, are nevertheless forced by the nature of their position to take a more discriminative view, and hence their expressions of opinion may be actually helpful to us in making discriminations of our own. At least I shall go on that presumption.

Myself, after discounting as well as I can my own factor of envy, I find that my uncritical, workingman's response to Lowell's achievement changes from time to time but generally hovers between the two extremes. In each stage of his poetic evolution, Lowell has written a few poems that seem to me extremely fine, and he has also written poems that seem to me mannered, pointless, incomplete, and obscure. Indeed, try as I may—and I have tried again and again over the years—some of his poems, particularly his earliest and then again his latest, remain incomprehensible to me, as dark and profuse as a pot of Bostonian whistleberries. Moreover, I cannot escape the feeling that some of this obscurity has been purposely, even crassly laid on.* For me, this is the single largest detracting element in his work.

One point, however, I wish to make perfectly clear. Lowell's position of leadership seems to me not only to have been earned but to be altogether suitable. I say this on two counts. As a man, Lowell has given us more than enough evidence of his firmness and integrity—one thinks of his conscientious objection during the war and all that it entailed, his refusal to attend White House sociables, and many other such actions—to substantiate his moral fitness for the role. As a poet, he gives us this same integrity in art. When I read his poetry, however negative my response may be to its effect, I know I am in the presence of an artist *in extremis,* operating, I should say struggling, at the limits of sensibility and technique. This is a quality

* Lowell has admitted as much. See his *Paris Review* interview.

which we consider peculiarly American, a kind of hardrock Yankee pertinacity, and to me it is peculiarly attractive. Who was it that said he would fight it out on this line if it took all summer? An American military man, I believe. When I read Lowell's lines, I feel that he has fought it out upon them for years. This is tough and homely and American. It is admirable. It is what leads me to place Lowell alongside William Carlos Williams, rather than in the company of older poets to whom he bears a closer superficial resemblance.

It is also what leads me, in the perennial confrontation of artists and the rest of the world, to rest content under his leadership. If my standing behind him will add to the strength of his position, he may be sure I am there.

III

So much for preliminary considerations. The phases of Lowell's poetic evolution are so well-known that I need indicate them only briefly. We may dismiss his first book, *Land of Unlikeness,* which was published in a limited edition that few people have seen; Lowell himself effectively dismissed it when he republished its main poems, considerably revised, in *Lord Weary's Castle,* the book that established him with one shot as a leader of his generation. Written in the first flush of enthusiasm after his conversion to Catholicism, the poems were highly charged devotional lyrics mixed with autobiographical elements, presented in an elaborate formal dress: close rhymes, exact meters, a heavy reliance on couplets, and an equally heavy reliance on the rhetoric of allusion. It was a virtuoso performance. At its best, in perhaps a fourth of the poems, it showed a young poet writing with genuine spontaneity in the strict forms of the English metaphysical convention, while bringing to them his own distinct voice and idiosyncratic manner. In short, Lowell had done what everyone had been saying could not be done: he had invented a new style. In his next book, *The Mills of the Kavanaughs,* he stuck with it but most readers considered the book a falling-off, especially the long title poem. What this poem, a dramatic narrative in monologue, showed was that the ability to sustain narrative tension across the librations of discrete pentameter couplets is lost to us: the suspension bridge has replaced the viaduct.

Lowell waited eight years to publish his next book. Then, in 1959, he presented us with a change of appearance so radical that it seemed a reversal. The formal manner was gone; no pentameters, no rhymes, no ornate rhetoric. The book, called *Life Studies,* which more than recouped his reputation, gave us instead poems in open, loose measures, without rhyme, in a diction that seemed easy and almost insouciant. The heart of the book was a group of autobiographical poems so intensely candid that critics immediately called them "confessional"; an unfortunate choice of terms. It implied that Lowell was engaged in public breast-beating, a kind of refreshing new psycho-exotic pastime, or in a shallow exercise of "self-expression," long ago discredited; whereas in fact his aim was far more serious than that.

The following two collections of poems, *For the Union Dead* in 1964 and *Near the Ocean* this year, have continued to explore themes of autobiographical candor, but have gradually reverted toward formalism. Not the conventional formalism of *Lord Weary's Castle,* however. Now the meters, though basically iambic, are cast in rough lines of trimeter and tetrameter, punctuated with purposefully inexact rhymes. The diction is more extreme, more peculiar and concise, than in *Life Studies,* and the syntax has become progressively more taut, split up into smaller and smaller units. This has gone so far in the latest poems that one can scarcely find a complete sentence from stanza to stanza, but only phrases, expletives, stabs of meaning. The effect, although entirely different from the high style of *Lord Weary's Castle,* nevertheless brings us back to an obscurity and artifice that seem to denote another reversal; the simplicity of *Life Studies* has been jettisoned.

In effect, Lowell made, in *Life Studies,* a considerable leap into a new area of poetic experience, which he has been exploring, since then, through increasingly elaborate means. Why he did this, what was in his mind, are questions readers must try to answer if they would understand the actual meaning of Lowell's experiment.

I have said nothing about the translations, perhaps because they are a source of embarrassment to me. Over the years Lowell has made a good many, including a couple of long ones and a whole book of short ones, from many languages, called *Imitations*. When this book was published in 1961, I reviewed it enthusiastically. The density and tonicity of the best translations took hold of me and persuaded me that Lowell had reached far toward the intrinsic qualities of the original poems, especially in his Baudelaires. Since then, my friends who know Baudelaire better than I have informed me with cogency that this is not true, and that I had no business reviewing such a book in the first place. Well, they are right on both counts, as I have ruefully come to see. Aside from the intended alterations of sequence and literal meaning which Lowell acknowledges, there is, for instance, the way in which Baudelaire's characteristic elegance, deriving from the fluent, almost sinuous build-up of stanzas and longer passages, is fragmented and rigidified in Lowell's choppy phrasings. And there is the way, too, in which Baudelaire's post-romantic sense of beauty is both reduced and roughened in its passage through Lowell's anguish-ridden, New Englander's sensibility; the flowers of evil become merely evil flowers—a considerable difference when you stop to think about it. Lowell's detractors seize on these points, and others, as ammunition for their campaign, which is made easier by the evident inferiority, when judged against any standard, of some of the translations. The Villons are quite bad, the Rimbauds and Pasternaks barely passable. But I continue to feel that the best of the Baudelaires, Rilkes, and Montales are excellent Lowells indeed, and this is all he had claimed for them. He does not call them translations, but imitations. Perhaps he should have gone further and specified that what he was imitating was not the poetry of Baudelaire or Rilke or the rest, but the poetry of Lowell; perhaps he should have chosen another title, e.g., *Appropriations* or *Assimilations*. No matter; the point is that Lowell has made a perfectly legitimate effort to consolidate his own poetic view of reality by levying upon congenial authentications from other languages and cultures. The best of his translations go together with the best of *Life Studies* and *For the Union Dead* to comprise the nucleus of his mature work, the organic unity of which must be apprehended by those who wish to form reliable judgments.

IV

Even at the most superficial level of technique, the prosodic level, Lowell's evolution, both his successes and his failures, offers a fascinating study to people who are interested in the disciplines of poetry. This is usually the case when important poets change styles. Consider Lowell's commonest prosodic device, the suspended or Hopkinsian upbeat produced by ending a line on the first syllable of a new unit of syntax, a phrase or sentence. He made it work well, not to say famously, in his early poems, but when he abandoned strict pentameters he had more trouble with it. How do you employ this very useful concept of metrical enjambment when your line-structure has been purposely unfixed? It is the old story: you can't have your cake and eat it too. Simple as it appears, this is a crucial problem, perhaps *the* crucial problem, of contemporary unmetered poetry, which different poets have met in many different ways. Some have adopted the practice of reading their poems with abrupt pauses at the end of each line, but this is an oral stratagem that seems to have little connection with the actual dynamics of the poem. Denise Levertov has gone further by developing her concept of "organic form," which appears, however, to be incompletely worked out at this stage.* Like her, Lowell has preferred to work on the page, i.e., within the poem's prosodic structure; but with indifferent success in many instances. Conceivably such a simple matter as this, which is nevertheless extremely important in terms of Lowell's natural style,

---

* Miss Levertov assumes a base in Charles Olson's "projective verse," of course, but to my mind Olson's ideas are even more unfulfilled (and unfulfillable).

lies behind his recent return to more exact, or more exacting, meters.

But that is a topic for another discussion. What I am interested in here is something prior to poetry. Before a man can create a poem he must create a poet. Considered from the limited perspective of artistry, this is the primal creative act.

Imagine Lowell seated at his work-table on some ordinary morning in 1950. *Lord Weary's Castle* has been out for four years; already its triumph is a burden. The poems in *The Mills of the Kavanaughs,* now at the press, have been finished for a year or more, and are beginning to slip into the past, to seem stale, remote, and incidental—like the verses of one's friends. Now I have no idea what Lowell would be doing in such circumstances, probably brooding and daydreaming like the rest of us, but for the moment let me ascribe to him a simple, orderly, godlike self-mastery that neither he nor you nor I nor Charles de Gaulle can claim in actuality. In 1950, given that marvelous perspicacity, he would have had to ask himself two questions. In essence, what is my theme? In general, what is my defect?

One does not ask these questions once and then go on to something else, one asks them over and over, as one asks all unanswerable questions. A serious poet moves progressively toward his essential theme, though he can never reach it, by means of exclusions, peeling away, from poem to poem, the inessential, working down to bedrock; and he examines every word he writes for clues to his defect. In the case of Lowell we cannot doubt that he works in such a state of constant tension and self-interrogation. Yet it seems clear to me, even so, that at some point around 1950 he must have asked these questions with special intentness. Nothing else can account for the change of poetic stance so strikingly evident in *Life Studies.*

What had Lowell set out to do in his first poems? He had set out explicitly, I think, though ingenuously, to build on the Donne-to-Hopkins tradition of devotional poetry in English, to write poems of faith. The evidence, in the poems themselves, is unmistakable. Consequently he had produced a rather large number of set pieces in a high style, such as the poems about Jonathan Edwards and other historical figures or events, affirming a public, devotional aspiration. This is what all young poets do, isn't it? They begin, or at least they try to begin, where the mature poets they admire left off. They do this in the compulsion of their literary zeal, in spite of the evident unfeasibility of it, owing to the irremediable disparity of experience. At the same time Lowell interspersed among his devotional pieces various autobiographical elements, usually disguised and highly wrought, set out in the same taut, allusive, difficult style as the rest, but genuine autobiography nevertheless. I think it must have become evident to him by 1950 that in spite of the very great but purely literary success of the devotional set pieces, these autobiographical poems were the more alive, the more interesting, and ultimately the more comprehensible.

Poems like "Mr. Edwards and the Spider" and "After the Surprising Conversions" are good specimens of their kind, but like all their kind they are sententious. That is to say, a large part of their meaning is a stable and predictable element of the general cultural situation, with which the poems are, so to speak, invested. (And under "meaning" I intend the entire affective and cognitive experience of the poem.) But the autobiographical poems or partly autobiographical poems, like "Mary Winslow" and "At the Indian Killer's Grave," work themselves out in their own terms, within their own language; and in spite of the high gloss of artifice that remains upon them, they speak with urgency.

All this is even more evident today, fifteen years later. The most prominent motifs of the poems in *Lord Weary's Castle* are the Christ, the Crucifix, and the Virgin; they are repeated on almost every page. Yet they remain inert. They are not personal realizations, they are not symbols, they are merely tokens (which perhaps, in the tradition Lowell had chosen, is all they can be). The personal motifs, on the other hand—personal guilt, personal death, personal time, personal violence and desire—are what carry the poet along, and they are connected, not with devotional aspirations, but with his experienced life. He returns to them again and again in poems about himself, about his mother and the Winslow family, and about his father, Commander Lowell. In *Life Studies* he simply relinquished one set of motifs, the former, and took up the other. The resulting augmentation of his poetic stature—his personal stature as creator within the domain of his poetic materials—was enormous.

As I say, Lowell cannot discover the precise specifications of his theme, which is lucky for him. If he were to do so, he would be clapped into silence instantly. Nor can we do it for him, which is equally lucky. All we can do is brood, as he does, over his lines and the shadows behind them, tracking down the motifs to see where they lead. In my own recent brooding I turn especially to two lines from the poem called "Night Sweat" in *For the Union Dead*:

> always inside me is the child who died,
> always inside me is his will to die . . .

Simple enough; explicit enough. They are one expression of the radical guilt which took form like any other, leaving aside psychoanalytical factors: first from elements of generalized cultural guilt, in Lowell's case the New Englander's shame over the Indians and the Salem women, which has exercised an obviously powerful influence on his imagination; then from guilt that all men feel, with deep necessity, for the deaths of their own fathers; and finally from the horrendous events of contemporary history. But what is the punishment for the crimes that produce this pervading guilt? It is personal death. We all know this, from the first moment of our mortal recognition. Yet against this Lowell casts again and again his instinctive belief in the remission of sin, or rather his knowledge, his feeling, of his own undiminished innocence. Then what can our death be? What is our guilt? There is only one answer, outside of absurdity. Our death is our sin, for which we pay in advance through our guilt. Our death is a crime against every good principle in the universe: nature, God, the human heart. Yet we, the innocent, are the responsible ones—this is the idea Lowell cannot forego. We carry this crime, like a seed, within us. Our bodies are going to commit it, do what we will. They are going to carry out this murder, inexorably, while we stand by, helpless and aghast.

This is the ultimate Yankee metonymy, you might say. Puritan death as punishment for sin contracts, under the paradox of benign Transcendentalism, to death as sin. Naturally it is a theological monstrosity. It is impossible. Yet in the human and poetic sphere, it is a validity of staggering force.

Well, all this is highly conjectural, of course. There are scores of other, doubtless better ways to approach Lowell's theme, I'm sure. Yet I feel this progressive identification of sin, guilt, and death can be traced fairly directly from such poems as "At the Indian Killer's Grave" to "Night Sweat" and beyond. The two lines I have quoted strike close to it. They are literal. When Lowell says "inside" I think he means inside: he is carrying this sin-death around in him like a monstrous illegitimate pregnancy. I would almost bet that if he suffers the common nightmare of artists, the dream of male parturition, it is a dead thing that comes out (at which point, if he hasn't awakened, his dream may be suffused with bliss).

Meanwhile Lowell has his defect, for which he should give thanks. It permits him to relax into the mercy of technical self-criticism. Not that it is easy to deal with; quite the contrary. Like all fundamental defects, it is a function of his personality, and hence wears many faces. I call it the defect of pervasive extraneity; but it could have other names. One aspect of it was quite clear, however, in *Lord Weary's Castle:* the laid-on metaphysical obscurity. This was the fashion of poetry at the time, and Lowell accommodated himself to it easily and naturally; and without the least poetic infidelity. We must bear in mind in considering fashion that a fashion during the period of its ascendancy is not a fashion; it is merely what is right. In composing the poems of *Lord Weary's Castle,* Lowell had no sense, I'm certain, of doing anything but what was necessary. He had no sense of *doing* anything at all, except writing poetry as it is written. Nevertheless, the obscurity, like the ornate style and the use of inert

figures from a general cultural conspectus, was clearly extraneous to
his main themes and objectives, as he could see five or six years later,
and he gave it up; this was his defect and he chopped off its head.
But it sprang up elsewhere, hydra-like. Other aspects of it were more
difficult to see. For instance, in the title poem from *The Mills of the
Kavanaughs,* he had shown his inability to sustain the long units of
poetry, and at the same time his great talent for the short units:
the line and phrase and isolated image. These are his forte. Lowell can
rap out a single sharp line with extraordinary facility. The trouble
is that these brilliant strokes may contribute nothing to the whole
fabric and intention of a poem; they may be merely extraneous—
pervasively extraneous because in spite of their irrelevance, they do
sit within the total structure and they cannot be eradicated once the
poem has acquired a certain degree of distinctness.

In a poem called "The Scream" from *For the Union Dead,* Lowell
writes of the time when his mother gave up her mourning:

> One day she changed to purple,
> and left her mourning. At the fitting,
> the dressmaker crawled on the floor,
> eating pins, like Nebuchadnezzar
> on his knees eating grass.

We have all seen this, of course, a woman crawling on the floor, her
mouth full of pins, to adjust another woman's hem, and so we are
struck by the originality of Lowell's simile. It seems to me absolutely
genuine; I have never encountered it before. Hence the pins and grass
collapse together spontaneously in my mind like a perfect
superimposition of images. I am charmed. Only when I stop to think
do I realize that Nebuchadnezzar and what he stands for have only
the remotest connection with this scene, and that the dressmaker
herself is a figure of no importance in the poem. As an image,
this is a brilliant extraneity: the defect at work.

And what shall we say about the appearance of the new book, its crass and confused ostentation? This is gross extraneity and nothing else.

In short, Lowell's defect is a temptation to mere appearance, to effects, trappings—to the extraneous. And it arises, I believe, from a discrete imagination, i.e., an imagination which works best in disjunctive snatches. I suppose some people would call it an analytic, rather than a synthetic, imagination. His problem as a poet during the past fifteen or twenty years has been to continue digging deeper toward his essential theme, while at the same time turning, if it is possible, his defect into an advantage.

V

So far I have been writing about Lowell as if he were an isolated case, but the reverse is the truth. He is a poet of his time. The shift of focus in his poetry has been one part, a very small part, of a general shift in artistic values and intentions during the past quarter-century.

When was the last time in our western civilization that a writer at his work-table could look at a piece of writing and call it finished, self-enclosed and self-sustaining, autonomous—a work of art in the original sense? I'd say in poetry it must have been at the time of Pope, and in fiction, since the novel lags behind, perhaps as late as Flaubert or Turgenev; but actually no one could draw the lines so precisely. The change from one notion of art to another was very gradual. All we can say with certainty is that sometime during the nineteenth century—that changeful time!—the old idea of the enclosed work of art was dislocated in the minds of serious artists: Heine, Rimbaud, Strindberg. Such men began to see that art is always unfinished; and from this arose the concept of its a priori unfinishability, i.e., its limitlessness. For a time—quite a time—the two concepts ran side-by-side; many artists tried by various means to combine them. In the forepart of our century, for instance, we got the idea of the circularity of artistic structure, from which derived the work of art that was both limitless and enclosed: *The Waste Land* and *Finnegans*

Wake. These were grandiose conceptions. They made art into something it had not been before, a world in itself.* They were helped along by the general collapse of values in the post-Nietzschean cultures of Europe. Some artists, despairing of their own painful nihilism, even tried to substitute for the reality of the world the anti-reality of art—or of style, the word, or whatever—believing that only by this means could they create a bearable plane upon which to enact human existence and build a consistent scheme of values. I am thinking of such men as Gottfried Benn, Céline, and Wyndham Lewis, or in a different way of Breton and the Surréalistes. Of course Hitler's war smashed all that, proving the ugliness and irresponsibility of it. Reality was reality after all. We came out of the war badly shaken, clinging to the idea of existential engagement. Henceforth, contrite as we were, we would be responsible and free, creative within the real world. Yet what could this mean in a reality over which we had no control, a reality in which we, the conscious element, possessed nothing but the lunatic knowledge of our own super-erogation, to use Auden's terms? If anti-reality were denied us by our own responsibility, and if reality were denied us by our own alienation, what could we create? We decided—and to my mind the inevitability of it is beautiful— that what we could create was life. Human life.

It was not a retreat to anti-reality. In looking back we saw that, after Nietzsche, we had been living in a crisis of intellectual evolution, a terrible blockage and confusion; we had been absorbing what Jaspers calls "the preparing power of chaos." Now we were ready to go forward. Now, in freedom and responsibility, we began to see the meaning of what we had known all along, that a life is more than a bundle of determined experiential data. (For the biggest horror of our crisis had been the complex but empty enticements of Freudian

* An extreme statement; in one sense art had always been a world apart. But in another the enclosed *and* limitless masterpieces of 1910–1940 did raise the possibility of an art that was not only distinct from "objective reality" but contradistinct; thus engendering a philosophical departure far more serious than the shallow Yellow-Book estheticism from which it partly sprang.

positivism.) A life is what we make it. In its authenticity it is our own interpretation and re-organization of experience, structured metaphorically. It is the result of successive imaginative acts—it is a work of art! By conversion, a work of art is life, *provided it be true to the experiential core*. Thus in a century artists had moved from an Arnoldian criticism of life to an Existential creation of life, and both the gains and the losses were immense.

The biggest loss perhaps was a large part of what we thought we had known about art. For now we saw in exactly what way art is limitless. It is limitless because it is free and responsible: it is a life. Its only end is the adventitious cutting off that comes when a heart bursts, or a sun. Still, the individual "piece" of art must be objective in some sense; it lies on the page, on the canvas. Practically speaking, what is a limitless object? It is a fragment; a random fragment; a fragment without intrinsic form, shading off in all directions into whatever lies beyond. And this is what our art has become in the past two decades: random, fragmentary, and open-ended.

Hence in literature any particular "work" is linear rather than circular in structure, extensible rather than terminal in intent, and at any given point inclusive rather than associative in substance; at least these are its tendencies. And it is autobiographical, that goes without saying. It is an act of self-creation by an artist within the tumult of experience.

This means that many of our ideas about art must be re-examined and possibly thrown out. I have in mind not our ideas of technique, derived from the separate arts, but our esthetic generalizations derived from all the arts. Such notions as harmony, dynamism, control, proportion, even style in its broadest sense. How do these criteria apply to a work which is not a work at all, conventionally considered, but a fragment? I do not say they do not apply; I say the applications must be radically re-determined.

As readers, where does this leave us? In a mere subjective muddle? Sometimes it seems so. For that matter, why should we read another person's poems at all? Our life is what concerns us, not his. Is he a

better observer than we, a better imaginer, a better creator? Can his
self-creation of his life assist us in ours, assuming a rough equivalence
of human needs and capacities? Perhaps; but these too are subjective
criteria. What then?

All I can say is that the most progressive criticism we have now *is*
subjective, resolutely so and in just these ways. It asks what a poem can
do for us. The reason we have so little of it is that we are unused to
such methods and fearful of them, and we do not know upon what
principles to organize them. Our critics are years behind our artists,
still afraid of the personal, ideal, moral, and contingent. For strangely
enough, these four qualities are just what we preserve in fragments
but destroy in wholes. Working philosophers know this. In a grave
correspondence to human limits, an apothegm is better philosophy
than an organon.

Still, I see some evidence, here and there, that the critics are
beginning to stir themselves.

VI

What Lowell thinks of all this he hasn't said. He has written almost
no criticism, and apparently does not intend to write any. I salute him!
But at all events we know that he has been working for twenty years
in the heart of the movement I have described, among eastern writers
and artists. He has been associated with the painters who gave their
work the unfortunate names of abstract expressionism and action
painting, and with theatrical people who have used such concepts as
the happening and non-acting acting; these being half-understood
designations for the artist's life-constructing function. This has been
Lowell's milieu. Of course he has shared it with many other writers;
what I have been discussing in terms of Lowell's work is a shift or
tightening of artistic intention which cuts across every line. And
one thing more is certain. Whatever the rationale, or whether or not
there is any rationale, we cannot read Lowell's autobiographical
writing, from *Life Studies* to *Near the Ocean,* without seeing that we
are in touch with a writer who is in fact making his life as he goes

along, and with a degree of seriousness and determination and self-awareness that surpasses the artistic confidence of any previous generation. He has resolved to accept reality, all reality, and to take its fragments indiscriminately as they come, forging from them this indissoluble locus of metaphoric connections that is known as Robert Lowell. No wonder he is enthusiastic.

Hence we see that in his translations, and for that matter in all his work, Lowell's methods are distinct from those of Ezra Pound. This is a distinction we must be careful to draw, I think, because Pound's methods have become so much second-nature to us all that they blur our recognition of the principal fact about the two poets, viz. that the historical gulf separating them is enormous. Thus when Pound wrenches and distorts Propertius in the translations from the Elegies, or when he capsulates writing from many sources in the *Cantos,* he does so in the interest of a general program of cultural aggrandisement conducted from a base of personal security. There is no uncertainty of values in the *Cantos;* in this respect the poem is as old-fashioned as *Candide* or Boethius. Nor is there any uncertainty of poetic personality. The writer—"ego, scriptor"—is a steady and reliable, if sometimes rudimentary, presence. Pound's work, in effect, is an Arnoldian criticism of life on a very grand scale, which is only possible because the critic looks out from the secure bastion of his own personality founded on a stable scheme of values. Lowell, on the other hand, is a poetic ego without fixtures: in a sense neither being nor becoming, but a sequence of fragments, like the individual frames of a movie film, propelled and unified by its own creative drive. This does not mean that Lowell's work lacks values; his poems are as strenuously moral as anyone's. But his objective is not critical, nor even broadly cultural; it is personal; and the moral elements of his poetry are used, not as precepts, but as the hypotheses of an experimental venture in self-validation. In his autobiographical work, both translations and original poems, Lowell employs many of Pound's devices, perhaps most of them, but his ends are his own—and this makes all the difference. It means a radically different creative outlook, issuing in new poetic justifications and criteria.

And so I return to my starting-place; for I am sure everyone knows that the hypothetical reviewer with whom I began is really myself, and that all this speculation springs from the moment when my review copy of *Near the Ocean* arrived in the mail. I have already said that I do not like the sequence of autobiographical poems which forms the heart of this new book. Let me add to this three further points.

1. Why has Lowell moved progressively away from the simplicity of *Life Studies* toward a new formalism? Is it only a reversionary impulse? Is it an attempt to give greater objectivity to the random, fragmentary materials of his autobiography by reintroducing elements of fixative convention? Is it from a desire to make fuller use of his talent, i.e., to turn his defect to advantage by emphasizing prosody and syntax? No doubt all these reasons, and others, are at work. But the result is a too great concentration of effort upon the verbal surface—to my mind very unfortunate. We now have poems which are compositions of brilliant minutiae, like mosaics in which the separate tiles are so bright and glittering that we cannot see the design. A mosaic is fine, it is the model *par excellence* for poetry in our time, but if we are to see the pattern, the separate pieces must be clear and naturally arranged; and in the best mosaics the colors are subdued rather than gaudy.

2. In point of substance I ask, still in a firmly subjective mode: what are the most useful parts of autobiography? To my mind the most interesting of Lowell's poems are those from his present, concerning his wife, divorce, children, illness, etc., but these are few and small compared to the great number about his youth and childhood, his ancestors, his visits to the family graveyard. I detect a faint odor of degenerate Freudian sentimentalism. Have we not had enough of this, and more? We are interested in the man, the present, unfinished, lively being. If the term "confessional" is to be applied to Lowell's work, although I have said why I think it is inadequate, then I suggest he has not confessed enough. In particular one topic is lacking, unless I am mistaken: his conversion to the Church of Rome and his subsequent—should I say recusancy? I hardly know. He was in and then he was out, and the rest for us is a mystery. Surely this touches

the man. And surely it touches many issues of our time: justice, probity, the individual and the mass, the role of love in society, even peace and war. In effect, I advocate a stiffening up of autobiographical substance, a colder and more realistic view. Let the rigor now reserved for verbal superficies be applied to the exact new content of experience.

3. But judgment fails. In this art it has not found its place. If I were to suggest one ultra-technical criterion still available to a poet in Lowell's circumstances, I would say: relevance. Be random, yes, fragmentary and open-ended—these are the conditions of life—but scrutinize every component of your act of creation for its relevance. The advantage of random observation is not only in what comes but in what is let go. Avoid the extraneous like the plague. Lowell does not always manage it, and his defect is not the advantage it might be. His style, though more deeply in-wrought than before, is still too much like a shell, a carapace, an extraneity. We see again and again that the most difficult work of imagination is not when it soars in fantasy but when it plods in fact. And what a force of imagination has gone into these poems! A man's being, fought for, fragment by fragment, there on the page: this we can recognize. And we know that in such poetry the risk of failure is no longer a risk, but a surety. It must be taken, eaten. The very poem which seems most awkward to us may be the one that will wrench us away, finally, from the esthetic fixatives of the conventions of irresponsibility, and release us into responsible creation. If we read Lowell's new poems in the light of the problems he is facing, we will know that although we must, since we are human, judge them, our judgment is not something superior or separate, it is a part of his struggle, as his struggle is a part of ours. In this knowledge we may discover what we have been groping toward for centuries: not humility, which we don't need, nor magnanimity, which I hope we already have, but the competence of human freedom.

Norman Mailer
from *The Steps of the Pentagon*

We find, therefore, Lowell and Mailer ostensibly locked in converse.
In fact, out of the thousand separate enclaves of their very separate
personalities, they sensed quickly that they now shared one enclave
to the hilt: their secret detestation of liberal academic parties to
accompany worthy causes. Yes, their snobbery was on this mountainous
face close to identical—each had a delight in exactly the other kind of
party, a posh evil social affair, they even supported a similar vein of
vanity (Lowell with considerably more justice) that if they were
doomed to be revolutionaries, rebels, dissenters, anarchists, protesters,
and general champions of one Left cause or another, they were also,
in private, *grands conservateurs,* and if the truth be told, poor damn
émigré princes. They were willing if necessary (probably) to die for
the cause—one could hope the cause might finally at the end have
an unexpected hint of wit, a touch of the Lord's last grace—but wit or
no, grace or grace failing, it was bitter rue to have to root up one's
occupations of the day, the week, and the weekend and trot down to
Washington for idiot mass manifestations which could only drench one
in the most ineradicable kind of mucked-up publicity and have for
compensation nothing at this party which might be representative of
some of the Devil's better creations. So Robert Lowell and Norman
Mailer feigned deep conversation. They turned their heads to one
another at the empty table, ignoring the potentially acolytic drinkers at
either elbow, they projected their elbows out in fact like flying

buttresses or old Republicans, they exuded waves of Interruption Repellent from the posture of their back, and concentrated on their conversation, for indeed they were the only two men of remotely similar status in the room. . . .

Lowell, whose personal attractiveness was immense (since his features were at once virile and patrician and his characteristic manner turned up facets of the grim, the gallant, the tender, and the solicitous as if he were the nicest Boston banker one had ever hoped to meet) was not concerned too much about the evening at the theater. "I'm just going to read some poems," he said. "I suppose you're going to speak, Norman."

"Well, I will."

"Yes, you're awfully good at that."

"Not really."

Harrumphs, modifications, protestations and denials of the virtue of the ability to speak.

"I'm no good at all at public speaking," said Lowell in the kindest voice. He had indisputably won the first round. Mailer the younger, presumptive, and self-elected prince was left to his great surprise—for he had been exercised this way many times before—with the unmistakable feeling that there was some faint strain of the second-rate in this ability to speak on your feet.

Then they moved on to talk of what concerned them more. It was the subject first introduced to Mailer by Mitch Goodman. Tomorrow, a group of draft resisters, led by William Sloane Coffin, Jr., Chaplain at Yale, were going to march from their meeting place at a church basement to the Department of Justice, and there a considerable number of draft cards would be deposited in a bag by individual students representing themselves, or their groups at different colleges, at which point Coffin and a selected few would walk into the Department of Justice, turn the cards over to the Attorney General, and await his reply.

"I don't think there'll be much trouble at this, do you?" asked Lowell.

"No, I think it'll be dull, and there'll be a lot of speeches."

"Oh, no," said Lowell with genuine pain, "Coffin's not that kind of fool."

"It's hard to keep people from making speeches."

"Well, you know what they want us to do?" Lowell explained. He had been asked to accompany a draft resister up to the bag in which the draft cards were being dropped. "It seems," said Lowell, with a glint of the oldest Yankee light winging off like a mad laser from his eye, "that they want us to be *big buddy*."

It was agreed this was unsuitable. No, Lowell suggested, it would be better if they each just made a few remarks. "I mean," said Lowell, beginning to stammer a little, "we could just get up and say we respect their action and support it, just to establish, I suppose, that we're there and behind them and so forth."

Mailer nodded. He felt no ease for any of these suggestions. He did not even know if he truly supported the turning in of draft cards. It seemed to him at times that the students who disliked the war most should perhaps be the first to volunteer for the Army in order that their ideas have currency in the Army as well. Without them, the armed forces could more easily become Glamour State for the more mindless regions of the proletariat if indeed the proletariat was not halfway to Storm Troop Junction already. The military could make an elite corps best when the troops were homogenized. On the other hand, no soldier could go into combat with the secret idea that he would not fire a gun. If nothing else, it was unfair to friends in his outfit; besides it suggested the suicidal. No, the irony of the logic doubtless demanded that if you disapproved of the war too much to shoot Vietcong, then your draft card was for burning. But Mailer arrived at this conclusion somewhat used up as we have learned from the number of decisions he had had to make at various moral crossroads en route and so felt no enthusiasm whatsoever for the preliminary demonstration at the Department of Justice tomorrow in which he would take part. To the contrary, he wondered if he would burn or surrender his own draft card if he were young enough to own one, and he did not really know the answer. How then could he advise others to take the action, or even associate his name? Still, he was going to be there.

He started to talk of these doubts with Lowell, but he could hear the sound of his own voice, and it offended him. It seemed weak, plaintive, as if his case were—no less incriminating word—phony, he did not quite know why. So he shut up.

A silence.

"You know, Norman," said Lowell in his fondest voice, "Elizabeth and I really think you're the finest journalist in America."

Mailer knew Lowell thought this—Lowell had even sent him a postcard once to state the enthusiasm. But the novelist had been shrewd enough to judge that Lowell sent many postcards to many people—it did not matter that Lowell was by overwhelming consensus judged to be the best, most talented, and most distinguished poet in America— it was still necessary to keep the defense lines in good working order. A good word on a card could keep many a dangerous recalcitrant in the ranks.

Therefore, this practice annoyed Mailer. The first card he'd ever received from Lowell was on a book of poems, *Deaths for the Ladies (and other disasters)* it had been called, and many people had thought the book a joke which, whatever its endless demerits, it was not. Not to the novice poet at least. When Lowell had written that he liked the book, Mailer next waited for some word in print to canonize his thin tome; of course it never came. If Lowell were to begin to award living American poets in critical print, two hundred starving worthies could with fairness hold their bowl out before the escaped novelist would deserve his turn. Still, Mailer was irked. He felt he had been part of a literary game. When the second card came a few years later telling him he was the best journalist in America, he did not answer. Elizabeth Hardwick, Lowell's wife, had just published a review of *An American Dream* in *Partisan Review* which had done its best to disembowel the novel. Lowell's card might have arrived with the best of motives, but its timing suggested to Mailer an exercise in neutralismanship—neutralize the maximum of possible future risks.

Mailer was not critically equipped for the task, but there was always the distant danger that some bright and not unauthoritative voice, irked at Lowell's enduring hegemony might come along with a long lance and presume to tell America that posterity might judge Allen Ginsberg the greater poet.

This was all doubtless desperately unfair to Lowell, who, on the basis of two kind cards, was now judged by Mailer to possess an undue unchristian talent for literary logrolling. But then Mailer was prickly. Let us hope it was not because he had been beaten a little too often by book reviewers, since the fruit of specific brutality is general suspicion.

Still Lowell now made the mistake of repeating his remark. "Yes, Norman, I really think you are the best journalist in America."

The pen may be mightier than the sword, yet at their best, each belongs to extravagant men. "Well, Cal," said Mailer, using Lowell's nickname for the first time, "there are days when I think of myself as being the best writer in America."

The effect was equal to walloping a roundhouse right into the heart of an English boxer who has been hitherto right up on his toes. Consternation, not Britannia, now ruled the waves. Perhaps Lowell had a moment when he wondered who was guilty of declaring war on the minuet. "Oh, Norman, oh, certainly," he said, "I didn't mean to imply, heavens no, it's just I have such *respect* for good journalism."

"Well, I don't know that I do," said Mailer. "It's much harder to write"—the next said with great and false graciousness— "a good poem."

"Yes, of course."

Chuckles. Headmastersmanship.

Chuckles. Fellow headmastersmanship.

They were both now somewhat spoiled for each other. Mailer got up abruptly to get a drink. He was shrewd enough to know that Lowell, like many another aristocrat before him, respected abrupt departures. The pain of unexpected rejection is the last sweet vice left to an aristocrat (unless they should happen to be not aristocrats, but secret monarchs—then watch for your head!). . . .

So Mailer gave his introduction to Macdonald.* It was less than he would have attempted if the flight had not been grounded, but it was certainly respectable. Under the military circumstances, it was a decent cleanup operation. For about a minute he proceeded to introduce Macdonald as a man with whom one might seldom agree, but could never disrespect because he always told the truth as he saw the truth, a man therefore of the most incorruptible integrity. "Pray heaven, I am right," said Mailer to himself, and walked past Macdonald who was on his way to the mike. Both men nodded coolly to each other. . . .

Lowell sat in a mournful hunch on the floor, his eyes peering over his glasses to scrutinize the metaphysical substance of his boot, now hide? now machine? now, where the joining and to what? foot to boot, boot to earth——cease all speculations as to what was in Lowell's head. "The one mind a novelist cannot enter is the mind of a novelist superior to himself," said once to Mailer by Jean Malaquais. So, by corollary, the one mind a minor poet may not enter . . .

Lowell looked most unhappy. Mailer, minor poet, had often observed that Lowell had the most disconcerting mixture of strength and weakness in his presence, a blending so dramatic in its visible sign of conflict that one had to assume he would be sensationally attractive to women. He had something untouchable, all insane in its force; one felt immediately there were any number of causes for which the man would be ready to die, and for some he would fight, with an axe in his hand and a Cromwellian light in his eye. It was even possible that physically he was very strong—one couldn't tell at all—he might be fragile, he might have the sort of farm mechanic's strength which could manhandle the rear axle and differential off a car and into the back of a pickup. But physical strength or no, his nerves were all too apparently delicate. Obviously spoiled by everyone for years, he seemed nonetheless to need the spoiling. These nerves—the nerves of a consummate poet—were not turned to any battering. The squalls of the mike, now riding up a storm on the erratic piping breath of

* Dwight Macdonald, literary critic and political commentator.

Macdonald's voice, seemed to tear along Lowell's back like a gale. He
destested tumult—obviously. And therefore saw everything which
was hopeless in a rife situation: the dank middle-class depths of the
audience, the strident squalor of the mike, the absurdity of talent
gathered to raise money—for what, dear God? who could finally know
what this March might convey, or worse, purvey, and worst of all—
to be associated now with Mailer's butcher-boy attack. Lowell's eyes
looked up from the shoe, and passed one withering glance by the
novelist, saying much, saying, "Every single bad thing I have ever
heard about you is not exaggerated."

Mailer, looking back, thought bitter words he would not say:
"You, Lowell, beloved poet of many, what do you know of the dirt
and the dark deliveries of the necessary? What do you know of dignity
hard-achieved, and dignity lost through innocence, and dignity lost
by sacrifice for a cause one cannot name? What do you know about
getting fat against your will, and turning into a clown of an arriviste
baron when you would rather be an eagle or a count, or rarest of all,
some natural aristocrat from these damned democratic states? No, the
only subject we share, you and I, is that species of perception which
shows that if we are not very loyal to our unendurable and most
exigent inner light, then some day we may burn. How dare you
condemn me! You know the diseases which inhabit that audience in
this accursed psychedelic house. How dare you scorn the explosive
I employ?"

And Lowell with a look of the greatest sorrow as if all this *mess*
were finally too shapeless for the hard Protestant smith of his own
brain, which would indeed burst if it could not forge his experience
into the iron edge of the very best words and the most unsinkable
relation of words, fell backward, his head striking the floor with no last
instant hesitation to cushion the blow, but like a baby, downright
sudden savagely to himself, as if from the height of a foot he had
taken a pumpkin and dropped it splat on the floor. "There, much
regarded, much-protected brain you have finally taken a blow,"
Lowell might have said to himself, for he proceeded to lie there,

resting quietly, while Macdonald went on reading from "The White Man's Burden," Lowell seeming as content as if he had just tested the back of his cranium against a policeman's club. What a royal head they had all to lose!

II

The evening went on. It was in fact far from climax. Lowell resting in the wing on the floor of the stage, Lowell recuperating from the crack he had given his head, was a dreamy figure of peace in the corner of the proscenium, a reclining shepherd contemplating his flute, although a Washington newspaper was to condemn him on Saturday in company with Mailer for "slobbish behavior" at this unseemly lounging. . . .

The novelist gave a fulsome welcome to the poet. He did not speak of his poetry (with which he was not conspicuously familiar) nor of his prose, which he thought excellent—Mailer told instead of why he had respect for Lowell as a man. A couple of years ago, the poet had refused an invitation from President Johnson to attend a garden party for artists and intellectuals, and it had attracted much attention at the time for it was one of the first dramatic acts of protest against the war in Vietnam, and Lowell was the only invited artist of first rank who had refused. Saul Bellow, for example, had attended the garden party. Lowell's refusal could not have been easy, the novelist suggested, because artists were attracted to formal afternoons of such elevated kind since that kind of experience was often stimulating to new perception and new work. So, an honorific occasion in full panoply was not easy for the mature artist to eschew. Capital! Lowell had therefore bypassed the most direct sort of literary capital. Ergo, Mailer respected him—he could not be certain he would have done the same himself, although, of course, he assured the audience he would not probably have ever had the opportunity to refuse. (Hints of merriment in the crowd at the thought of Mailer on the White House lawn.)

If the presentation had been formal up to here, it had also been somewhat graceless. On the consequence, our audience's amusement tipped the slumbering Beast. Mailer now cranked up a vaudeville clown for finale to Lowell's introduction. "Ladies and gentlemen, if novelists come from the middle class, poets tend to derive from the bottom and the top. We all know good poets at the bot'—ladies and gentlemen, here is a poet from the top, Mr. Robert Lowell." A large vigorous hand of applause, genuine enthusiasm for Lowell, some standing ovation.

But Mailer was depressed. He had betrayed himself again. The end of the introduction belonged in a burlesque house—he worked his own worst veins, like a man on the edge of bankruptcy trying to collect hopeless debts. He was fatally vulgar! Lowell passing him on the stage had recovered sufficiently to cast him a nullifying look. At this moment, they were obviously far from friends.

Lowell's shoulders had a slump, his modest stomach was pushed forward a hint, his chin was dropped to his chest as he stood at the microphone, pondering for a moment. One did not achieve the languid grandeurs of that slouch in one generation—the grandsons of the first sons had best go through the best troughs in the best eating clubs at Harvard before anyone in the family could try for such elegant note. It was now apparent to Mailer that Lowell would move by instinct, ability, and certainly by choice, in the direction most opposite from himself.

"Well," said Lowell softly to the audience, his voice dry and gentle as any New England executioner might ever hope to be, "this has been a zany evening." Laughter came back, perhaps a little too much. It was as if Lowell wished to reprove Mailer, not humiliate him. So he shifted, and talked a bit uneasily for perhaps a minute about very little. Perhaps it was too little. Some of the audience, encouraged by earlier examples, now whistled. "We can't hear you," they shouted, "speak louder."

Lowell was annoyed. "I'll bellow," he said, "but it won't do any good." His firmness, his distaste for the occasion, communicated some subtle but impressive sense of his superiority. Audiences are moved by many cues but the most satisfactory to them is probably the voice of their abdomen. There are speakers who give a sense of security to the abdomen, and they always elicit the warmest kind of applause. Mailer was not this sort of speaker; Lowell was. The hand of applause which followed this remark was fortifying. Lowell now proceeded to read some poetry.

He was not a splendid reader, merely decent to his own lines, and he read from that slouch, that personification of ivy climbing a column, he was even diffident, he looked a trifle helpless under the lights. Still, he made no effort to win the audience, seduce them, dominate them, bully them, amuse them, no, they were there for him, to please *him,* a sounding board for the plucked string of his poetic line, and so he endeared himself to them. They adored him—for his talent, his modesty, his superiority, his melancholy, his petulance, his weakness, his painful, almost stammering shyness, his noble strength—there was the string behind other strings.

> O to break loose, like the chinook
> salmon jumping and falling back,
> nosing up to the impossible
> stone and bone-crushing waterfall—
> raw-jawed, weak-fleshed there, stopped by ten
> steps of the roaring ladder, and then
> to clear the top on the last try,
> alive enough to spawn and die.

Mailer discovered he was jealous. Not of the talent. Lowell's talent was very large, but then Mailer was a bulldog about the value of his own talent. No, Mailer was jealous because he had worked for this audience, and Lowell without effort seemed to have stolen them: Mailer did not know if he was contemptuous of Lowell for playing *grand maître,* or admiring of his ability to do it. Mailer knew his own version of *grand maître* did not compare. Of course no one would be there to accept his version either. The pain of bad reviews was not in the sting, but in the subsequent pressure which, like water on a joint, collected over the decade. People who had not read your books in fifteen years were certain they were missing nothing of merit. A buried sorrow, not very attractive, (for bile was in it and the bitterness of unrequited literary injustice) released itself from some ducts of the heart, and Mailer felt hot anger at how Lowell was loved and he was not, a pure and surprising recognition of how much emotion, how much simple and childlike bitter sorrowing emotion had been concealed from himself for years under the manhole cover of his contempt for bad reviews.

> Pity the planet, all joy gone
> from this sweet volcanic cone;
> peace to our children when they fall
> in small war on the heels of small
> war—until the end of time
> to police the earth, a ghost
> orbiting forever lost
> in our monotonous sublime.

They gave Lowell a good standing ovation, much heartiness in it, much obvious pleasure that they were there on a night in Washington when Robert Lowell had read from his work—it was as nice as that— and then Lowell walked back to the wings, and Mailer walked forward. Lowell did not seem particularly triumphant. He looked still modest, still depressed, as if he had been applauded too much for too little and so the reservoir of guilt was still untapped.

Nonetheless, to Mailer it was now *mano a mano*. Once, on a vastly larger scale of applause, perhaps people had reacted to Manolete not unlike the way they reacted to Lowell, so stirred by the deeps of sorrow in the man, that the smallest move produced the largest emotion. If there was any value to the comparison then Mailer was kin to the young Dominguin, taking raucous chances, spitting in the eye of the bull, an excess of variety in his passes. But probably there was no parallel at all. He may have felt like a matador in the flush of full competition, going out to do his work after the other torero has had a triumph, but for fact he was probably less close in essence now to the bullfighter than the bull. We must not forget the Beast. He had been sipping the last of the bourbon out of the mug. He had been delayed, piqued, twisted from his purpose, and without anything to eat in close to ten hours. He was on the hunt. For what, he hardly knew. It is possible the hunt existed long before the victim was ever conceived. . . .

III

Next morning, Macdonald and Lowell met Mailer in the dining room of the Hay-Adams for breakfast . . . there was a crowd about now. . . . "It was a good day, wasn't it, Norman," Lowell kept asking. In the best of gentle moods, his nerves seemed out of their rack, and his wit had plays of light, his literary allusions, always near to private, were now full of glee. In one sprawling bar-restaurant where they went at random to drink, a plump young waitress with a strong perfume, who looked nonetheless a goddess of a bucket for a one-night stand, caught Mailer the novelist's eye—he flirted with the sense of gravity Buddhists reserve for the cow. "Good God, Norman, what do you see in her?" Macdonald had to know. Mailer, conceivably, could have told him, but they talked instead of cheap perfume—why it was offensive to some, aphrodisiac to others.

Lowell remarked, "I like cheap perfume, Norman, don't you?" But he said this last as if he was talking about some grotto in Italy he had blundered into all by himself. It was a difficult remark to make without some faint strain of dry-as-sachet faggotry, but Lowell brought it off. The mixture of integrity (Cromwellian axe of light in the eye!) in company with his characteristic gentleness, enabled him to make just about any remark without slithering. It was as if he had arrived at the recognition, nothing lost, that cheap perfume might be one of the hundred odd scents of mystery in the poet's apothecary—let us not, however, forget the smell of gasoline which Mailer in his turn had pondered. Gasoline and cheap perfume—half the smell in American adventure.

But in fact what must have been contributing to his good mood was the knowledge that Norman Mailer seemed to like him. Robert Lowell gave off at times the unwilling haunted saintliness of a man who was repaying the moral debts of ten generations of ancestors. So his guilt must have been a tyrant of a chemical in his blood always ready to obliterate the best of his moods. Just as danger is a Turk to a coward and the snub a disembowelment to the social climber, so Lowell was vulnerable to not being liked by anyone remotely a peer. In the poet's loneliness—the homely assumption is that all talent is lonely to the degree it is exalted—Lowell was at the mercy of anyone he considered of value, for only they might judge his guilt, and so relieve the intolerable dread which accompanies this excessive assumption of the old moral debts of the ancestors. Who knows what they might be? We may only be certain that the moral debt of the Puritan is no mean affair: agglutinations of incest, abominations upon God, kissing the *sub cauda* of the midnight cat—Lowell's brain at its most painful must have been equal to an overdose of Halloween on LSD.

There had been, however, a happy conversation somewhat earlier and it had made a difference in Lowell's good mood. As they were coming down the steps from the Department of Justice in the now late cold October afternoon, Lowell had said, "I was most impressed with your speech, Norman."

"Well, glad you liked it, Cal," Mailer said, "for I think your speech produced it."

"My speech did?"

"I was affected by what you said. It took me out of one mood and put me in another."

"What sort of mood, Norman?"

"Well, maybe I was able to stop brooding over myself. I don't know, Cal, your speech really had a most amazing impact on me." Mailer drawled the last few words to drain any excessive sentimental infection, but Lowell seemed hardly to mind.

"Well, Norman, I'm delighted," he said, taking Mailer's arm for a moment as if, God and knightdom willing, Mailer had finally become a Harvard dean and could be addressed by the appropriate limb. "I'm delighted because I liked *your* speech so much."

These repetitions would have been ludicrous if not for the simplicity of feeling they obviously aroused in so complex a man as Lowell. Through the drinks and the evening at dinner, he kept coming back to the same conversation, kept repeating his pleasure in Mailer's speech in order to hear Mailer doggedly reaffirm his more than equal pleasure in Lowell's good words. Mailer was particularly graceless at these ceremonious repetitions by which presumably New England mandarins (like old Chinese) ring the stately gong of a new friendship forming.

In fact the dinner was what delivered Lowell's decision to remain for the March on the Pentagon. On the whole, he had come down for the event at the Department of Justice, he had in fact a dinner party at his home in New York on Saturday night, and he did not wish to miss it. That was obvious. For whatever reason, Lowell had evidently been looking forward for days to Saturday evening.

"I wonder if I could get the plane back by six tomorrow," he kept asking aloud. "If we're arrested, I don't suppose there's much chance of that at all."

Mailer had not forgotten the party to which he was, in his turn, invited. Repeat: It had every promise of being wicked, tasty, and rich. "I think if we get arrested early," he said, "we can probably be released among the first."

"By six?"

"No, Cal," said Mailer, the honest soul, "if you get arrested, you had better plan on not making dinner before nine."

"Well, should we get arrested? What do you think of the merits?"

They talked about it for a while. It was Mailer's firm conclusion that this was probably the way they could best serve the occasion. "If the three of us are arrested," he said, "the papers can't claim that hippies and hoodlums were the only ones guilty."

IV

Now, here, after several years of the blandest reports from the religious explorers of LSD, vague Tibetan lama goody-goodness auras of religiosity being the only publicly announced or even rumored fruit from all trips back from the buried Atlantis of LSD, now suddenly an entire generation of acid-heads seemed to have said goodbye to easy visions of heaven, no, now the witches were here, and rites of exorcism, and black terrors of the night—hippies being murdered. Yes, the hippies had gone from Tibet to Christ to the Middle Ages, now they were Revolutionary Alchemists. Well, thought Mailer, that was all right, he was a Left Conservative himself. "Out, demons, out! Out, demons, out!"

"You know I like this," he said to Lowell.

Lowell shook his head. He looked not untroubled. "It was all right for awhile," he said, "but it's so damn repetitious."

And Macdonald had a harsh glee in his pale eye as if he were half furious but half diverted by the meaninglessness of the repetitions. Macdonald hated meaninglessness even more than the war in Vietnam; on the other hand, he lived for a new critical stimulation: Here it might be.

But to Lowell it was probably not meaninglessness. No, probably Lowell reacted against everything which was hypnotic in that music. Even if much of his poetry could be seen as formal incantations, halfway houses on the road to hypnosis and the oceans of contemplation beyond,

> O to break loose, like the chinook
> salmon jumping and falling back,
> nosing up the impossible
> stone and bone-crushing waterfall—

yes, even if Lowell's remarkable sense of rhythm drew one deep into the poems, nonetheless hypnotic they resolutely were not, for the language was particular, with a wicked sense of names, details and places.

> . . . Remember playing
> Marian Anderson, Mozart's *Shepherd King,*
> *il re pastore?* Hammerheaded shark,
> the rainbow salmon of the world—your hand

a rose . . . And at the Mittersill, you topped
the ski-run . . .

Lowell's poetry gave one the sense of living in a well, the echoes were
deep, and sound was finally lost in moss on stone; down there the light
had the light of velvet, and the ripples were imperceptible. But one
lay on one's back in this well, looking up at the sky, and stars were
determinedly there at night, fixed points of reference; nothing in the
poems ever permitted you to turn on your face and try to look down
into the depths of the well, it was enough you were in the well—now,
look up! The world dazzled with its detail.

Lowell, drawn to hypnosis, would resist it, resist particularly these
abstract clackety sounds like wooden gears in a noisemaker, "Hari,
hari, hari, hari, rama, rama, Krishna, hari, rama, Krishna," and the
whoop of wild Indians in "out, demons, out!" Nothing was more
dangerous to the poet than hypnosis, for the *style* of one's entrance to that
plain of sleep where all ideas coalesced into one, was critical—enter
by any indiscriminate route, "Om, Om, Om," and who knows what
finely articulated bones of future prosody might be melted in these
undifferentiated pots—no, Lowell's good poetry was a reconnaissance
into the deep, and for that, pirate's patrols were the best—one went
down with the idea one would come back with more, but one did not
immerse oneself with open guru Ginsberg arms crying, "Baa, baa,
slay this sheep or enrich it, Great Deep," no, one tiptoed in and made a
raid and ideally got out good. . . .

But of course Lowell's final distaste was for the attraction itself of
these sounds (which were incidentally lifting Mailer into the happiest
sense of comradeship—without a drink in him, he was nonetheless
cheering up again at the thought of combat, and deciding it would be
delightful to whack a barricade in the company of Ed Sanders with
the red-gold beard who had brought grope-freak talk to the Village
and always seemed to Mailer a little over-liberated, but now suitable,
yes, the novelist was working up all steam in the "Out, demons, out."

INTERVIEW

Frederick Seidel
An Interview
with Robert Lowell

*On one wall of Mr. Lowell's study was a large portrait of Ezra Pound,
the tired, haughty outlines of the face concentrated as in the raised
outlines of a ring seal in an enlargement. Also bearded, but on
another wall, over the desk, James Russell Lowell looked down from a
gray old-fashioned photograph on the apex of the triangle thus formed,
where his great-grand-nephew sat and answered questions.*

*Mr. Lowell had been talking about the classes he teaches at
Boston University.*

*Four floors below the study window, cars whined through the early
spring rain on Marlborough Street toward the Boston Public Garden.*

INTERVIEWER: What are you teaching now?

LOWELL: I'm teaching one of these poetry-writing classes and a course
in the novel. The course in the novel is called Practical Criticism.
It's a course I teach every year, but the material changes. It could be
anything from Russian short stories to Baudelaire, a study of the
New Critics, or just fiction. I do whatever I happen to be working
on myself.

INTERVIEWER: Has your teaching over the last few years meant
anything to you as a writer?

From *The Paris Review*, No. 25 (Winter-Spring, 1961). The interview has also
been included in *Writers at Work: The Paris Review Interviews, Second Series*,
published by The Viking Press, Inc., and Martin Secker & Warburg, Ltd.
By permission of the publishers. Copyright © 1963 by The Paris Review, Inc.

LOWELL: It's meant a lot to me as a human being, I think. But my teaching is part time and has neither the merits nor the burdens of real teaching. Teaching is entirely different from writing. You're always up to it, or more or less up to it; there's no question of it's clogging, of it's not coming. It's much less subjective, and it's a very pleasant pursuit in itself. In the kind of teaching I do, conversational classes, seminars, if the students are good, which they've been most of the time, it's extremely entertaining. Now, I don't know what it has to do with writing. You review a lot of things that you like, and you read things that you haven't read or haven't read closely, and read them aloud, go into them much more carefully than you would otherwise; and that must teach you a good deal. But there's such a jump from teaching to writing.

INTERVIEWER: Well, do you think the academic life is liable to block up the writer-professor's sensitivity to his own intuitions?

LOWELL: I think it's impossible to give a general answer. Almost all the poets of my generation, all the best ones, teach. I only know one, Elizabeth Bishop, who doesn't. They do it for a livelihood, but they also do it because you can't write poetry all the time. They do it to extend themselves, and I think it's undoubtedly been a gain to them. Now the question is whether something else might be more of a gain. Certainly the danger of teaching is that it's much too close to what you're doing—close and not close. You can get expert at teaching and be crude in practice. The revision, the consciousness that tinkers with the poem—that has something to do with teaching and criticism. But the impulse that starts a poem and makes it of any importance is distinct from teaching.

INTERVIEWER: And protected, you think, from whatever you bring to bear in the scrutiny of parts of poems and aspects of novels, etc?

LOWELL: I think you have to tear it apart from that. Teaching may make the poetry even more different, less academic than it would be otherwise. I'm sure that writing isn't a craft, that is, something for which you learn the skills and go on turning out. It must come from some deep impulse, deep inspiration. That can't be taught, it can't be

what you use in teaching. And you may go further afield looking
for that than you would if you didn't teach. I don't know, really; the
teaching probably makes you more cautious, more self-conscious,
makes you write less. It may make you bolder when you do write.

INTERVIEWER: You think the last may be so?

LOWELL: The boldness is ambiguous. It's not only teaching, it's growing
up in this age of criticism which we're all so conscious of, whether
we like it or don't like it, or practice it or don't practice it. You
think three times before you put a word down, and ten times about
taking it out. And that's related to boldness; if you put words down
they must do something, you're not going to put clichés. But then
it's related to caution; you write much less.

INTERVIEWER: You yourself have written very little criticism, haven't
you? You did once contribute to a study of Hopkins.

LOWELL: Yes, and I've done a few omnibus reviews. I do a review or
two a year.

INTERVIEWER: You did a wonderful one of Richards' poems.

LOWELL: I felt there was an occasion for that, and I had something to
say about it. Sometimes I wish I did more, but I'm very anxious in
criticism not to do the standard analytical essay. I'd like my essay
to be much sloppier and more intuitive. But my friends are critics,
and most of them poet-critics. When I was twenty and learning to
write, Allen Tate, Eliot, Blackmur, and Winters, and all those people
were very much news. You waited for their essays, and when a good
critical essay came out it had the excitement of a new imaginative
work.

INTERVIEWER: Which is really not the case with any of the critics
writing today, do you think?

LOWELL: The good critics are almost all the old ones. The most brilliant
critic of my generation, I think, was Jarrell, and he in a way connects
with that older generation. But he's writing less criticism now than
he used to.

INTERVIEWER: In your schooling at St. Mark's and Harvard— we can
talk about Kenyon in a minute—were there teachers or friends who

had an influence on your writing, not so much by the example of their own writing as by personal supervision or direction—by suggesting certain reading, for instance?

LOWELL: Well, my school had been given a Carnegie set of art books, and I had a friend, Frank Parker, who had great talent as a painter but who'd never done it systematically. We began reading the books and histories of art, looking at reproductions, tracing the Last Supper on tracing paper, studying dynamic symmetry, learning about Cézanne, and so on. I had no practical interest in painting, but that study seemed rather close to poetry. And from there I began. I think I read Elizabeth Drew or some such book on modern poetry. It had free verse in it, and that seemed very simple to do.

INTERVIEWER: What class were you in then?

LOWELL: It was my last year. I'd wanted to be a football player very much, and got my letter but didn't make the team. Well, that was satisfying but crushing too. I read a good deal, but had never written. So this was a recoil from that. Then I had some luck in that Richard Eberhart was teaching there.

INTERVIEWER: I'd thought he'd been a student there with you.

LOWELL: No, he was a young man about thirty. I never had him in class, but I used to go to him. He'd read aloud and we'd talk, he was very pleasant that way. He'd smoke honey-scented tobacco, and read Baudelaire and Shakespeare and Hopkins—it made the thing living——and he'd read his own poems. I wrote very badly at first, but he was encouraging and enthusiastic. That probably was decisive, that there was someone there whom I admired who was engaged in writing poetry.

INTERVIEWER: I heard that a very early draft of "The Drunken Fisherman" appeared in the St. Mark's magazine.

LOWELL: No, it was the Kenyon college magazine that published it. The poem was very different then. I'd been reading Winters, whose model was Robert Bridges, and what I wanted was a rather distant, quiet, classical poem without any symbolism. It was in four-foot couplets as smooth as I could write them. The *Kenyon Review* had published a poem of mine and then they'd stopped. This was the one time they said, if you'd submitted this we'd have taken it.

INTERVIEWER: Then you were submitting other poems to the Review?

LOWELL: Yes, and that poem was rather different from anything else I did. I was also reading Hart Crane and Thomas and Tate and Empson's *Seven Types of Ambiguity;* and each poem was more difficult than the one before, and had more ambiguities. Ransom, editing the *Kenyon Review,* was impressed, but didn't want to publish them. He felt they were forbidding and clotted.

INTERVIEWER: But finally he did come through.

LOWELL: Well, after I'd graduated. I published when I was a junior, then for about three years no magazine would take anything I did. I'd get sort of pleasant letters—"One poem in this group interests us, if you can get seven more." At that time it took me about a year to do two or three poems. Gradually I just stopped, and really sort of gave it up. I seemed to have reached a great impasse. The kind of poem I thought was interesting and would work on became so cluttered and overdone that it wasn't really poetry.

INTERVIEWER: I was struck on reading *Land of Unlikeness* by the difference between the poems you rejected for *Lord Weary's Castle* and the few poems and passages that you took over into the new book.

LOWELL: I think I took almost a third, but almost all of what I took was rewritten. But I wonder what struck you?

INTERVIEWER: One thing was that almost all the rejected poems seemed to me to be those that Tate, who in his introduction spoke about two kinds of poetry in the book, said were the more strictly religious and strictly symbolc poems, as against the poems he said were perhaps more powerful because more experienced or relying more on your sense of history. What you took seemed really superior to what you left behind.

LOWELL: Yes, I took out several that were paraphrases of early Christian poems, and I rejected one rather dry abstraction, then whatever seemed to me to have a messy violence. All the poems have religious imagery, I think, but the ones I took were more concrete. That's what the book was moving toward: less symbolic imagery. And as I say, I tried to take some of the less fierce poems. There seemed to be too much twisting and disgust in the first book.

INTERVIEWER: I wondered how wide your reading had been at the time. I wondered, when I read in Tate's introduction that the stanza in one of your poems was based on the stanza in "The Virginian Voyages," whether someone had pointed out Drayton's poem to you.

LOWELL: Tate and I started to make an anthology together. It was a very interesting year I spent with Tate and his wife. He's a poet who writes in spurts, and he had about a third of a book. I was going to do a biography of Jonathan Edwards and he was going to write a novel, and our wives were going to write novels. Well, the wives just went humming away. "I've just finished three pages," they'd say at the end of the day; and their books mounted up. But ours never did, though one morning Allen wrote four pages to his novel, very brilliant. We were in a little study together separated by a screen. I was heaping up books on Jonathan Edwards and taking notes, and getting more and more numb on the subject, looking at old leather-bound volumes on freedom of the will and so on, and feeling less and less a calling. And there we stuck. And then we decided to make an anthology together. We both liked rather formal, difficult poems, and we were reading particularly the Sixteenth and Seventeenth centuries. In the evening we'd read aloud, and we started a card catalogue of what we'd make for the anthology. And then we started writing. It seems to me we took old models like Drayton's Ode——Tate wrote a poem called "The Young Proconsuls of the Air" in that stanza. I think there's a trick to formal poetry. Most poetry is very formal, but when a modern poet is formal he gets more attention for it than old poets did. Somehow we've tried to make it look difficult. For example, Shelley can just rattle off terza rima by the page, and it's very smooth, doesn't seem an obstruction to him—you sometimes wish it were more difficult. Well, someone does that today and in modern style it looks as though he's wrestling with every line and may be pushed into confusion, as though he's having a real struggle with form and content. Marks of that are in the finished poem. And I think both Tate and I felt that we wanted our formal patterns to seem a hardship and something that we couldn't rattle off easily.

INTERVIEWER: But in *Lord Weary's Castle* there were poems moving toward a sort of narrative calm, almost a prose calm—"Katherine's Dream," for example, or the two poems on texts by Edwards, or "The Ghost"—and then, on the other hand, poems in which the form was insisted upon and maybe shown off, and where the things that were characteristic of your poetry at that time—the kind of enjambments, the rhyming, the meters, of course—seem willed and forced, so that you have a terrific log jam of stresses, meanings, strains.

LOWELL: I know one contrast I've felt, and it takes different forms at different times. The ideal modern form seems to be the novel and certain short stories. Maybe Tolstoi would be the perfect example— his work is imagistic, it deals with all experience, and there seems to be no conflict of the form and content. So one thing is to get into poetry that kind of human richness in rather simple descriptive language. Then there's another side of poetry: compression, something highly rhythmical and perhaps wrenched into a small space. I've always been fascinated by both these things. But getting it all on one page in a few stanzas, getting it all done in as little space as possible, revising and revising so that each word and rhythm though not perfect is pondered and wrestled with—you can't do that in prose very well, you'd never get your book written. "Katherine's Dream" was a real dream. I found that I shaped it a bit, and cut it, and allegorized it, but still it was a dream someone had had. It was material that ordinarily, I think, would go into prose, yet it would have had to be much longer or part of something much longer.

INTERVIEWER: I think you can either look for forms, you can do specific reading for them, or the forms can be demanded by what you want to say. And when the material in poetry seems under almost unbearable pressure you wonder whether the form hasn't cookie-cut what the poet wanted to say. But you chose the couplet, didn't you, and some of your freest passages are in couplets.

LOWELL: The couplet I've used is very much like the couplet Browning uses in "My Last Duchess," in *Sordello,* run-on with its rhymes buried. I've always, when I've used it, tried to give the impression that I had as much freedom in choosing the rhyme word as I had in any of the other words. Yet they were almost all true rhymes, and maybe half the time there'd be a pause after the rhyme. I wanted something as fluid as prose; you wouldn't notice the form, yet looking back you'd find that great obstacles had been climbed. And the couplet is pleasant in this way—once you've got your two lines to rhyme, then that's done and you can go on to the next. You're not stuck with the whole stanza to round out and build to a climax. A couplet can be a couplet or can be split and left as one line, or it can go on for a hundred lines; any sort of compression or expansion is possible. And that's not so in a stanza. I think a couplet's much less lyrical than a stanza, closer to prose. Yet it's an honest form, its difficulties are in the open. It really is pretty hard to rhyme each line with the one that follows it.

INTERVIEWER: Did the change of style in *Life Studies* have something to do with working away from that compression and pressure by way of, say, the kind of prose clarity of "Katherine's Dream"?

LOWELL: Yes. By the time I came to *Life Studies* I'd been writing my autobiography and also writing poems that broke meter. I'd been doing a lot of reading aloud. I went on a trip to the West Coast and read at least once a day and sometimes twice for fourteen days, and more and more I found that I was simplifying my poems. If I had a Latin quotation I'd translate it into English. If adding a couple of syllables in a line made it clearer I'd add them, and I'd make little changes just impromptu as I read. That seemed to improve the reading.

INTERVIEWER: Can you think of a place where you added a syllable or two to an otherwise regular line?

LOWELL: It was usually articles and prepositions that I added, very slight little changes, and I didn't change the printed text. It was just done for the moment.

INTERVIEWER: Why did you do this? Just because you thought the most important thing was to get the poem over?

LOWELL: To get it over, yes. And I began to have a certain disrespect for the tight forms. If you could make it easier by adding syllables, why not? And then when I was writing *Life Studies,* a good number of the poems were started in very strict meter, and I found that, more than the rhymes, the regular beat was what I didn't want. I have a long poem in there about my father, called "Commander Lowell," which actually is largely in couplets, but I originally wrote perfectly strict four-foot couplets. Well, with that form it's hard not to have echoes of Marvell. That regularity just seemed to ruin the honesty of sentiment, and became rhetorical; it said, "I'm a poem"— though it was a great help when I was revising having this original skeleton. I could keep the couplets where I wanted them and drop them where I didn't; there'd be a form to come back to.

INTERVIEWER: Had you originally intended to handle all that material in prose?

LOWELL: Yes. I found it got awfully tedious working out transitions and putting in things that didn't seem very important but were necessary to the prose continuity. Also, I found it hard to revise. Cutting it down into small bits, I could work on it much more carefully and make fast transitions. But there's another point about this mysterious business of prose and poetry, form and content, and the reasons for breaking forms. I don't think there's any very satisfactory answer. I seesaw back and forth between something highly metrical and something highly free; there isn't any one way to write. But it seems to me we've gotten into a sort of Alexandrian age. Poets of my generation and particularly younger ones have gotten terribly proficient at these forms. They write a very musical, difficult poem with tremendous skill, perhaps there's never been such skill. Yet the writing seems divorced from culture somehow. It's become too much something specialized that can't handle much experience. It's become a craft, purely a craft, and there must be some breakthrough back into life. Prose is in many ways better off than poetry. It's quite hard to think of a young poet who has the vitality, say, of Salinger or Saul Bellow. Yet prose tends to be very diffuse. The novel is really a much more difficult form than it seems; few people have the wind to write anything that long. Even a short story demands almost poetic perfection. Yet on the whole prose is less cut off from life than poetry is. Now, some of this Alexandrian poetry is very brilliant, you would not have it changed at all. But I thought it was getting increasingly stifling. I couldn't get my experience into tight metrical forms.

INTERVIEWER: So you felt this about your own poetry, your own technique, not just about the general condition of poetry?

LOWELL: Yes, I felt that the meter plastered difficulties and mannerisms on what I was trying to say to such an extent that it terribly hampered me.

INTERVIEWER: This then explains, in part anyway, your admiration for Elizabeth Bishop's poetry. I know that you've said the qualities and the abundance of its descriptive language reminded you of the Russian novel more than anything else.

LOWELL: Any number of people are guilty of writing a complicated poem that has a certain amount of symbolism in it and really difficult meaning, a wonderful poem to teach. Then you unwind it and you feel that the intelligence, the experience, whatever goes into it, is skin-deep. In Elizabeth Bishop's "Man-Moth" a whole new world is gotten out and you don't know what will come after any one line. It's exploring. And it's as original as Kafka. She's gotten a world, not just a way of writing. She seldom writes a poem that doesn't have the exploratory quality; yet it's very firm, it's not like beat poetry, it's all controlled.

INTERVIEWER: What about Snodgrass? What you were trying to do in *Life Studies* must have something to do with your admiration for his work.

LOWELL: He did these things before I did, though he's younger than I am and had been my student. He may have influenced me, though people have suggested the opposite. He spent ten years at the University of Iowa, going to writing classes, being an instructor; rather unworldly, making little money, and specializing in talking to other people writing poetry, obsessed you might say with minute technical problems and rather provincial experience—and then he wrote about just that. I mean, the poems are about his child, his divorce, and Iowa City, and his child is a Dr. Spock child—all handled in expert little stanzas. I believe that's a new kind of poetry. Other poems that are direct that way are slack and have no vibrance. His experience wouldn't be so interesting and valid if it weren't for the whimsy, the music, the balance, everything revised and placed and pondered. All that gives light to those poems on agonizing subjects comes from the craft.

INTERVIEWER: And yet his best poems are all on the verge of being slight and even sentimental.

LOWELL: I think a lot of the best poetry is. Laforgue—it's hard to think of a more delightful poet, and his prose is wonderful too. Well, it's on the verge of being sentimental, and if he hadn't dared to be sentimental he wouldn't have been a poet. I mean, his inspiration was that. There's some way of distinguishing between false sentimentality, which is blowing up a subject and giving emotions that you don't feel, and using whimsical minute, tender, small emotions that most people don't feel but which Laforgue and Snodgrass do. So that I'd say he had pathos and fragility—but then that's a large subject too. He has fragility along the edges and a main artery of power going through the center.

INTERVIEWER: Some people were disappointed with *Life Studies* just because earlier you had written a kind of heroic poetry, an American version of heroic poetry, of which there had been none recently except your own. Is there any chance that you will go back to that?

LOWELL: I don't think that a personal history can go on forever, unless you're Walt Whitman and have a way with you. I feel I've done enough personal poetry. That doesn't mean I won't do more of it, but I don't want to do more now. I feel I haven't gotten down all my experience, or perhaps even the most important part, but I've said all I really have much inspiration to say, and more would just dilute. So that you need something more impersonal, and other things being equal it's better to get your emotions out in a Macbeth than in a confession. Macbeth must have tons of Shakespeare in him. We don't know where, nothing in Shakespeare's life was remotely like Macbeth, yet he somehow gives the feeling of going to the core of Shakespeare. You have much more freedom that way than you do when you write an autobiographical poem.

INTERVIEWER: These poems, I gather from what you said earlier, did take as much working over as the earlier ones.

LOWELL: They were just as hard to write. They're not always factually true. There's a good deal of tinkering with fact. You leave out a lot, and emphasize this and not that. Your actual experience is a complete flux. I've invented facts and changed things, and the whole balance of the poem was something invented. So there's a lot of artistry, I hope, in the poems. Yet there's this thing: if a poem is autobiographical—and this is true of any kind of autobiographical writing and of historical writing—you want the reader to say, this is true. In something like Macaulay's *History of England* you think you're really getting William III. That's as good as a good plot in a novel. And so there was always that standard of truth which you wouldn't ordinarily have in poetry—the reader was to believe he was getting the *real* Robert Lowell.

INTERVIEWER: I wanted to ask you about this business of taking over passages from earlier poems and rewriting them and putting them in new contexts. I'm thinking of the passage at the end of the "Cistercians in Germany," in *Land of Unlikeness,* which you rewrote into those wonderful lines that end "At the Indian Killer's Grave." I know that Hart Crane rewrote early scraps a great deal and used most of the rewrites. But doesn't doing this imply a theory of poetry that would talk much more about craft than about experience?

LOWELL: I don't know, it's such a miracle if you get lines that are halfway right; it's not just a technical problem. The lines must mean a good deal to you. All your poems are in a sense one poem, and there's always the struggle of getting something that balances and comes out right, in which all parts are good, and that has experience that you value. And so if you have a few lines that shine in a poem or are beginning to shine, and they fail and get covered over and drowned, maybe their real form is in another poem. Maybe you've mistaken the real inspiration in the original poem and they belong in something else entirely. I don't think that violates experience. The "Cistercians" wasn't very close to me, but the last lines seemed felt; I dropped the Cistercians and put a Boston graveyard in.

INTERVIEWER: But in Crane's "Ode to an Urn," a poem about a personal friend, there are lines which originally applied to something very different, and therefore, in one version or the other, at least can't be called personal.

LOWELL: I think we always bring over some unexplained obscurities by shifting lines. Something that was clear in the original just seems odd and unexplained in the final poem. That can be quite bad, of course; but you always want—and I think Chekhov talks about this—the detail that you can't explain. It's just there. It seems right to you, but you don't have to have it; you could have something else entirely. Now if everything's like that you'd just have chaos, but a few unexplained difficult things—they seem to be the life-blood of variety—they may work. What may have seemed a little odd, a little difficult in the original poem, gets a little more difficult in a new way in the new poem. And that's purely accidental, yet you may gain more than you lose——a new suggestiveness and magic.

INTERVIEWER: Do you revise a very great deal?

LOWELL: Endlessly.

INTERVIEWER: You often use an idiom or a very common phrase either for the sake of irony or to bear more meaning than it's customarily asked to bear—do these come late in the game, do you have to look around for them?

LOWELL: They come later because they don't prove much in themselves, and they often replace something that's much more formal and worked-up. Some of my later poetry does have this quality that the earlier doesn't: several lines can be almost what you'd say in conversation. And maybe talking with a friend or with my wife I'd say, "This doesn't sound quite right," and sort of reach in the air as I talked and changed a few words. In that way the new style is easier to write; I sometimes fumble out a natural sequence of lines that will work. But a whole poem won't come that way; my seemingly relaxed poems are just about as hard as the very worked-up ones.

INTERVIEWER: That rightness and familiarity, though, is in "Between the Porch and the Altar" in several passages which are in couplets.

LOWELL: When I am writing in meter I find the simple lines never come right away. Nothing does. I don't believe I've ever written a poem in meter where I've kept a single one of the original lines. Usually when I was writing my old poems I'd write them out in blank verse and then put in the rhymes. And of course I'd change the rhymes a lot. The most I could hope for at first was the rhymed version wouldn't be much inferior to the blank verse. Then the real work would begin, to make it something much better than the original out of the difficulties of the meter.

INTERVIEWER: Have you ever gone as far as Yeats and written out a prose argument and then set down the rhymes?

LOWELL: With some of the later poems I've written out prose versions, then cut the prose down and abbreviated it. A rapidly written prose draft of the poem doesn't seem to do much good, too little pain has gone into it; but one really worked on is bound to have phrases that are invaluable. And it's a nice technical problem: how can you keep phrases and get them into meter?

INTERVIEWER: Do you usually send off your work to friends before publishing it?

LOWELL: I do it less now. I always used to do it, to Jarrell and one or two other people. Last year I did a lot of reading with Stanley Kunitz.

INTERVIEWER: At the time you were writing the poems for *Lord Weary's Castle,* did it make a difference to you whether the poet to whom you were sending your work was Catholic?

LOWELL: I don't think I ever sent any poems to a Catholic. The person I was closest to then was Allen Tate, who wasn't a Catholic at the time; and then later it became Jarrell, who wasn't at all Catholic. My two close Catholic writer friends are prose writers, J. F. Powers and Flannery O'Connor, and they weren't interested in the technical problems of poems.

INTERVIEWER: So you feel that the religion is the business of the poem that it's in and not at all the business of the Church or the religious person.

LOWELL: It shouldn't be. I mean, a religion ought to have objective validity. But by the time it gets into a poem it's so mixed up with technical and imaginative problems that the theologian, the priest, the serious religious person isn't of too much use. The poem is too strange for him to feel at home and make any suggestions.

INTERVIEWER: What does this make of the religious poem as a religious exercise?

LOWELL: Well, it at least makes this: that the poem tries to be a poem and not a piece of artless religious testimony. There is a drawback. It seems to me that with any poem, but maybe particularly a religious one where there are common interests, the opinion of intelligent people who are not poets ought to be useful. There's an independence to this not getting advice from religious people and outsiders, but also there's a narrowness. Then there is a question whether my poems are religious, or whether they just use religious imagery. I haven't really any idea. My last poems don't use religious imagery, they don't use symbolism. In many ways they seem to me more religious than the early ones, which are full of symbols and references to Christ and God. I'm sure the symbols and the Catholic framework didn't make the poems religious experiences. Yet I don't feel my experience changed very much. It seems to me it's clearer to me now than it was then, but it's very much the same sort of thing that went into the religious poems—the same sort of struggle, light and darkness, the flux of experience. The morality seems much the same. But the symbolism is gone; you couldn't possibly say what creed I believed in. I've wondered myself often. Yet what made the earlier poems valuable seems to be some recording of experience, and that seems to be what makes the later ones.

INTERVIEWER: So you end up saying that the poem does have some integrity and can have some beauty apart from the beliefs expressed in the poem.

LOWELL: I think it can only have integrity apart from the beliefs; that no political position, religious position, position of generosity, or what have you, can make a poem good. It's all to the good if a poem *can* use politics, or theology, or gardening, or anything that has its own validity aside from poetry. But these things will never *per se* make a poem.

INTERVIEWER: The difficult question is whether when the beliefs expressed in a poem are obnoxious the poem as a whole can be considered to be beautiful—the problem of the *Pisan Cantos*.

LOWELL: The *Pisan Cantos* are very uneven, aren't they? If you took what most people would agree are maybe the best hundred passages, would the beliefs in those passages be obnoxious? I think you'd get a very mixed answer. You could make quite a good case for Pound's good humor about his imprisonment, his absence of self-pity, his observant eye, his memories of literary friends, for all kinds of generous qualities and open qualities and lyrical qualities that anyone would think were good. And even when he does something like the death of Mussolini, in the passage that opens the *Pisan Cantos,* people debate about it. I've talked to Italians who were partisans, and who said that this is the only poem on Mussolini that's any good. Pound's quite wily often: Mussolini hung up like an ox—his brutal appearance. I don't know whether you could say the beliefs there are wrong or not. And there are other poems that come to mind: in Eliot, the Jew spelled with a small j in "Gerontion," is that anti-Semitism or not? Eliot's not anti-Semitic in any sense, but there's certainly a dislike of Jews in those early poems. Does he gain in the fierceness of writing his Jew with a small j? He says you write what you have to write and in criticism you can say what you think you should believe in. Very ugly emotions perhaps make a poem.

INTERVIEWER: You were on the Bollingen Committee at the time the award was made to Pound. What did you think of the great ruckus?

LOWELL: I thought it was a very simple problem of voting for the best book of the year; and it seemed to me Pound's was. I thought the *Pisan Cantos* was the best writing Pound had ever done, though it included some of his worst. It is a very mixed book: that was the question. But the consequences of not giving the best book of the year a prize for extraneous reasons, even terrible ones in a sense— I think that's the death of art. Then you have Pasternak suppressed and everything becomes stifling. Particularly in a strong country like ours you've got to award things objectively and not let the beliefs you'd like a man to have govern your choice. It was very close after the war, and anyone must feel that the poetry award was a trifling thing compared with the concentration camps. I actually think they were very distant from Pound. He had no political effect whatsoever and was quite eccentric and impractical. Pound's social credit, his Fascism, all these various things, were a tremendous gain to him; he'd be a very Parnassan poet without them. Even if they're bad beliefs—and some were bad, some weren't, and some were just terrible, of course—they made him more human and more to do with life, more to do with the times. They served him. Taking what interested him in these things gave a kind of realism and life to his poetry that it wouldn't have had otherwise.

INTERVIEWER: Did you become a translator to suit your own needs or because you wanted to get certain poems, most of them not before translated, into English? Or was it a matter of both, as I suppose it usually is, and as it was for Pound?

LOWELL: I think both. It always seemed to me that nothing very close to the poems I've translated existed in English; and on the other hand, there was some kind of closeness, I felt a kinship. I felt some sort of closeness to the Rilke and Rimbaud poems I've translated, yet they were doing things I couldn't do. They were both a continuation of my own bias and a release from myself.

INTERVIEWER: How did you come to translate Propertius—in fact, how did you come to have such a great interest in Roman history and Latin literature?

LOWELL: At Harvard my second year I took almost entirely English courses—the easiest sort of path. I think that would have been a disaster. But before going to Kenyon I talked to Ford Madox Ford and Ransom, and Ransom said you've just got to take philosophy and logic, which I did. The other thing he suggested was classics. Ford was rather flippant about it, said of course you've got to learn classics, you'll just cut yourself off from humanity if you don't. I think it's always given me some sort of yardstick for English. And then the literature was amazing, particularly the Greek; there's nothing like Greek in English at all. Our plays aren't formally at all like Aeschylus and Sophocles. Their whole inspiration was unbelievably different, and so different that you could hardly think of even the attempt to imitate them, great as their prestige was. That something like *Antigone* or *Oedipus* or the great Achilles moments in the *Iliad* would be at the core of a literature is incredible for anyone brought up in an English culture—Greek wildness and sophistication all different, the women different, everything. Latin's of course much closer. English is a half-Latin language, and we've done our best to absorb the Latin literature. But a Roman poet is much less intellectual than the Englishman, much less abstract. He's nearer nature somehow—somewhat what we feel about a Frenchman but more so still. And yet he's very sophisticated. He has his way of doing things, though the number of forms he explored is quite limited. The amount he could take from the Greeks and yet change is an extraordinary piece of firm discipline. Also, you take almost any really good Roman poet—Juvenal, or Vergil, or Propertius, Catullus—he's much more raw and direct than anything in English, and yet he has this blocklike formality. The Roman frankness interests me. Until recently our literature hasn't been as raw as the Roman, translations had to have stars. And their history has a terrible human frankness that isn't customary with us— corrosive attacks on the establishment, comments on politics and the decay of morals, all felt terribly strongly, by poets as well as historians. The English writer who reads the classics is working at one thing, and his eye is on something else that can't be done. We will always have the Latin and Greek classics, and they'll never be absorbed. There's something very restful about that.

INTERVIEWER: But, more specifically, how did Latin poetry—your study of it, your translations—affect your measure of English poetry?

LOWELL: My favorite English poetry was the difficult Elizabethan plays and the Metaphysicals, then the nineteenth century, which I was aquiver about and disliked but which was closer to my writing than anything else. The Latin seemed very different from either of these. I immediately saw how Shelley wasn't like Horace and Vergil or Aeschylus—and the Latin was a mature poetry, a realistic poetry, which didn't have the contortions of the Metaphysicals. What a frail, bony, electric person Marvell is compared with Horace!

INTERVIEWER: What about your adaptation of Propertius?

LOWELL: I got him through Pound. When I read him in Latin I found a kind of Propertius you don't get in Pound at all. Pound's Propertius is a rather Ovidian figure with a great deal of Pound's fluency and humor and irony. The actual Propertius is a very excited, tense poet, rather desperate; his line is much more like parts of Marlowe's *Faustus*. And he's of all the Roman poets the most like a desperate Christian. His experiences, his love affair with Cynthia, are absolutely rending, destroying. He's like a fallen Christian.

INTERVIEWER: Have you done any other translations of Latin poems?

LOWELL: I did a monologue that started as a translation of Vergil and then was completely rewritten, and there are buried translations in several other poems. There's a poem called "To Speak of Woe That Is in Marriage" in my last book that started as a translation of

Catullus. I don't know what traces are left, but it couldn't have been written without the Catullus.

INTERVIEWER: You've translated Pasternak. Do you know Russian?

LOWELL: No, I have rewritten other English translations, and seldom even checked with Russian experts. I want to get a book of translations together. I read in the originals, except for Russian, but I have felt quite free to alter things, and I don't know that Pasternak would look less close than the Italian, which I have studied closely. Before I publish, I want to check with a Russian expert.

INTERVIEWER: Can I get you back to Harvard for a minute? Is it true you tried out for the Harvard *Advocate,* did all the dirty work for your candidacy, and then were turned down?

LOWELL: I nailed a carpet down. I forget who the editor was then, but he was a man who wrote on Frost. At that time people who wrote on Frost were quite different from the ones who write on him now; they tended to be conservative, out of touch. I wasn't a very good writer then, perhaps I should have been turned down. I was trying to write like William Carlos Williams, very simple, free verse, imagistic poems. I had a little group I was very proud of which was set up in galleys; when I left Harvard it was turned down.

INTERVIEWER: Did you know any poets at the time?

LOWELL: I had a friend, Harry Brown, who writes dialogue for movies and has been in Hollywood for years. He was a terribly promising poet. He came to Harvard with a long correspondence with Harriet Monroe and was much more advanced than anyone else. He could write in the style of Auden or Webster or Eliot or Crane. He'd never graduated from high school, and wasn't a student, but he was the person I felt closest to. My other friends weren't writers.

INTERVIEWER: Had you met any older poets—Frost, for instance, who must have been around?

LOWELL: I'd gone to call on Frost with a huge epic on the First Crusade, all written out in clumsy longhand on lined paper. He read a page of that and said, "You have no compression." Then he read me a very short poem of Collins, "How Sleep the Brave," and

said, "That's not a great poem, but it's not too long." He was very
kindly about it. You know his point about the voice coming into
poetry: he took a very unusual example of that, the opening of
Hyperion; the line about the Naiad, something about her pressing a
cold finger to her cold lips, which wouldn't seem like a voice passage
at all. And he said, "Now Keats comes alive here." That was a
revelation to me; what had impressed me was the big Miltonic
imitation in *Hyperion.* I don't know what I did with that, but I
recoiled and realized that I was diffuse and monotonous.

INTERVIEWER: What decided you to leave Harvard and go to Kenyon?

LOWELL: I'd made the acquaintance of Merrill Moore, who'd been at
Vanderbilt and a Fugitive. He said that I ought to study with a man
who was a poet. He was very close to Ransom, and the plan was
that I'd go to Vanderbilt; and I would have, but Ransom changed
to Kenyon.

INTERVIEWER: I understand you left much against the wishes of your
family.

LOWELL: Well, I was getting quite morose and solitary, and they sort
of settled for this move. They'd rather have had me a genial social
Harvard student, but at least I'd be working hard this way. It
seemed to them a queer but orderly step.

INTERVIEWER: Did it help you that you had had intellectual and literary
figures in your family?

LOWELL: I really didn't know I'd had them till I went to the South.
To my family, James Russell Lowell was the ambassador to England,
not a writer. Amy seemed a bit peculiar to them. When I began
writing I think it would have been unimaginable to take either Amy
or James Russell Lowell as models.

INTERVIEWER: Was it through Ransom that you met Tate?

LOWELL: I met them at more or less the same time, but actually stayed
with Tate before I knew Ransom very well.

INTERVIEWER: And Ford Madox Ford was there at some time, wasn't
he?

LOWELL: I met Ford at a cocktail party in Boston and went to dinner with him at the Athens Olympia. He was going to visit the Tates, and said, "Come and see me down there, we're all going to Tennessee." So I drove down. He hadn't arrived, so I got to know the Tates quite well before his appearance.

INTERVIEWER: Staying in a pup-tent.

LOWELL: It's a terrible piece of youthful callousness. They had one Negro woman who came in and helped, but Mrs. Tate was doing all the housekeeping. She had three guests and her own family, and was doing the cooking and writing a novel. And this young man arrived, quite ardent and eccentric. I think I suggested that maybe I'd stay with them. And they said, "We really haven't any room, you'd have to pitch a tent on the lawn." So I went to Sears, Roebuck and got a tent and rigged it on their lawn. The Tates were too polite to tell me that what they'd said had been just a figure of speech. I stayed two months in my tent and ate with the Tates.

INTERVIEWER: And you were showing him your work all the while.

LOWELL: Oh, I became converted to formalism and changed my style from brilliant free verse, all in two months. And everything was in rhyme, and it still wasn't any good. But that was a great incentive. I poured out poems and went to writers' conferences.

INTERVIEWER: What about Ford?

LOWELL: I saw him out there and took dictation from him for a while. That was hell, because I didn't know how to type. I'd take the dictation down in longhand, and he rather mumbled. I'd ask him what he'd said, and he'd say, "Oh, you have no sense of prose rhythm," and mumble some more. I'd get most of his words, then I'd have to improvise on the typewriter.

INTERVIEWER: So for part of Ford's opus we're indebted to you.

LOWELL: A handful of phrases in *The March of Literature,* on the Provençal poets.

INTERVIEWER: That was the summer before you entered Kenyon; but most of the poems in *Land of Unlikeness* were written after you'd graduated, weren't they?

LOWELL: Yes, they were almost all written in a year I spent with the

Tates, though some of them were earlier poems rewritten. I think becoming a Catholic convert had a good deal to do with writing again. I was much more interested in being a Catholic than in being a writer. I read Catholic writers but had no intention of writing myself. But somehow, when I started again, I won't say the Catholicism gave me subject matter, but it gave me some kind of form, and I could begin a poem and build it to a climax. It was quite different from what I'd been doing earlier.

INTERVIEWER: Why, then, did you choose to print your work in the small liberal magazines whose religious and political positions were very different from yours? Have you ever submitted to the *New Yorker* or the *Atlantic Monthly?*

LOWELL: I think I may have given something to the *Atlantic* on Santayana; the *New Yorker* I haven't given anything. I think the *New Yorker* does some of the best prose in the country, in many ways much more interesting than the quarterlies and little magazines. But poems are lost in it; there's no table of contents, and some of their poetry is light verse. There's no particular continuity of excellence. There just seems no point in printing there. For a while the little magazines, whose religious-political positions *were* very different from mine, were the only magazines that would publish me, and I feel like staying with them. I like magazines like the *New Statesman,* the *Nation,* the *New Republic*—something a little bit off the track.

INTERVIEWER: Just because they are off the track?

LOWELL: I think so. A political position I don't necessarily agree with which is a little bit adverse seems to me just more attractive than a time-serving, conventional position. And they tend to have good reviews, those magazines. I think you write for a small audience, an ardent critical audience. And you know Graves says that poets ought to take in each other's washing because they're the only responsible audience. There's a danger to that—you get too specialized—but I pretty much agree that's the audience you do write for. If it gets further, that's all fine.

INTERVIEWER: There is, though, a certain inbred, in-group anemia to those magazines, at least to the literary quarterlies. For instance, it would have been almost inconceivable for *Partisan Review,* which is the best of them, I think, to give your last book a bad review or even a sharp review.

LOWELL: I think no magazine likes to slam one of its old contributors. *Partisan* has sometimes just not reviewed a book by someone they liked very much and their reviewer didn't. I know Shapiro has been attacked in *Partisan* and then published there, and other people have been unfavorably reviewed and made rather a point of sending them something afterwards. You want to feel there's a certain degree of poorer writing that wouldn't get published in the magazine your work appears in. The good small magazine may publish a lot of rather dry stuff, but at least it's serious, and if it's bad it's not bad by trying to be popular and put something over on the public. It's a wrenched personal ineptitude that will get published rather than a public slickness. I think that has something to do with good reviews coming out in the magazine. We were talking about *Partisan's* not slamming one of its contributors, but *Partisan* has a pretty harsh, hard standard of reviewing, and they certainly wouldn't praise one of their contributors who'd gone to pot.

INTERVIEWER: What poets among your contemporaries do you most admire?

LOWELL: The two I've been closest to are Elizabeth Bishop—I spoke about her earlier—and Jarrell, and they're different. Jarrell's a great man of letters, a very informed man, and the best critic of my generation, the best professional poet. He's written the best war poems, and those poems are a tremendous product of our culture, I feel. Elizabeth Bishop's poems, as I said, are more personal, more something she did herself, and she's not a critic but has her own tastes, which may be very idiosyncratic. I enjoy her poems more than anybody else's. I like some of Shapiro very much, some of Roethke and Stanley Kunitz.

INTERVIEWER: What about Roethke, who tries to do just about everything you don't try to do?

LOWELL: We've read to each other and argued, and may be rather alike in temperament actually, but he wants a very musical poem and always would quarrel with my ear as I'd quarrel with his eye. He has love poems and childhood poems and startling surrealistic poems, rather simple experience done with a blaze of power. He rejoices in the rhetoric and the metrics, but there's something very disorderly working there. Sometimes it will smash a poem and sometimes it will make it. The things he knows about I feel I know nothing about, flowers and so on. What we share, I think, is the exultant moment, the blazing out. Whenever I've tried to do anything like his poems, I've felt helpless and realized his mastery.

INTERVIEWER: You were apparently a very close friend of Delmore Schwartz's.

LOWELL: Yes, and I think that I've never met anyone who has somehow as much seeped into me. It's a complicated personal thing to talk about. His reading was very varied, Marx and Freud and Russell, very catholic and not from a conservative position at all. He sort of grew up knowing those things and has a wonderful penetrating humorous way of talking about them. If he met T. S. Eliot his impressions of Eliot would be mixed up with his impressions of Freud and what he'd read about Eliot; all these things flowed back and forth in him. Most of my writer friends were more specialized and limited than Schwartz, most of them took against-the-grain positions which were also narrow. Schwartz was a revelation. He felt the poet who had experience was very much better than the poet with polish. Wordsworth would interest him much more than Keats—he wanted openness to direct experience. He said that if you got people talking in a poem you could do anything. And his own writing, *Coriolanus* and *Shenandoah,* is interesting for that.

INTERVIEWER: Isn't this much what you were saying about your own hopes for *Life Studies?*

LOWELL: Yes, but technically I think that Delmore and I are quite different. There have been very few poets I've been able to get very much from technically. Tate has been one of the closest to me.

My early poems I think grew out of my admiration for his poems.

INTERVIEWER: What about poets in the past?

LOWELL: It's hard for me to imitate someone; I'm very self-conscious about it. That's an advantage perhaps—you don't become too imitative—but it's also a limitation. I tremble when I feel I'm being like someone else. If it's Rilke or Rimbaud or Propertius, you know the language is a big bar and that if you imitate you're doing something else. I've felt greater freedom that way. I think I've tried to write like some of the Elizabethans.

INTERVIEWER: And Crane? You said you had read a good deal of Crane.

LOWELL: Yes, but his difficult style is one I've never been able to do much with. He can be very obscure and yet write a much more inspired poem than I could by being obscure. There's a relationship between Crane and Tate, and for some reason Tate was much easier for me. I could see how Tate was done, though Tate has a rhythm that I've never been able to imitate. He's much more irregular than I am, and I don't know where the rhythm comes from, but I admire it very much. Crane said somewhere that he could write five or six good lines but Tate could write twelve that would hang together, and you'd see how the twelve were built. Tate was somehow more of a model: he had a lot of wildness and he had a lot of construction. And of course I knew him and never knew Crane. I think Crane is the great poet of that generation. He got out more than anybody else. Not only is it the tremendous power there, but he somehow got New York City; he was at the center of things in the way that no other poet was. All the chaos of his life missed getting sidetracked the way other poets' did, and he was less limited than any other poet of his generation. There was a fullness of experience; and without that, if you just had his mannerisms, and not his rather simple writing—which if done badly would be sentimental merely—or just his obscure writing, the whole thing would be merely verbal. It isn't with Crane. The push of the whole man is there. But his style never worked for me.

INTERVIEWER: But something of Crane does seem to have gotten into your work—or maybe it's just that sense of power thrashing about. I thought it had come from a close admiring reading of Crane.

LOWELL: Yes, some kind of wildness and power that appeals to me, I guess. But when I wrote difficult poems they weren't meant to be difficult, though I don't know that Crane meant his to be. I wanted to be loaded and rich, but I thought the poems were all perfectly logical. You can have a wonderful time explaining a great poem like "Voyages II," and it all can be explained, but in the end it's just a love poem with a great confusion of images that are emotionally clear; a prose paraphrase wouldn't give you any impression whatever of the poem. I couldn't do that kind of poem, I don't think; at least I've never been able to.

INTERVIEWER: You said that most of the writers you've known have been against the grain. What did you mean?

LOWELL: When I began writing most of the great writers were quite unpopular. They hadn't reached the universities yet, and their circulation was small. Even Eliot wasn't very popular then. But life seemed to be there. It seemed to be one of those periods when the lid was still being blown. The great period of blowing the lid was the time of Schönberg and Picasso and Joyce and the early Eliot, where a power came into the arts which we perhaps haven't had since. These people were all rather traditional, yet they were stifled by what was being done, and they almost wrecked things to do their great works—even rather minor but very good writers such as Williams or Marianne Moore. Their kind of protest and queerness has hardly been repeated. They're wonderful writers. You wouldn't see anyone as strange as Marianne Moore again, not for a long while. Conservative and Jamesian as she is, it was a terrible, private, and strange revolutionary poetry. There isn't the motive to do that now. Yet those were the classics, and it seems to me they were all against the grain, Marianne Moore as much as Crane. That's where life was for the small audience. It would be a tremendous subject to say whether the feelings were against the grain too, and whether they were purifying, nihilistic, or both.

INTERVIEWER: Have you had much contact with Eliot?

LOWELL: I may have seen him a score of times in my life, and he's always been very kind. Long before he published me he had some of my poems in his files. There's some kind of New England connection.

INTERVIEWER: Has he helpfully criticized your work?

LOWELL: Just very general criticism. With the first book of mine Faber did he had a lot of little questions about punctuation, but he never said he liked this or disliked that. Then he said something about the last book—"These are first-rate, I mean it"—something like that that was very understated and gratifying. I feel Eliot's less tied to form than a lot of people he's influenced, and there's a freedom of the twenties in his work that I find very sympathetic. Certainly he and Frost are the great New England poets. You hardly think of Stevens as New England, but you have to think of Eliot and Frost as deeply New England and puritanical. They're a continuation and a criticism of the tradition, and they're probably equally great poets. Frost somehow put life into a dead tradition. His kind of poetry must have seemed almost unpublishable, it was so strange and fresh when it was first written. But still it was old-fashioned poetry and really had nothing to do with modern writing—except that he is one of the greatest modern writers. Eliot was violently modern and unacceptable to the traditionalist. Now he's spoken of as a literary dictator, but he's handled his position with wonderful sharpness and grace, it seems to me. It's a narrow position and it's not one I hold particularly, but I think it's been held with extraordinary honesty and finish and development. Eliot has done what he said Shakespeare had done: all his poems are one poem, a form of continuity that has grown and snowballed.

INTERVIEWER: I remember Jarrell in reviewing *Mills of the Kavanaughs* said that Frost had been doing narrative poems with ease for years, and that nobody else had been able to catch up.

LOWELL: And what Jarrell said is true: nobody except Frost can do a sort of Chaucerian narrative poem that's organized and clear. Well, a lot of people do them, but the texture of their verse is so limp and uninspired. Frost does them with great power. Most of them were done early, in that *North of Boston period*. That was a miracle, because except for Robinson—and I think Frost is a very much greater poet than Robinson—no one was doing that in England or America.

INTERVIEWERS But you hadn't simply wanted to tell a story in *Mills of the Kavanaughs*.

LOWELL: No, I was writing an obscure, rather Elizabethan, dramatic and melodramatic poem. I don't know quite how to describe this business of direct experience. With Browning, for instance, for all his gifts—and there is almost nothing Browning couldn't use— you feel there's a glaze between what he writes and what really happened, you feel the people are made up. In Frost you feel that's just what the farmers and so on were like. It has the virtue of a photograph but all the finish of art. That's an extraordinary thing; almost no other poet can do that now.

INTERVIEWER: What do you suppose are the qualities that go into that ability?

LOWELL: I don't know. Prose writers have it much more, and quite a few prose writers have it. It's some kind of sympathy and observation of people. It's the deep, rather tragic poems that I value most. Perhaps it's been overdone with Frost, but there's an abundance and geniality about those poems that isn't tragic. With this sense of rhythm and words and composition, and getting into his lines language that is very much like the language he speaks—which is also a work of art, much better than other people's ordinary speech and yet natural to him; he has that continuity with his ordinary self and his poetic self—he's made what with anyone else would be just flat. A very good prose writer can do this and make something of it. You get it quite often in Faulkner. Though he's an Elizabethan sort of character, rather unlike Frost, he can get this amazing immediacy and simplicity. When it comes to verse the form is so hard that all of that gets drained out. In a very conventional old-fashioned writer, or someone who's trying to be realistic but also dramatic and inspired, though he may remain a good poet, most of that directness and realism goes. It's hard for Eliot to be direct that way, though you get it in bits of the *Wasteland,* that marvelous Cockney section. And he can be himself; I feel Eliot's real all through the *Quartets.* He can be very intelligent or very simple there, and *he's* there, but there are no other people in the *Quartets.*

INTERVIEWER: Have many of your poems been taken from real people and real events?

LOWELL: I think, except when I've used myself or occasionally named actual people in poems, the characters are purely imaginary. I've tried to buttress them by putting images I've actually seen and in indirect ways getting things I've actually experienced into the poem. If I'm writing about a Canadian nun the poem may have a hundred little bits of things I've looked at, but she's not remotely anyone I've ever known. And I don't believe anybody would think my nun was quite a real person. She has a heart and she's alive, I hope, and she has a lot of color to her and drama, and has some things that Frost's characters don't, but she doesn't have their wonderful quality of life. His Witch of Coös is absolutely there. I've gathered from talking to him that most of the *North of Boston* poems came from actual people he knew shuffled and put together. But then it's all-important that Frost's plots are so extraordinary, so carefully worked out though it almost seems that they're not there. Like some things in Chekhov, the art is very well hidden.

INTERVIEWER: Don't you think a large part of it is getting the right details, symbolic or not, around which to wind the poem tight and tighter?

LOWELL: Some bit of scenery or something you've felt. Almost the whole problem of writing poetry is to bring it back to what you really feel, and that takes an awful lot of maneuvering. You may feel the doorknob more strongly than some big personal event, and the doorknob will open into something that you can use as your own.

A lot of poetry seems to me very good in the tradition but just doesn't move me very much because it doesn't have personal vibrance to it. I probably exaggerate the value of it, but it's precious to me. Some little image, some detail you've noticed—you're writing about a little country shop, just describing it, and your poem ends up with an existentialist account of your experience. But it's the shop that started it off. You didn't know why it meant a lot to you. Often images and often the sense of the beginning and end of a poem are all you have—some journey to be gone through between those things; you know that, but you don't know the details. And that's marvelous; then you feel the poem will come out. It's a terrible struggle, because what you really feel hasn't got the form, it's not what you can put down in a poem. And the poem you're equipped to write concerns nothing that you care very much about or have much to say on. Then the great moment comes when there's enough resolution of your technical equipment, your way of constructing things, and what you can make a poem out of, to hit something you really want to say. You may not know you have it to say.

Jerome Mazzaro
Checklist: 1939-1968

(for Joseph N. Riddel)

When The Achievement of Robert Lowell: 1939–1959 *(1960) was published, I remarked that the current indexes of periodical literature were disastrously inadequate to the compiling of a checklist on Lowell. Nine years have done little to alleviate the situation. I must again report that this bibliography, as complete as it is, can make no claim to being entirely definitive and that the responsibility for gaps and errors that exist in it is mine. I should like to thank Karl Gay of the Lockwood Library and Kevin McCullough for their assistance in helping me put this checklist together. The abbreviations I have used for periodical titles are as follows:*

AQ	American Quarterly	NYTBR	New York Times Book Review
AS	American Scholar		
BPJ	Beloit Poetry Journal	PR	Partisan Review
CSM	Christian Science Monitor	PW	Publishers' Weekly
		RLC	Revue de Littérature Comparée
CTBT	Chicago Tribune Books Today	SA	Studi Americani
CTMB	Chicago Tribune Magazine of Books	SAQ	South Atlantic Quarterly
		Sat R	Saturday Review
CW	Catholic World	Se R	Sewane Review
Hud R	Hudson Review	SFSCTW	San Francisco Sunday Chronicle This World
KR	Kenyon Review		
LJ	Library Journal	SPe	Lo Spettatore Italiano
MR	Massachusetts Review	SRL	Saturday Review of Literature
Minn R	Minnesota Review		
NEQ	New England Quarterly	TDR	Tulane Drama Review
		TLS	Times Literary Supplemen
NMQ	New Mexico Quarterly		
NY	New Yorker	TSLL	Texas Studies in Lit-

NYHTBW	*New York Herald*		*erature and Language*
	Tribune Book Week	*VQR*	*Virginia Quarterly*
NYHTWBR	*New York Herald*		*Review*
	Tribune Weekly	*WLB*	*Wilson Library Bulletin*
	Book Review	*WSCL*	*Wisconsin Studies in*
NYRB	*New York Review of*		*Contemporary*
	Books		*Literature*
NYT	*New York Times*	*YR*	*Yale Review*

I. INTERVIEWS

1. Alvarez, A. "Robert Lowell in Conversation," London *Observer,* July 21, 1963, p. 19.

2. ———. "Robert Lowell in Conversation," *Review,* No. 8 (August 1963), pp. 36–40. Reprints portions of the *Observer* interview and adds new material.

3. ———. "Talk with Robert Lowell," *Encounter,* XXIV (February 1965), 39–43. Reprinted in *Under Pressure.* Penguin Books, 1966.

4. Billington, Michael. "Mr. Lowell on T. S. Eliot and the Theatre," *Times,* March 8, 1967, p. 10.

5. Brooks, Cleanth and Robert Penn Warren. *Conversations on the Craft of Poetry.* New York, 1961.

6. Carne-Ross, D. S. "Conversation with Robert Lowell," *Delos,* I (1968), 165–175.

7. Gilman, Richard. "Life Offers No Neat Conclusions," *NYT,* May 5, 1968, 11, pp. 1, 5.

8. Kunitz, Stanley. "Talk with Robert Lowell," *NYTBR,* October 4, 1964, p. 34+.

9. Seidel, Frederick. "Interview with Robert Lowell," *Paris Review,* XXV (Winter-Spring 1961), 56–95. Reprinted in *Writers at Work.* Second Series. New York, 1963.

II. BIBLIOGRAPHIES

10. Mazzaro, Jerome. "The Achievement of Robert Lowell: 1939–1959," *Fresco,* X (Winter-Spring 1960), 51–77. Expanded and reprinted as *The Achievement of Robert Lowell: 1939–1959.* Detroit, 1960.

11. ———. "A Checklist of Materials on Robert Lowell: 1939–1968," in Robert Lowell: A Portrait of the Artist in His Time, ed. Michael London and Robert Boyers. New York, 1970.

12. Staples, Hugh B. "Robert Lowell: Bibliography 1939-1959, with an Illustrative Critique," *Harvard Library Bulletin,* XIII (1959), 292–318. Expanded and

reprinted in the Appendix to *Robert Lowell: The First Twenty Years*. New York, 1962.

III. BIOGRAPHY

A. *General*:

13. "Issues in Alabama," *NYT*, May 12, 1963, IV, p. 10.

14. "Johnson Hails College Students as His 'Fellow Revolutionaries,'" *NYT*, August 5, 1965, p. 13.

15. "Lady with a Switchblade," *Life*, LV (September 20, 1963), 61–64.

16. "Lowell to Teach at Harvard," *NYT*, June 23, 1958, p. 21.

17. "The Lowells of Massachusetts," *Life*, XLII (March 18, 1957), 127–137.

18. "Marianne Moore to Open New School Poetry Series," *NYT*, May 28, 1962, p. 24.

19. "News Notes," *Poetry*, LXXXI (1953), 403–405. (Appointed Lecturer in the Poetry Workshop at State University of Iowa.)

20. "News Notes," *Poetry*, LXXXVI (1955), 306–309. (Member of Wheaton College's (Mass.) Modern Poetry Symposium, April 23, 1955.)

21. "News Notes," *Poetry*, LXXXVIII (1956), 411–412. (Speaker at Harvard University's Summer School's "The Little Magazine in America," July 30-August 1, 1956.)

22. "News Notes," *Poetry*, IC (1962), 395–396. (Visiting Professor at Harvard.)

23. "News Notes," *Poetry*, C (1962), 266–267. (Supported the publication of *Tropic of Cancer*.)

24. "News Notes," *Poetry*, CI (1963), 363–364. (Member of committee awarding Bolligen Prize to Robert Frost.)

25. "News Notes," *Poetry*, CIII (1963), 204–208. (Member of Board of Chancellors voting 1963 Fellowship of Academy of American Poets to Ezra Pound.)

26. "News Notes," *Poetry*, CV (1964), 141–143. (Member of Board of Chancellors voting Academy of American Poets' Fellowship to Elizabeth Bishop.)

27. "News Notes," *Poetry*, CVI (1965), 373–376. (Member of Board of Chancellors voting Academy of American Poets' Fellowship to Marianne Moore; awarded Litt. D., Williams College.)

28. "News Notes," *Poetry*, CIX (1967), 276–278. (Member of Board of Chancellors voting Academy of American Poets' Fellowship to John Berryman.)

29. "1947 Pulitzer Prize Poet to Lecture in Cincinnati," *NYT*, December 18, 1953, p. 6.

30. "Poets among Us," *Vogue*, CXXI (April 15, 1953), 90–91.

31. "Poets Pay Tribute to T. S. Eliot," *Times*, January 6, 1965, p. 8.

32. "Robert Lowell," *The International Who's Who*. 23rd Edition. London, 1959. Reprinted in 24th Edition (1960); revised for 25th Edition (1961); revised again for 26th Edition (1962); reprinted in 27th Edition (1963); revised for 28th

Edition (1964); revised for 29th Edition (1965); revised for 30th Edition (1966), revised for 31st Edition (1968).

33. "Robert Lowell," *The National Cyclopaedia of American Biography,* I (1953–1959). New York, 1960.

34. "Robert Lowell," *Who's Who in America,* XXVI (1950–1951). Chicago, 1950. Reprinted in XXVII (1952); revised for XXVIII (1954); revised again for XXIX (1956); revised for XXX (1958); revised for XXXI (1960); revised again for XXXII (1962); revised for XXXIII (1964); revised again for XXXIV (1966); reprinted in XXXV (1968).

35. "Robert Lowell," *Who's Who, 1967–1968.* New York, 1967.

36. "The Second Chance," *Time,* LXXXIX (June 2, 1967), 67–74.

37. "70 Attend Birthday Party for Marianne Moore, 75," *NYT,* November 15, 1962, p. 39.

38. "Soviet Poet Sees Literary Rebirth," *NYT,* April 30, 1967, p. 80.

39. Austin, Anthony. "Talk with Andrei Voznesensky," *NYTBR,* May 14, 1967, pp. 4–5.

40. Baker, M. J. "Classes with a Poet," *Madamoiselle,* XL (November 1954), 106+.

41. Berryman, John. "Randall Jarrell," in *Randall Jarrell, 1914–1965,* ed. Robert Lowell, Peter Taylor, and Robert Penn Warren. New York, 1967.

42. Bozman, E. F., ed. "Robert Lowell," *The Macmillan Everyman's Encyclopedia.* 4th Edition. New York, 1959. (The information in this volume is incorrect.)

43. Browning, D. C. "Robert Lowell," *Everyman's Dictionary of Literary Biography, English & American.* New York, 1958.

44. Detmold, John Hunter. "Arnold not Lowell," *NYT,* August 16, 1965, p. 26.

45. Ethridge, James M., ed. "Robert Lowell," *Contemporary Authors.* Vols. IX–X. Detroit, 1964.

46. Fitzgibbon, Constantine. *The Life of Dylan Thomas.* Boston, 1965.

47. Herzberg, Max J. "Robert Lowell," *The Reader's Encyclopedia of American Literature.* New York, 1962.

48. Holmes, John. "A Galaxy of Poets in Baltimore," *CSM,* November 9, 1961, p. 7.

49. Howe, Irving. "The Writer Can't Keep to His Attic," *NYT Magazine,* December 5, 1965, p. 43+.

50. Jarrell, Mrs. Randall. "The Group of Two," in *Randall Jarrell, 1914–1965,* ed. Robert Lowell, Peter Taylor, and Robert Penn Warren. New York, 1967.

51. Kunitz, Stanley, ed. "Robert Lowell," *Twentieth Century Authors: First Supplement.* New York, 1955.

52. ———. "Telling the Time," *Salmagundi*, I, iv (1966–67), 22–24.

53. McCormick, J. "Falling Asleep over Grillparzer," *Poetry*, LXXXI (1953), 269–279.

54. Newlove, Donald. "Dinner at the Lowells'," *Esquire*, LXXII (September 1969), 128+.

55. Plimpton, George. "The World Series with Marianne Moore," *Harper's*, CCXXIX (October 1964), 50–58.

56. Reck, Michael, *Ezra Pound*. New York, 1967.

57. Rexroth, Kenneth. "How Poets Make a Living, If Any," *Harper's*, CCXXXIV (February 1967), 90–101.

58. Richards, Robert Fulton. "Robert Lowell," *Concise Dictionary of American Literature*. New York, 1955.

59. Roethke, Theodore. *Selected Letters,* ed. Ralph J. Mills, Jr. Seattle, 1968.

60. Rosenthal, M. L. "Angst across the Sea," *Reporter*, XXXII (March 11, 1965), 41–42. (Review of *Under Pressure* with extensive Lowell quotes.)

61. Rothe, Anna, ed. "Robert Lowell," *Current Biography, 1947*. New York, 1948.

62. Scott, Walter D., et al., ed. "Robert Lowell," *The American Peoples Encyclopedia*. Vol. XII. Chicago, 1959.

63. Seager, Allan. *The Glass House*. New York, 1968.

64. ———. "An Evening with Ted Roethke," *Michigan Quarterly Review*, VI (1967), 227–234.

65. Sexton, Anne. "Classroom at Boston University," *Harvard Advocate*, CXLV (November 1961), 13–14.

66. Shapiro, Karl. "The Death of Randall Jarrell," in *Randall Jarrell, 1914–1965*, ed. Robert Lowell, Peter Taylor, and Robert Penn Warren. New York, 1967.

67. Slonim, Marc. "Writers in Moscow," *NYTBR*, May 21, 1967, pp. 18–20.

68. Smith, Hedrick. "Cairo Welcomes Frederic Marches," *NYT*, April 8, 1965, p. 43.

69. Spender, Stephen. "Journal Extracts," *Art & Literature*, No. 9 (Summer 1966), pp. 198–215.

70. Untermeyer, Louis. *Lives of the Poets*. New York, 1959.

B. *Draft Evasion* (1943)

71. "A 'Boston Lowell' Is a Draft Dodger," *NYT*, October 12, 1943, p. 29.

72. "Dodgers and Dissenters," *Time*, XLII (October 25, 1943), 68.

73. "Indicted as Draft Evader," *NYT*, October 2, 1943, p. 8.

74. "Nazi Draft Dodger Gets 3-Year Term," *NYT*, October 14, 1943, p. 13.

75. "To Act on Draft Evader," *NYT*, September 9, 1943, p. 27.

76. "Warrant for Draft Evader," *NYT*, October 8, 1943, p. 13.

C. *Bollingen Controversy* (1949)

77. "Pound, in Mental Clinic, Wins Prize for Poetry Penned in Treason Cell," *NYT*, February 20, 1949, p. 1+.

78. "Savants Deny 'Fascism,' " *NYT*, August 12, 1949, p. 9.

79. Auden, W. H., et al. "The Question of the Pound Award," *PR*, XVI (1949), 512–522. (See particularly the comments by Karl Shapiro.) Reprinted in *A Casebook on Ezra Pound*, ed. William Van O'Connor and Edward Stone. New York, 1959.

80. Barrett, William. "A Prize for Ezra Pound," *PR*, XVI (1949), 344–347.

81. Cousins, Norman and Harrison Smith. "More on Pound," *SRL*, XXXII (July 30, 1949), 22.

82. Deutsch, Albert. "Editorial," The New York *Post*, February 28, 1949.

83. Macdonald, Dwight. "Homage to Twelve Judges," *Politics*, VI (Winter 1949). Reprinted in his *Memoirs of a Revolutionist* (New York, 1957; Meridian Books, 1958) and in *A Casebook on Ezra Pound*, ed. William Van O'Connor and Edward Stone, New York, 1959.

84. Thomson, Ralph. "In and Out of Books," *NYTBR*, July 24, 1949, p. 8.

D. *Awards, Honors* (1946–1960)

85. "Amateur Wins Photo Honor in Award of Pulitzer Prizes," *NYT*, May 6, 1947, p. 1+.

86. "American Academy and National Institute Make Awards," *PW*, CLI (May 17, 1947), 2504.

87. "Arts Group Names Winners of Grants," *NYT*, May 8, 1947, p. 19.

88. "Books—Authors," *NYT*, October 21, 1947, p. 21.

89. "Five Are Elected to Arts Institute," *NYT*, February 10, 1954, p. 36.

90. "Franklin's Ideals Seen Lost Today," *NYT*, May 27, 1954, p. 25.

91. "Kenyon Installs Lund," *NYT*, October 5, 1958, p. 65.

92. "The Literary Life," *Time*, IL (May 19, 1947), 44.

93. "Monroe Poetry Award," *PW*, CLXII (July 19, 1952), 240.

94. "News Notes," *Poetry*, LXX (1947), 228–230. (Prizes for *Lord Weary's Castle;* Guggenheim Fellowship.)

95. "News Notes," *Poetry*, LXXI (1947), 168–170. (Appointed Consultant to the Library of Congress.)

96. "News Notes," *Poetry*, LXXII (1948), 113–114. (On jury for awarding of Bollingen Prize.)

97. "News Notes," *Poetry*, LXXVI (1950), 59. (Appointed to Bollingen Award Committee at Yale; to instruct at Kenyon School of English, Summer 1950.)

98. "News Notes," *Poetry*, LXXIX (1952), 152–153. (Awarded $500 Harriet Monroe Prize at University of Chicago, June 1952.)

99. "News Notes," *Poetry*, XC (1957), 59–60. (On jury for first Creative Arts awards.)

100. "News Notes," *Poetry*, XCV (1960), 319. (Guinness Poetry Award.)

101. "News Notes," *Poetry*, XCVI (1960), 61–63. (Longview Foundation Award.)

102. "News Notes," *Poetry*, XCVI (1960), 127–128. (Ford Foundation Grant, National Book Award, and Boston Arts Festival.)

103. " 'Prize Poet' Robert Lowell Wins the Pulitzer Prize," *Life* XXII (May 19, 1947), 91+.

104. "Pulitzer Prize Awarded to Authors and Journalists," *PW*, CLI (May 17, 1947), 2502–2504.

105. "The Pulitzer Prize Awards for 1946," *SRL*, XXX (May 17, 1947), 20–21.

106. "Storyteller, Biographer and Poet Win Book Awards," *NYT*, March 24, 1960, p. 24.

107. "Words, words," *NY*, XXXVI (April 2, 1960), 32–33.

108. "Year's Most Rewarded Poet," *Time*, IL (May 19, 1947), 44.

109. Frank, Stanley. "Mr. Pulitzer's Prize Hair Pull," *Saturday Evening Post*, CCIX (May 3, 1947), 26+.

110. Fuller, John G. "Trade Winds," *Sat R*, XLIII (April 9, 1960), 12+.

111. Nichols, Lewis. "In and Out of Books," *NYTBR*, March 20, 1960, p. 8.

112. ———. "In and Out of Books," *NYTBR*, April 3, 1960, p. 8.

113. Pack, Robert. "Introduction," *New Poets of England and America*, Second Series, ed. Donald Hall and Robert Pack. Cleveland, 1962.

114. Penland, Patrick R. "National Book Awards Presented," *LJ*, LXXXV (1960), 1421–1422.

E. *Helen Burlin Memorial Award Controversy* (1962)

115. "News Notes," *Poetry*, XCVIII (1961), 199.

116. "News Notes," *Poetry*, C (1962), 412–414.

117. "Poems in 'Y' Dispute Will Be Published," *NYT*, July 17, 1962, p. 22.

118. Knox, Sandra. "Poets' Jury Quits in Award Dispute," *NYT*, July 16, 1962, p. 25.

F. *White House Arts Festival* (1965)

119. "Lowell Refuses to Attend White House Arts Festival," *PW*, CLXXXVII (June 14, 1965), 77.

120. "Miller Sees Pen Growing Mightier," *NYT*, July 6, 1965, p. 30.

121. "News Notes," *Poetry*, CVI (1965), 373–376.
122. "The Occasion for Protest," *Nation*, CC (1965), 658–659.
123. "Paul Strand, Photographer, Declines White House Bid," *NYT*, June 14, 1965, p. 44.
124. "The Presidency," *Time*, LXXXV (June 11, 1965), 29.
125. "President and Poet," *NYT*, June 6, 1965, IV, p. 4.
126. "Rejection Slip," *Newsweek*, LXV (June 14, 1965), 68.
127. "Writers Support Robert Lowell," *Times*, June 5, 1965, p. 7.
128. Brandon, Henry. "Uneasy Alliance," *Sat R*, XLVIII (July 3, 1965), 8.
129. Ellison, Ralph. "A Very Stern Discipline," *Harper's*, CCXXXIV (March 1967), 76–95.
130. Gilroy, Harry. "2 in Arts Chided by Schlesinger," *NYT*, June 8, 1965, p. 46.
131. Goldman, E. F. "The White House and the Intellectuals," *Harper's*, CCXXXVIII (January 1969), 31–45; (March 1969), 4+. Excerpts from *The Tragedy of Lyndon Johnson*. New York, 1969.
132. Kempton, Murray. "Lessons from Lowell," *Spectator*, CCXV (1965), 745–747.
133. Macdonald, Dwight. "A Day at the White House," *NYRB*, V (July 15, 1965), 10–15.
134. ———. "Dwight Macdonald's Arts Statement," *NYT*, June 24, 1965, p. 34.
135. Maloff, Saul. "The White House Festival," *Commonweal*, CXXXII (1965), 485–487.
136. Raymont, Henry. "Historian's Book Recalls Furor at White House Arts Festival," *NYT*, December 22, 1968, p. 23.
137. Roth, Philip. "Festival of Arts Now?" *NYT*, June 15, 1965, p. 40.
138. Schlesinger, Arthur, Jr. "What Schlesinger Said," *NYT*, June 21, 1965, p. 28.
139. Shepard, Richard F. "Robert Lowell Rebuffs Johnson as Protest over Foreign Policy," *NYT*, June 3, 1965, p. 1+.
140. ———. "20 Writers and Artists Endorse Poet's Rebuff of the President," *NYT*, June 4, 1965, p. 2.
141. Taubman, Howard. "White House Salutes Culture in America," *NYT*, June 15, 1965, p. 1+.

G. *Oxford Chair* (1966)
142. "British Poet Calls Lowell, Oxford Loser, Best in Field," *NYT*, February 9, 1966, p. 36.
143. "Lowell Defeated for Oxford Chair," *NYT*, February 6, 1966, p. 18.

144. "Lowell Nominated at Oxford," *NYT*, January 19, 1966, p. 33.

145. "Mr. Blunden Wins Poetry Chair by 236 Votes," *Times*, February 7, 1966, p. 5.

146. "Mr. Lowell Nominated for Oxford Poetry Chair," *Times*, January 15, 1966, p. 10.

147. "Two Candidates for Chair of Poetry," *Times*, January 25, 1966, p. 10.

148. Coleman, Terry. "Poet's Professorship," Manchester *Guardian Weekly*, February 10, 1966, p. 13.

149. Conquest, Robert. "Letter," *Spectator*, CCXVI (1966), 136.

150. ———. "Letter," *Spectator*, CCXVI (1966), 225–226.

151. Duncan, Ronald. "Letter," *Spectator*, CCXVI (1966), 136.

152. Graves, Robert. "Letter," *Times*, February 16, 1966, p. 13.

153. Hudson, Derek. "Letter," *Spectator*, CCXVI (1966), 136–137.

154. ———. "Letter," *Spectator*, CCXVI (1966), 197.

155. Lewis, Anthony. "Oxford Politics: 2 Poets in a Race," *NYT*, February 1, 1966, p. 32.

156. Lucie-Smith, Edward. "An Address to the Electors of Oxford," *Spectator* CCXVI (1966), 107–108.

157. ———. "The Angus Maude of Literature," *Spectator*, CCXVI (1966), 166.

158. Parker, Derek. "Letter," *New Statesman*, LXXI (1966), 260.

159. Reeves, James. "Letter," *Spectator*, CCXVI (1966), 136.

160. Ricks, Christopher. "Lowell, Go Home," *New Statesman*, LXXI (1966), 199.

161. Spender, Stephen. "Letter," *New Statesman*," LXXI (1966), 260.

162. ———. "Letter," *Times*, February 8, 1966, p. 11.

163. Tripp, John. "Letter," *Spectator*, CCXVI (1966), 165–166.

164. Wain, John. "Electing a Poet," *Encounter*, XXVI (April 1966), 51–52.

165. Wightman, G. B. H. "Letter," *Spectator*, CCXVI (1966), 137.

166. ———. "Letter," *Spectator*, CCXVI (1966), 197.

H. *Lincoln Center Festival* (1967)

167. Handler, M. S. "Russian's Poems Read in Absentia," *NYT*, June 22, 1967, p. 36.

168. ———. "Soviet May Bar Voznesensky Trip," *NYT*, June 19, 1967, p. 29.

169. ———. "Soviet Poet Voznesensky Cancels His Visit Here," *NYT*, June 20, 1967, p. 5.

I. *Political Issues* (1966–1968)

170. "Crisis of Conscience in U.S. over President's Policy," *Times*, June 4, 1967, p. 10.

171. "Crowd Here Hails Monk from Vietnam," *NYT*, June 10, 1966, p. 9.

172. "McCarthy Takes Time Off to Visit Poet Robert Lowell," *NYT*, August 3, 1968, p. 10.

173. "News Notes," *Poetry*, CVIII (1966), 346–349. (Listed among poets participating in anti-war readings.)

174. "Robert Lowell Gives Reason for Not Signing War Plea," *NYT*, June 14, 1967, p. 3.

175. "Writers Appeal on Soviet Jews," *NYT*, May 21, 1967, p. 12.

176. Burks, Edward C. "320 Vow to Help Draft Resisters," *NYT*, September 27, 1967, p. 13.

177. Handler, M. S. "Lowell, at Voznesensky Recital Criticizes Both U.S. and Soviet," *NYT*, May 18, 1967, p. 43.

178. Holmstrom, David. "Politician and Poet on Platform," *CSM*, June 17, 1968, p. 13.

179. Kenworthy, E. W. "Poet and Politician Orchestrate McCarthy Overtures to Voters," *NYT*, March 29, 1968, p. 26.

180. ———. "Thousands Reach Capital to Protest Vietnam War," *NYT*, October 21, 1967, p. 1+

181. Lask, Thomas. "18 Leading Poets and Writers Give Reading Stressing Peace," *NYT*, November 13, 1967, p. 60.

182. Lowell, Robert. "Letter," *NYRB*, X (February 29, 1968), 32. (On Vietnam.)

183. ———. "Letter," *NYRB*, XI (July 11, 1968), 43. (On Yale Degree.)

184. ———. "Letter," *NYRB*, XI (January 2, 1969), 42–43. (On Czechoslovakia.)

185. ———. "Why I'm For McCarthy," *New Republic*, CLVIII (April 13, 1968), 22.

186. ——— and Diana Trilling. "Liberalism & Activism," *Commentary*, LXXIV (April 1969), 19–20, 22

187. ——— and others. "Letter," *NYRB*, XII (March 27, 1969), 46. (On arrests in Spain.)

188. ———. "Liberalism & Columbia," *Commentary*, LXXIV (March 1969), 4+.

189. Mailer, Norman. "The Steps of the Pentagon," *Harper's*, CCXXXVI (March 1968), 47+. Reprinted in *The Armies of the Night*. New York, 1968.

190. Miller, Arthur. "Literature and Masse Communications," *World Theatre*, XV (1966), 164–167.

191. Reed, Roy. "Critics on Vietnam Divided by Appeal on Israel," *NYT*, June 12, 1967, p. 5.

192. Roberts, Steven B. "M'Carthy, Here, Offers War View," *NYT*, February 17, 1968, p. 12.

193. Simpson, Louis. "McCarthy as Poet: Irony and Moral Sense," *NYTBR*, August 4, 1968, p. 2+

J. *Awards, Honors* (1961–1968)

194. "Alti Premi," *Forum Italicum*, II (1968), 284.

195. "American Academy Adds Members," *NYT*, December 10, 1963, p. 50.

196. "Announcement of Prize Awards for 1963," *Poetry*, CIII (1963), 202–203. (Levinson Prize.)

197. "Bollingen Translation Prize," *WLB*, XXXVII (December 1962), 323.

198. "Bollingen Translation Prize of $2,500 Is Shared by Two," *NYT*, November 6, 1962, p. 39.

199. "Books—Authors," *NYT*, August 10, 1966, p. 38. (Sarah Josepha Hale Award.)

200. "14 Join National Arts Institute; American Academy Inducts 4," *NYT*, May 21, 1964, p. 41.

201. "News Notes," *Poetry*, XCVII (1961), 396–398. (Invited to White House.)

202. "News Notes," *Poetry*, IC (1962), 327–328. (Member of National Poetry Council.)

203. "News Notes," *Poetry*, CI (1963), 295–297. (Member, Board of Chancellors of Academy of American Poets.)

204. "News Notes," *Poetry*, CIII (1964), 272. (Elected to membership in American Academy of Arts and Letters.)

205. "News Notes," *Poetry*, CIV (1964), 268–269. (Inducted into Academy of Arts and Letters.)

206. "News Notes," *Poetry*, CV (1965), 343-344. (Member of National Advisory Board for the University of Texas' Ford Foundation granted Center for Translation.)

207. "Rutgers Awards Degrees to 4,100," *NYT*, June 10, 1965, p. 22.

208. "Temple's Graduates Hear Warning on 'Modern Idol,'" *NYT*, June 12, 1964, p. 72.

209. Borders, William. "Yale Awards 2,402 Degrees and Honors 14 at Commencement," *NYT*, June 11, 1968, p. 43.

210. Fenton, John H. "Harriman Extols Marshall Plan," *NYT*, June 17, 1966, p. 31.

211. Schumach, Murray. "Commencements: Disruption Assailed at Columbia," *NYT*, June 4, 1969, p. 30.

IV. CRITICISM

A. *General:*

212. "American Poetry To-Day," *TLS*, January 19, 1951, pp. 29–31.

213. "Applause for a Prize Poet," *Life*, LVIII (February 19, 1965), 49–58. Reprinted in *Life Educational Reprints 9.*

214. "Eternal Verities," *TLS*, November 6, 1959, p. xvii.

215. "Hearing Lowell Read," *Canadian Forum*, XLVIII (1969), 272.

216. "Now Read In . . ." *TLS*, May 12, 1966, p. 407.

217. "The Poet as Patron," *WLB*, XXXVI (January 1962), 365–372.

218. "Poetry in English: 1945–1962," *Time*, LXXIX (March 9, 1962), 92–95.

219. "Robert Lowell," *Atlantic Advocate*, LIX (March 1969), 59.

220. Alvarez, A. *The Shaping Spirit*. London, 1958.

221. ———. *Beyond All This Fiddle*. London, 1968. Reprints "Beyond All This Fiddle," *TLS* (March 23, 1967), 229–232.

222. Andress, Lyman. "Voices of America," *Times,* March 9, 1969, p. 56.

223. Arnavon, Cyrille, *Histoire Littéraire des États-Unis*. Paris, 1953.

224. Bayley, John. "Robert Lowell: The Poetry of Cancellation," *London Magazine*, VI (June 1966), 76–85.

225. Beccaro, Felice del. "Elegia marina di Robert Lowell," *Il Mattino dell' Italia Centrale*, August 7, 1951.

226. Berman, David. "Robert Lowell and the Aristocratic Tradition," *Harvard Advocate*, CXLV (November 1961), 15–19.

227. Bernlef, J. "Over Robert Lowell," *De Gids* 131, ii/iii:157–159.

228. Bly, Robert. "On Political Poetry," *Nation*, CCIV (1967), 522–524.

229. Bogan, Louise. *Achievement in American Poetry 1900–1950*. Chicago, 1951.

230. Bowen, Roger. "Confession and Equilibrium: Robert Lowell's Poetic Development," *Criticism*, XI (1969), 78–93.

231. Boyers, Robert and Michael London. Robert Lowell: A Portrait of the Artist in His Time. New York, 1970.

232. Braybrooke, Neville. "The Poetry of Robert Lowell," *CW*, CXCVIII (1964), 230–237. See also "Robert Lowell and the Unjust Steward."

233. ———. "Robert Lowell and the Unjust Steward," *Contemporary Review*, CCIV (November 1963), 242–247. Reprinted in *Dalhousie Review*, XLIV (Spring 1964), 28–34, and *Arena*, No. 64 (December 1965), pp. 14–19, 29.

234. Brown, Ashley. "Poets of a Silver Age," *Se R*, LXXII (1964), 519–526.

235. Brumleve, Sr. Eric Marie. "Permanence and Change in the Poetry of Robert Lowell," *TSLL*, X (1968), 143–153.

236. Calhoun, Richard J. "The Poetic Metamorphosis of Robert Lowell," *Furman Studies*, XIII, i, 7–17.

237. Cambon, Glauco. *Dante's Craft: Studies in Language and Style*. Minneapolis, 1969.

238. ———. *Recent American Poetry*. Minneapolis, 1962.

239. ———. *Tematica E Sviluppo della Poesia Americana*. Rome, 1958.

240. ———. "Dea Roma and Robert Lowell," *Accent*, XX (1960), 51–61.

241. ———. "Lowell e Roethke: Poesia in extremis," *SA*, X (1964), 429–435.

242. Carruth, Hayden. "A Meaning of Robert Lowell," *Hud R*, XX (1967), 429–447.

243. Ciardi, John. "Letter," *Poetry*, LXXII (1948), 261–263.

244. Coblentz, Stanton A. *The Poetry Circus*. New York, 1967.

245. Cory, Daniel. *Santayana: The Later Years*. New York, 1963.

246. Cott, Jonathan. "The New American Poetry," in *The New American Arts*, ed. Richard Kostelanetz. New York, 1965.

247. Cowley, Malcolm. "Who's to Take the Place of Hemingway and Faulkner," *NYTBR*, October 7, 1962, p. 4.

248. Davison, Peter. "The Difficulties of Being Major," *Atlantic*, CCXX (October 1967), 116–121.

249. Deutsch, Babette. *Poetry in Our Time*. New York, 1956.

250. Donoghue, Denis. *Connoisseurs of Chaos*. London, 1965.

251. Dorius, Joel, R. E. Garis and S. T. Johnson. "Colloquy on Robert Lowell," Harvard Advocate, CXXX (May 1947), 26–35.

252. Ehrenpreis, Irvin. "The Age of Lowell," in *American Poetry*, ed. I. Ehrenpreis. Stratford-upon-Avon Studies No. 7. London, 1965.

253. Elton, William. "A Note on Robert Lowell," *Poetry*, LXXI (1947), 138–140.

254. Fairfax, John. "Poems Threepence Each," *The Poetry Review*, LVII (1966), 43–45.

255. Feltham, Elizabeth. "Francis Webb and Robert Lowell: Self-Exploration and Poetic Control," *Quadrant*, VI (Spring 1962), 19–27.

256. Fitzgerald, Robert. "Notes on American Poetry after 1945," *American Review*, I (Autumn 1960), 127–135.

257. Frankenberg, Lloyd. *Pleasure Dome*. Boston, 1949.

258. French, A. L. "Robert Lowell: The Poetry of Abdication," *Oxford Review*, No. 9 (1968), pp. 5–20.

259. Fried, Michael. "The Achievement of Robert Lowell," *London Magazine*, n.s. I (October 1962), 54–64.

260. Goodwin, K. L. *The Influence of Ezra Pound*. London, 1966.

261. Greene, George. "Four Campus Poets," *Thought*, XXXV (Summer 1960), 223–246.

262. Gregory, Horace. "Poetry," *Sat R*, XXXVI (March 14, 1953), 13+.

263. Gross, Harvey. *Sound and Form in Modern Poetry*. Ann Arbor, 1964.

264. Gustafson, Richard. "The Voice of the Beep: The Middle Style in Modern American Verse," *Poet and Critic*, I (Fall 1964), 36–42.

265. Hall, Donald. "American Poets Since the War," *World Review*, n.s. No. 47 (January 1953), pp. 48–54. Reprinted in *American Literary Essays*, ed. Lewis Leary. New York, 1960.

266. ———. "The Battle of the Bards," *Horizon,* IV (September 1961), 116–121.

267. ———. "Introduction," *Contemporary American Poetry.* Penguin Books, 1962.

268. Hamilton, Ian. "Robert Lowell," *Review,* No. 3 (August-September 1962), pp. 15–23.

269. Hardison, O. B., Jr. "Robert Lowell: The Poet and the World's Body," *Shenandoah,* XIV (Winter 1963), 24–32.

270. Hart, James D. *The Oxford Companion to American Literature.* 3rd Edition. New York, 1956. Revised for 4th Edition (1965).

271. Heiney, Donald. *Recent American Literature.* Great Neck, N.Y., 1958.

272. Hughes, Daniel. "The Dream Song: Spells for Survival," *Southern Review* (Australia), II (1966), 5–17.

273. Jarrell, Randall. "Fifty Years of American Poetry," *Prairie Schooner,* XXXVII (Spring 1963), 1–27. Appears also in *National Poetry Festival: Proceedings.* Washington, D.C., 1964.

274. ———. "View from Parnassus," *Time,* LXXX (November 9, 1962), 100+.

275. Johnson, Geoffrey. "Modern American Poetry," *Literary Half-Yearly,* VII:2 (July 1966), pp. 40–44.

276. Jones, A. R. "Necessity and Freedom: The Poetry of Robert Lowell, Sylvia Plath and Anne Sexton," *Critical Quarterly,* VII (Spring 1965), 11–30.

277. Katz, Bill. "Poetry in Public Libraries," *LJ,* XCIII (1968), 2207.

278. Leibowitz, Herbert. "Robert Lowell: Ancestral Voices," *Salmagundi,* I, iv (1966–67), 25–43.

279. Lombard, C. F. "Lowell and French Romanticism," *RLC,* XXXVIII (1964), 582–588.

280. Lombardo, Agostino. "La poesia di Robert Lowell," *SPe,* VIII (June 1955), 238–244.

281. ———. "La 'Realta Americana' nella Tradizione," *La Fiera Letteraria,* VII (May 18, 1952), 1–2.

282. Lutyens, David Bulwer. *The Creative Encounter.* London, 1960.

283. Martz, William J. "Robert Lowell—'Which Way I Fly Is Hell,' " *The Achievement of Robert Lowell.* Glenview, Ill., 1966.

284. Mazzaro, Jerome. *The Poetic Themes of Robert Lowell.* Ann Arbor, 1965.

285. ———. "Robert Lowell and the Circle," *New Republic,* CLX (May 31, 1969), 31–33.

286. ———. "Robert Lowell's Early Politics of Apocalypse," in *Modern American Poetry: Essays in Criticism,* ed. Jerome Mazzaro. New York, 1970.

287. Miller, Terry. "The Prosodies of Robert Lowell," *Speech Monographs,* XXXV (1968), 425–434.

288. Mills, Ralph J., Jr. *Contemporary American Poetry*. New York, 1966.

289. ———. "A Note on the Personal Element in Recent American Poetry," *Chicago Circle Studies*, I (December 1965), 7–11.

290. Mizener, Arthur. "American Poetry in the Twentieth Century," in *The Arts at Mid-Century*, ed. Robert Richman. New York, 1954.

291. Mottram, E. N. W. "American Poetry," in *The Concise Encyclopedia of English and American Poets and Poetry*, ed. Stephen Spender and Donald Hall. New York, 1963.

292. Nyren, Dorothy. *A Library of Literary Criticism*. New York, 1960.

293. Ong, Walter J. *In the Human Grain*. New York, 1967.

294. Ostroff, Anthony. "The Sound of Poetry," *KR*, XXIII (1961), 343–351.

295. Parkinson, Thomas. *Robert Lowell: A Collection of Critical Essays*. Englewood Cliffs, N. J., 1968.

296. Pearson, Gabriel. "Robert Lowell," *Review*, No. 20 (March 1969), pp. 3–36.

297. Perloff, Marjorie. "Death by Water: The Winslow Elegies of Robert Lowell," *ELH*, XXXIV (1967), 116–140.

298. Podhoretz, Norman. *Making It*. New York, 1967.

299. Ransom, John C. "A Look Backward and a Note of Hope," *Harvard Advocate*, CXLV (November 1961), 22–24.

300. ———. "Robert Lowell," in *The Concise Encyclopedia of English and American Poets and Poetry*, ed. Stephen Spender and Donald Hall. New York, 1963.

301. Read, Sir Herbert. "American Bards and British Reviewers," in *National Poetry Festival: Proceedings*. Washington, D. C., 1964.

302. Riewald, J. G. *Autogene symbolen in de poëzie van Robert Lowell*. Groningen, 1967.

303. Rizzardi, Alfredo. *La Condizione Americana*. Bologna, 1959.

304. Rosenthal, M. L. *Modern Poets: A Critical Introduction*. New York, 1960.

305. ———. *New Poets*. New York, 1967.

306. Santayana, George. *The Letters of George Santayana*, ed. Daniel Cory. New York, 1955.

307. Seymour-Smith, Martin. *Bluff Your Way in Literature*. London, 1966.

308. Simon, John. "Abuse of Privilege: Lowell as Translator," *Hud R*, XX (1967–68), 543–562.

309. Stallworthy, Jon. "W. B. Yeats and the Dynastic Theme," *Critical Quarterly*, VII (Autumn 1965), 247–265.

310. Staples, Hugh B. *Robert Lowell: The First Twenty Years*. New York, 1962.

311. ———. "Beyond Charles River to the Acheron: An Introduction to the Poetry of Robert Lowell," in *Poets in Progress,* ed. E. B. Hungerford. Evanston, Ill., 1962.

312. ———. "A Graph of Revelations," *Northwestern University Tri-Quarterly,* I (Winter 1959), 7–12.

313. Stepanchev, Stephen. *American Poetry Since 1945.* New York, 1965.

314. ———. "A Look at Recent American Poetry," *Shenandoah,* XV (Summer 1964), 70–77.

315. Stiehl, Harry. "Achievement in American Catholic Poetry," *Ramparts,* I (November 1962), 26–38.

316. Strickland, Geoffrey. "Un rimeur aux abois," *Delta* (Montreal), (Summer 1964), pp. 30–34.

317. Tate, Allen. "Robert Lowell," *Harvard Advocate,* CXLV (November 1961), 5.

318. Thorp, Willard. *American Writing in the Twentieth Century.* Cambridge, Mass., 1960.

319. Tulip, James. "Robert Lowell and James Dickey," *Poetry Australia,* No. 24 (October 1968), pp. 39–47.

320. Wagner, Linda W. "Ancient and Moderns, Some Similarities," *East-West Review,* III (1967–68), 273–280.

321. Wilder, Amos N. *Modern Poetry and the Christian Tradition.* New York, 1952.

322. Williams, William Carlos. *I Wanted to Write a Poem,* ed. Edith Heal. Boston, 1958.

323. ———. *The Selected Letters,* ed. John C. Thirlwall. New York, 1957.

324. Wilson, Edmund. "Books—An Interview," *NY,* XXXVIII (June 2, 1962), 118–128.

B. *Land of Unlikeness* (1944)

325. Aiken, Conrad. "Varieties of Poetic Statement," *New Republic,* CXI (1944), 528–530. Reprinted in *A Reviewer's ABC.* New York, 1958.

326. Blackmur, R. P. "Notes on Eleven Poets," *KR,* VII (1945), 339–352. Reprinted in *Form & Value in Modern Poetry.* New York, 1952.

327. Devlin, Denis. "Twenty-Four Poets," *Se R,* LIII (1945), 457–466.

328. Donaghy, William A. "Recent Poetry," *America,* LXXII (1944–45), 295–297.

329. Drew, Elizabeth. "Challenging Vitality," *NYHTWBR,* December 17, 1944, p. 18.

330. Dupee, F. W. "Some Young Poets and a New Genre," *Nation,* CLX (1945), 159–161.

331. Flint, F. Cudworth. "Comments on Recent Poetry," *VQR,* XXI (1945), 293–301.

332. Jarrell, Randall. "Poetry in War and Peace," *PR*, XII (1945), 120–126.

333. Mizener, Arthur. "Recent Poetry," *Accent*, V (1944–45), 114–120.

334. Nims, John Frederick. "Two Catholic Poets," *Poetry*, LXV (1944–45), 264–268.

335. Rosenberger, Coleman. "Lowell, Schwartz, Gustafson," *Voices*, No. 121 (Spring 1945), pp. 49–51.

336. Swallow, Alan. "A Review of Some Current Poetry," *NMQ*, XV (1945), 73–77.

337. Tate, Allen. "Introduction," in *Land of Unlikeness*. Cummington, Mass., 1944.

C. *Lord Weary's Castle* (1946)

338. "Books Received," *Christian Century*, LXIII (1946), 1473.

339. Adams, Walter W. "A Great Tradition and a Minor One," *Voices*, No. 128 (Winter 1947), pp. 49–51.

340. Akey, John. "Lowell's 'After Surprising Conversions,'" *Explicator*, IX (June 1951), 53.

341. Berryman, John. "Lowell, Thomas, &c" *PR*, XIV (1947), 73–85.

342. Blackmur, R. P. "Religious Poetry in America," in *Religion in American Life*, ed. James W. Smith. 4 vols. Princeton, 1961.

343. Bogan, Louise. "Experiment and Post-Experiment," *AS*, XVI (1947), 237–252.

344. ———. "Verse," *NY*, XXII (November 30, 1946), 129–132.

345. ———. *Selected Criticism*. New York, 1955.

346. Brégy, Katherine. "Review of *Lord Weary's Castle*," *CW*, CLXIV (1946–47), 374–375.

347. Cambon, Glauco. "Robert Lowell and the Sense of History," *Papers of the Michigan Academy of Science, Arts, and Letters*, XLVII (1962), 571–578. Reprinted in *The Inclusive Flame*. Bloomington, Ind., 1963.

348. Davidson, Eugene. "New Volumes of Poetry," *YR*, XXXVI (1946–47), 539–542.

349. Deutsch, Babette. "In These Home Waters," *NYHTWBR*, November 24, 1946, p. 16.

350. Doyno, Victor. "Poetic Language and Transformation," *Style*, I (1967), 151–157.

351. Duffy, John. "Review of *Lord Weary's Castle*," *Spirit* XIV (1947), 24–27.

352. Eberhart, Richard. "Four Poets," *Se R*, LV (1947), 324–336.

353. Engle, Paul. "Five Years of Pulitzer Poets," *English Journal*, XXXVIII (1949), 59–66.

354. Fein, Richard. "Mary and Bellona: The War Poetry of Robert Lowell," *Southern Review*, n.s. I (1965), 820–834.

355. ———. "Modern War Poetry," *Southwest Review*, XLVII (Autumn 1962), 279–288.

356. Fiedler, Leslie A. "The Believing Poet and the Infidel Reader," *New Leader*, XXX (May 10, 1947), 12.

357. Flint, F. Cudworth. "Diversity among the Poets," *VQR*, XXIII (1947), 287–296.

358. Flint, R. W. "Robert Lowell: The Tradition and the Technique of Revolt," *New Leader*, XXX (December 27, 1947), 11–12.

359. Fremantle, Anne. "Review of *Lord Weary's Castle*," *Commonweal*, XLV (1946–47), 283–284.

360. Friedmann, A. E. "The Equal Generation," *Poetry Broadside*, I (Winter 1957–58), 6+.

361. Giovannini, G. "Lowell's 'After Surprising Conversions,'" *Explicator*, IX (June 1951), 53.

362. Golffing, Francis C. "Two Volumes of Verse," *Western Review*, XI (1946–47), 111–112.

363. Grady, Rev. Thomas. "A First-Rate Poet Says Father Grady," *Books on Trial*, V (February 1947), 167.

364. Hall, Donald. "Lord Weary in 1947," *Harvard Advocate*, CXLV (November 1961), 20–21.

365. Harrigan, Anthony. "American Formalists," *SAQ*, IL (1950), 483–489.

366. Hazo, Samuel. "Poetry of Contact," *Commonweal*, LXXIII (1960), 116–118.

367. Ingalls, Jeremy. "Poets in Family Circles," *SRL*, XXIX (November 16, 1946), 16–17.

368. Jarrell, Randall. "From the Kingdom of Necessity," *Nation*, CLXIV (1947), 74–77. Reprinted in *Poetry and the Age*. New York, 1955.

369. ———. "On Lowell's 'Where the Rainbow Ends,'" in *Readings for a Liberal Education*, ed. L. G. Locke, W. M. Gibson, and G. W. Arms. 2nd Edition. New York, 1952. II, 279–280.

370. Jumper, W. C. "Whom Seek Ye?" *Hud R*, IX (1956), 117–125.

371. Laros, Fred. "Method and Metaphor," *Perspective*, I (Autumn 1947), 61–64.

372. McAleer, John J. "Lowell's 'Mary Winslow,'" *Explicator*, XVIII (February 1960), 29.

373. McCluhan, John, Jr. "Lowell's 'After Surprising Conversions,'" *Explicator*, IX (June 1951), 53.

374. McElroy, Walter. "Review of *Lord Weary's Castle*," *Chimera*, V (1946–47), 58–60.

375. Moss, Howard. "Ten Poets," *KR*, IX (1947), 290–298.

376. O'Connor, William Van. *Sense and Sensibility in Modern Poetry,* Chicago, 1948.

377. O'Malley, Frank. "The Blood of Robert Lowell," *Renascence,* II (1949), 3–9.

378. Palmer, Orvile, "Review of *Lord Weary's Castle,*" *Imagi,* III (Summer-Fall 1947), 15–16.

379. Pearce, Roy Harvey. "Lowell's 'After Surprising Conversions,'" *Explicator,* IX (June 1951), 53.

380. Rink, Sr. Mary Terese. "The Sea in Lowell's 'Quaker Graveyard in Nantucket,'" *Renascence,* XX (1967), 39–43.

381. Rodman, Selden. "Boston Jeremiads," *NYTBR,* November 3, 1946, p. 7+.

382. Schlauch, Margaret. *Modern English and American Poetry.* London, 1956.

383. Standerwick, De Sales. "Notes on Robert Lowell," *Renascence,* VIII (1955–56), 75–83.

384. Swallow, Alan. "A Review of Some Current Poetry," *NMQ,* XVI (1946), 491–496.

385. Viereck, Peter. "Poets versus Readers," *Atlantic,* CLXXX (July 1947), 109–112.

386. Warren, Austin. "A Double Discipline," *Poetry,* LXX (1947), 262–265.

387. Weatherhead, A. Kingsley. "Imagination and Fancy: Robert Lowell and Marianne Moore," *TSLL,* VI (Summer 1964), 188–199. Reprinted in *The Edge of the Image.* Seattle, 1967.

388. Wellsheim, Mother Anita von. "Imagery in Modern Marian Poetry," *Renascence,* X (1957–58), 176–186.

389. Wiebe, Dallas E. "Mr. Lowell and Mr. Edwards," *WSCL,* III (1962), 21–31.

D. *Poems, 1938–1949* (1950)

390. "Review of *Poems, 1938–1949,*" *Listener,* XLIV (1950), 605–606.

391. "Review of *Poems, 1938–1949,*" *World Review,* n.s. No. 19 (September 1950), p. 70.

392. "A Scrupulous Verse," *TLS,* August 11, 1950, p. 496.

393. B., C. "Poetry Review," *English,* VIII (Autumn 1950), 155–157.

394. Bayliss, John. "Americana," *The Poetry Review,* XLI (1950), 280–282.

395. Bethell, Samuel L. "Review of *Poems, 1938–1949,*" *Poetry: London,* V (February 1951), 24–26.

396. Bewley, Marius. "Aspects of Modern American Poetry," *Scrutiny,* XVII (1950), 334–352. Reprinted in *The Complex Fate.* London, 1952.

397. Breton, M. Le. "Review of *Poems, 1938–1949,*" *Etudes Anglais,* XV (1962), 319.

398. Enright, D. J. "Poetry and Passion," *Month*, n.s. V (1951), 247–249.

399. Jones, T. H. "The Poetry of Robert Lowell," *Month*, n.s. IX (1953), 133–142.

400. M., P. W. "Review of *Poems 1938–1949*," *The Dublin Magazine*, n.s. XXV (October-December 1950), 65–66.

401. Moore, Nicholas. "Boston Cod," *Nine*, II (Autumn 1950), 348–349.

402. Muir, Sir Edwin. "Review of *Poems, 1938–1949*," London *Observer*, January 14, 1951, p. 7

403. Murphy, Richard. "A New American Poet," *Spectator*, CLXXXV (1950), 480.

404. Painter, George D. "New Poetry," *New Statesman and Nation*, XL (1950), 439–440.

405. Piper, Henry Dan. "Modern American Classics," *Sat R*, XLV (February 17, 1962), 20.

406. Sitwell, Edith. "Preface," *The American Genius*. London, 1951.

E. *The Mills of the Kavanaughs* (1951)

407. Arrowsmith, William. "Five Poets," *Hud R*, IV (1951–52), 619–627.

408. Baro, Gene. "New Richness from an American Poet," *NYHTWBR*, April 22, 1951, p. 4.

409. Bogan, Louise. "Verse," *NY*, XXVII (June 9, 1951), 94–97.

410. Brégy, Katherine. "Review of *The Mills of the Kavanaughs*," *CW*, CLXXIV (1951–52), 76–77.

411. Clancy, J. P. "Review of *The Mills of the Kavanaughs*," *America*, LXXXVI (1951), 47–48.

412. Daiches, David. "Some Recent Poetry," *YR*, XLI (1951), 153–157.

413. Eberhart, Richard. "Five Poets," *KR*, XIV (1952), 168–176.

414. Engle, Paul. "Poems in Which You Hear Human Voices," *CTMB*, June 10, 1951, p. 4.

415. Feldman, Steve. "Review of *The Mills of the Kavanaughs*," *Gambit*, I (1952), 15–17.

416. Fitts, Dudley. "Review of *The Mills of the Kavanaughs*," *Furioso*, VI (1951), 76–78.

417. Flint, F. Cudworth. "Let the Snake Wait," *VQR*, XXVII (1951), 471–480.

418. Frankenberg, Lloyd. "The Year in Poetry," *Harper's*, CCIII (October 1951), 108–112.

419. Gray-Lewis, Stephen W. "Too Late for Eden—An Examination of Some Dualisms in 'The Mills of the Kavanaughs,'" *Cithara*, V (1966), 41–51.

420. Humphries, Rolfe. "Verse Chronicle," *Nation*, CLXXIII (1951), 76–77.

421. Jarrell, Randall. "A View of Three Poets," *PR*, XVIII (1951), 691–700. Reprinted in *Poetry and the Age*. New York, 1955.

422. Johnson, Manly. "Five Poets," *Hopkins Review,* V (Winter 1952), 108–113.

423. Mandelbaum, Allen. "A Catholic Vision of America," *Commentary,* XII (1951), 400–402.

424. Mazzaro, Jerome. "Robert Lowell and the Kavanaugh Collapse," *University of Windsor Review,* V (Autumn 1969), 1–24.

425. McDonald, Gerald D. "Review of *The Mills of the Kavanaughs,*" *LJ,* LXXVI (June 15, 1951), 1029.

426. Nerber, John. "A Posthumous Collection and Two Others," *Voices,* No. 147 (January-April 1952), pp. 51–52.

427. O'Malley, Frank. "Review of *The Mills of the Kavanaughs,*" *Renascence,* IV (1951), 105–106.

428. Poore, Charles. "Books of the Times," *NYT,* May 12, 1951, p. 19.

429. Therese, Sr. M. "Review of *The Mills of the Kavanaughs,*" *Books on Trial,* X (June 1951), 28.

430. Unterecker, John. "No Time for Poetry," *New Leader,* XXXIV (December 17, 1951), 24–25.

431. Vazakas, Byron. "Eleven Contemporary Poets," *NMQ,* XXII (1952), 213–230.

432. Viereck, Peter. "Technique and Inspiration," *Atlantic,* CLXXXIX (January 1952), 81–83.

433 Walsh, James P. "Of Tragedy and Nobility," *Spirit,* XVIII (1951), 122–123.

434. West, Ray B., Jr. "The Tiger in the Wood: Five Contemporary Poets," *Western Review,* XVI (1951–52), 76–84.

435. Williams, William Carlos. "In a Mood of Tragedy," *NYTBR,* April 22, 1951, p. 6. Reprinted in *Selected Essays.* New York, 1954.

F. *Poesie, 1942–1953* (1955)

436. Anzilotti, Rolando. "Introduzione," *Poesie* di Robert Lowell, a cura di Rolando Anzilotti. Edizioni Fussi. Firenze, 1955.

437. Hughes, Merritt Y. "Review of *Poesie, 1942–1953,*" *Comparative Literature,* VII (1955), 285.

438. Mottram, E. N. W. "Review of *Poesie, 1942–1953,*" *English Studies,* XXXVII (1956), 39–40.

439. Rizzardi, Alfredo. "Note Anglo-Americane," *Letterature Moderne,* VI (1956), 345–356.

440. ———. "La Poesia di Robert Lowell," *SA,* II (1956), 219–230.

G. *Life Studies* (1959)

441. "The Destructive Element," *TLS,* October 14, 1960, p. 660.

442. "Modern Poets Look Outside Themselves for a Theme," *Times*, August 6, 1959, p. 11.

443. "Review of *Life Studies*," *College English*, XXI (1960), 358.

444. "Uncollected," *TLS*, January 25, 1968, p. 85.

445. Aiken, Conrad. "An Interview," *Paris Review*, XLII (Winter/Spring 1968), 122.

446. Alvarez, A. "Something New in Verse," London *Observer*, April 12, 1959, p. 22. Reprinted in *Beyond All This Fiddle*. London, 1968.

447. Bateson, F. W. "The Language of Poetry," *TLS*, July 27, 1967, pp. 688–689.

448. Bennett, Joseph. "Two Americans, a Brahmin and the Bourgeoisie," *Hud R*, XII (1959), 431–439.

449. Berryman, John. "On Robert Lowell's 'Skunk Hour,'" in *The Contemporary Poet as Artist and Critic*, ed. Anthony Ostroff. Boston, 1964. It appeared originally in *New World Writing #21*.

450. Bly, Robert. "Books of Poetry Published in 1959," *Sixties*, No. 4 (Fall 1960), p. 57.

451. ———. "Prose vs. Poetry," *Choice*, No. 2 (1962), pp. 65–80.

452. ———. "A Wrong Turning in American Poetry," *Choice*, No. 3 (1962), pp. 33–47.

453. Bogan, Louise. "Verse," *NY*, XXXV (October 24, 1959), 194–196.

454. Burns, John. "Review of *Life Studies*," *Catholic Library World*, XXXI (June 1960), 519–521.

455. Calhoun, Richard J. "Lowell's 'My Last Afternoon with Uncle Devereux Winslow,'" *Explicator*, XXIII (January 1965), 38.

456. Coblentz, Stanton A. "Review of *Life Studies*," *Wings*, XIV (Winter 1960), 21–23.

457. Connolly, Francis X. "With Compassion," *Spirit*, XXVI (1960), 187–188.

458. Cook, Albert. *Prisms*. Bloomington, 1967.

459. Dale, Peter. "Auden, Lowell, Snodgrass, and Stafford," *Agenda*, VII:2 (Spring 1969), pp. 79–81.

460. Davie, Donald. "Review of *Life Studies*," *The Twentieth Century*, CLXVI (1959), 116–118.

461. ———. "Sincerity and Poetry," *Michigan Quarterly Review*, V (January 1966), 3–8.

462. Davison, Peter. "New Poetry," *Atlantic*, CCIV (July 1959), 73–76.

463. Dickinson, Peter. "More and More Poems," *Punch*, CCXXXXVI (1959), 659.

464. Dupee, F. W. "The Battle of Robert Lowell," *PR*, XXVI (1959), 473–475. Reprinted in *The King of the Cats*. New York, 1965.

465. Eberhart, Richard. "A Poet's People," *NYTBR*, May 3, 1959, p. 4+.

466. Ehrenpreis, Irvin. "Unamerican Editions," *TLS*, January 18, 1968, p. 61.

467. Engle, Paul. "A Great Year for Poetry and Light," *CTMB*, November 29, 1959, p. 24.

468. Farmer, A. J. "Review of *Life Studies*," *Etudes Anglais*, XIV (1961), 263–264.

469. Fiedler, Leslie A. "A Kind of Solution: The Situation of Poetry Now," *KR*, XXVI (1964), 54–79. Reprinted in *Waiting for the End*. New York, 1964.

470. Fitts, Dudley. "New Verse for Midsummer Night Dreamers," *Sat R*, XLII (July 25, 1959), 14–16.

471. Fraser, G. S. "I, They, We," *New Statesman*, LVII (1959), 614–615.

472. Fuller, Roy. "Review of *Life Studies*," *London Magazine*, VI (August 1959), 68–73.

473. Gregory, Horace. "A Life Study As an Illumination of Life Conflicts," *Commonweal*, LXX (1959), 356–357.

474. Gunn, Thom. "Excellence and Variety," *YR*, IL (1960), 295–305.

475. Hoffman, Daniel G. "Arrivals and Rebirths," *Se R*, LXVIII (1960), 118–137.

476. Hollander, John. "Robert Lowell's New Book," *Poetry*, XCV (1959), 41–46.

477. Johnson, Geoffrey. "The Whole and the Sick," *The Poetry Review*, L (1959), 173–174.

478. Jones, LeRoi. "Putdown of the Whore of Babylon," *Yugen*, No. 7 (1961), pp. 4–5.

479. Kazin, Alfred. "In Praise of Robert Lowell," *Reporter*, XX (June 25, 1959), 41–42. Reprinted in *Contemporaries*. New York, 1962.

480. Kenny, Herbert A. "Review of *Life Studies*," *The Critic*, XVIII (August-September 1959), 49.

481. Kermode, Frank. "Talent and More," *Spectator*, CCII (1959), 628.

482. Kunitz, Stanley. "American Poetry's Silver Age," *Harper's*, CCXIX (October 1959), 173–179.

483. ———. "The New Books," *Harper's*, CCXXI (September 1960), 96–104.

484. Larkin, Philip. "Collected Poems," Manchester *Guardian Weekly*, May 21, 1959, p. 10.

485. Linenthal, Mark. "The New Poetry," *Arts in Society*, III (1965), 214–221.

486. Lowell, Robert. "On 'Skunk Hour,'" in *The Contemporary Poet as Artist and Critic*, ed. Anthony Ostroff. Boston, 1964. It appeared originally in *New World Writing #21*.

487. Lucie-Smith, Edward and Peter Porter. "Talent and More," *Spectator*, CCII (1959), 702.

488. MacCraig, Norman. "Book Review: Poetry," *Saltire Review*, VI (Autumn 1959), 70–72.

489. Mathias, Roland. "Review of *Life Studies*," *Anglo-Welsh Review*, X (1959), 114–117.

490 Montague, John "American Pegasus," *Studies*, XLVIII (Summer 1959), 183–191.

491. Montieth, Charles. "Uncollected," *TLS*, February 1, 1968, p. 109.

492. Nims, John Frederick. "On Robert Lowell's 'Skunk Hour,'" in *The Contemporary Poet as Artist and Critic*, ed. Anthony Ostroff. Boston, 1964. It appeared originally in *New World Writing #21*.

493. Nowlan, Alden A. "Ten Books of Poetry," *Tamarack Review*, No. 16 (Summer 1960), pp. 71–79.

494. Offen, Ronald. "Review of *Life Studies*," *Odyssey*, II (December 1959), 35–38.

495. Phelps, Robert. "A Book of Revelations," *National Review*, VII (August 29, 1959), 307–308.

496. Poore, Charles. "Books and the Times," *NYT*, April 30, 1959, p. 29.

497. Reeves, James. "Three Poets," *Time and Tide*, XL (1959), 601–602.

498. Rosenthal, M. L. "Poetry as Confession," *Nation*, CXC (1959), 154–155.

499. ———. "Poetic Theory of Some Contemporary Poets," *Salmagundi*, I,iv (1966–67), 69–77.

500. Simpson, Louis. "Review of *Life Studies*," *AS*, XXVIII (1959), 535.

501. Smith, William Jay. "Some New Poetry: From Last August to This," *Harper's*, CCXXVIII (August 1964), 99–103.

502. Sorrentino, Gilbert. "Review of *Life Studies*," *Yugen*, No. 7 (1961), pp. 5–7.

503. Spender, Stephen. "Robert Lowell's Family Album," *New Republic*, CXL (June 8, 1959), 17.

504. Standerwick, De Sales. "Pieces too Personal," *Renascence*, XIII (1960), 53–56.

505. Steiner, George. "A Literature Enters the Sixties," *Time and Tide*, XL (1959), 927–928.

506. Stern, Richard G. "A Poet's Self-Portrait," *Commentary*, XXVIII (1959), 272–274.

507. Thompson, John. "Two Poets," *KR*, XXI (1959), 482–490.

508. Walsh, Chad. "Robert Lowell Looking Back," *NYHTWBR*, June 7, 1959, p. 6.

509. Wilbur, Richard. "On Robert Lowell's 'Skunk Hour,'" in *The Contemporary Poet as Artist and Critic*, ed. Anthony Ostroff. Boston, 1964. It appeared originally in *New World Writing #21*.

510. Willy, Margaret. "Poetry Review," *English* XII (Summer 1959), 193–196.

H. *Phaedra* (1961)

511. "Contemporary Poets Who Deserve a Reading," *Times*, March 14, 1963, p. 17.

512. "French With/Without Tears," *Time*, LXXVII (April 28, 1961), 100–103.

513. "Racine Rendered," *TLS*, July 26, 1963, p. 560.

514. "Review of *Phaedra*," BPJ, XII (Fall 1961), p. 39.

515. "Review of *Phaedra*," VQR, XXXVIII (Spring 1962), lvi.

516. Adams, Phoebe. "Review of *Phaedra*," *Atlantic*, CCVIII (August 1961), 99.

517. Bayley, John. "Book Review," *Agenda*, III (August-September 1963), 9–13.

518. Bentley, Eric. "Comment," *KR*, XXIV (1962), 143–144.

519. Bermel, Albert. "Comment," *KR*, XXIV (1962), 144–145.

520. Bishop, Morris. "Questions of Text and Style," *Poetry*, C (1962), 41–43.

521. Bogan, Louise. "Verse," *NY*, XXXVII (October 7, 1961), 204–208.

522. Clurman, Harold. "Ignorance Is a Betrayal of Pleasure," *NYTBR*, May 28, 1961, p. 5.

523. Cruttwell, Patrick. "Six Phaedras in Search of One Phèdre," *Delos*, I:2 (1968), 198–211.

524. Fein, Richard. "The Trying-Out of Robert Lowell," *Se R*, LXXII (1964), 131–139.

525. Fitts, Dudley. "Translation and Re-creation," *AS*, XXXI (1961–62), 144+.

526. Kenner, Hugh. "Memory Refreshed: New Translations of Racine," *National Review*, XI (1961), 385–386.

527. Kerr, Walter. "Theatre: Robert Lowell's 'Phaedra' in Philadelphia," *NYT*, May 22, 1967, p. 50.

528. Kunitz, Stanley. "Some Poets of the Year and Their Language of Transformation," *Harper's*, CCXXIII (August 1961), 86–91.

529. Lucie-Smith, Edward. "Review of *Phaedra*," *Listener*, LXIX (1963), 722.

530. Mercier, Vivian. "Great Racine," *Commonweal*, LXXIV (1961), 184–185.

531. Poisson, Philippe L. "A Handful of Translations," *Drama Survey*, II (1962–63), 217–219.

532. Sergeant, Howard. "Poetry Review," *English*, XIV (1963), 250–251.

533. Seymour, William Kean. "Drama in Poetry," *The Poetry Review*, LIV (1963), 194–198.

534. Solomon, Samuel. "Letter," *TDR*, XI (Summer 1967), 159–161. (Summary of his article in *London Magazine* which is accompanied by a reply by Robert Lowell on pages 161 and 163.)

535. ———. "Racine and Lowell," *London Magazine*, VI (October 1966), 29–42.

536. Spurling, Hilary. "John Bull and Naked Passion," *Spectator,* CCXVI (1966), 41–42.

537. Steiner, George. "Reply," *KR,* XXIV (1962), 145.

538. ———. "Two Translations," *KR,* XXIII (1961), 714–721.

539. Williams, Raymond. "Classic European Plays," *MR,* IV (1962), 219–222.

I. *Imitations* (1961), including reviews of *The Voyage and Other Versions of Poems by Baudelaire* (1968)

540. "The Limits of Imitation," *Time, LXXVIII* (November 3, 1961), 86.

541. "Poet of an Ousted Aristocracy," *TLS,* June 15, 1962, p. 447.

542. "Review of *Imitations,*" *BPJ,* XII (Summer 1962), 38.

543. "Review of *Imitations,*" *The Booklist,* LIX (1961), 187.

544. "Review of *Imitations,*" *NY,* XXXVII (January 20, 1962), 120.

545. Adams, Phoebe. "Review of *Imitations,*" *Atlantic,* CCVIII (December 1961), 112, 114.

546. Baro, Gene. "Poet as Partner," *NYHTWBR,* February 4, 1962, p. 11.

547. Belitt, Ben. "*Imitations:* Translation as Personal Mode," *Salmagundi,* I, iv (1966–67), 44–56.

548. Cambon, Glauco. "Review of *Imitations,*" *East-West Review,* I (Spring 1964), 86–91.

549. Carne-Ross, D. S. "The Two Voices of Translation," in *Robert Lowell: A Collection of Critical Essays,* ed. Thomas Parkinson. Englewood Cliffs, N. J., 1968.

550. Carruth, Hayden. "Toward, Not Away From . . ." *Poetry,* C (1962), 43–47.

551. Chadwick, C. "Meaning and Tone," *Essays in Criticism,* XIII (1963), 432–435.

552. Cluysenaar, Anne. "Review of *Imitations,*" *The Dubliner,* I (July-August 1962), 65–66.

553. Cookson, William. "Review of *Imitations,*" *Agenda,* II (September-October 1962), 21–24.

554. Dickinson, Peter. "Some Are More Imitative Than Others," *Punch,* CCXLII (1962), 917.

555. Ehrenpreis, Irvin. "Four Poets and Others," *Minn R,* II (1962), 397–410.

556. Enright, D. J. "Common Market," *New Statesman,* LXIII (1962), 901–902.

557. Fitts, Dudley. "It's Fidelity to the Spirit That Counts," *NYTBR,* November 12, 1961, p. 5+.

558. Fulton, Robin. "Lowell and Ungaretti," *Agenda,* VI:3–4 (1968), pp. 118–123.

559. Gifford, Henry. "Review of *Imitations*," *Critical Quarterly*, V (Spring 1963), 94–95.

560. Gunn, Thom. "Imitations and Originals," *YR*, LI (1962), 480–489.

561. Hecht, Roger. "Rilke in Translation," *Se R*, LXXI (1963), 513–522.

562. Hill, Geoffrey. "Robert Lowell: 'Contrasts and Repetitions,'" *Essays in Criticism*, XIII (1963), 188.

563. Holmes, Richard. "Campbell, Lowell, Herbert, Sexton, Barker," *Times*, March 2, 1968, p. 21.

564. Horgan, Paul. "The Revolving Bookstand," *AS*, XXXIV (1965), 482, 484.

565. Hughes, Daniel. "Arms and the Poet: Eight Books of Verse," *MR*, IV (1963), 606–616.

566. Hughes, Robert. "You Know It Well," *Spectator*, CCXX (1968), 334–335.

567. Hughes, Ted. "Review of *Imitations*," *Listener*, LXVIII (1962), 185.

568. Jackson, Katherine Gauss. "Review of *Imitations*," *Harper's*, CCXXIII (December 1961), 107.

569. Jerome, Judson. "Review of *Imitations*," *Antioch Review*, XXIII (1963), 117.

570. Kenny, Herbert A. "Review of *Imitations*," *The Critic*, XX (December 1961-January 1962), 89–90.

571 Levi, Peter. "Americanizations," *Spectator*, CCVIII (1962), 758.

572. Lowell, Robert. "The State of Translation," *Delos*, I:2 (1968), 46–47.

573. Mazzaro, Jerome. "The Poem in Large Type," *Nation*, CCVII (1968), 698–699.

574. McAleer, John J. "Robert Lowell's *Imitations*," *America*, CVI (1962), 452.

575. Morse, Samuel French. "Poetry 1961," *WSCL*, III (Winter 1962), 49–64.

576. O'Connor, William Van. "The Recent Contours of the Muse," *Sat R*, XLIV (January 6, 1962), 68–71, 84.

577. Pugh, Griffith T. "Review of *Imitations*," *English Journal*, LI (1962), 375–376.

578. Rizzardi, Alfredo. "Introduzione," *Poesie di Montale*, tr. Robert Lowell. Bologna, 1960. Translated by Frances Frenaye and printed as "Notes Between Two Poets," *Odyssey Review*, II (March 1962), 50–65.

579. ———. "Leopardi tradotto da Robert Lowell," *SA*, VII (1961), 443–463.

580. Rosenthal, M. L. "Found in Translation," *Reporter*, XXV (December 21, 1961), 36–38.

581. Rovit, Earl. "Review of *Imitations*," *Books Abroad*, XXXVI (1962), 435–436.

582. Schevill, James. "Contemporary Poetry—Lowell, Wilbur, Gunn and Others," *SFSCTW*, December 3, 1961, pp. 31–32.

583. Sergeant, Howard. "Poetry Review," *English*, XIV (Autumn 1962), 118–119.

584. Simpson, Louis. "Matters of Tact," *Hud R*, XIV (1961–62), 614–617.

585. Smith, Hal. "Review of *Imitations*," *Epoch*, XI (Winter 1962), 260–263.

586. Smith, Ray. "Review of *Imitations*," *LJ*, LXXXVI (1961), 4191.

587. Symons, Julian. "MacSpaunday," *New Statesman*, LXXV (1968), 276.

588. Tomlinson, Charles. "Reviews," *NMQ*, XXXIII (1963–64), 457–460.

589. Whittemore, Reed. "Packing Up for Devil's Island," *KR*, XXIV (1962), 372–377.

590. Williams, William Carlos. "Robert Lowell's Verse Translation into the American Idiom," *Harvard Advocate*, CXLV (December 1961), 12. Reprinted in *Harvard Advocate Centennial Anthology*, ed. Jonathan D. Culler. Cambridge, Mass., 1966.

J. *For the Union Dead* (1964)

591. "Eastern Personal Time," *TLS*, July 1, 1965, p. 558.

592. "Farrar, Straus Becomes Farrar, Straus and Giroux," *PW*, CLXXXVI (September 28, 1964), 89.

593. "In Bounds," *Newsweek*, LXIV (October 12, 1964), 120–122.

594. "Poems for the Good Heart," *Times*, November 4, 1965, p. 15.

595. "Poet of the Particular," *Time*, LXXXIV (October 16, 1964), 121–127.

596. "Review of *For the Union Dead*," *BPJ*, XV (Winter 1964–65), 39.

597. "Review of *For the Union Dead*," *The Booklist*, LXI (1964), 291–292.

598. "Review of *For the Union Dead*," *Choice*, I (1965), 556.

599. "Review of *For the Union Dead*," *Christian Century*, LXXXI (1964), 1244.

600. "Review of *For the Union Dead*," *VQR*, XLI (Winter 1965), xiv.

601. Alvarez, A. "Review of *For the Union Dead*," London *Observer*, March 14, 1965, p. 26.

602. Bly, Robert. "The Dead World and the Live World," *Sixties*, No. 8 (1966), pp. 2–7.

603. ———. "Robert Lowell's 'For the Union Dead,'" *Sixties*, No. 8 (1966), pp. 93–96.

604. Bogan, Louise. "Verse," *NY*, XLI (April 10, 1965), 193–196.

605. Booth, Philip. "Lowell's Elegy for a Puritan Past," *CSM*, October 15, 1964, p. 11.

606. Carruth, Hayden. "Freedom and Style," *Poetry*, CVI (1965), 358–360.

607. Curran, Mary Doyle. "Poems Public and Private," *MR*, VI (1965), 411–415.

608. Dale, Peter. "Review of *For the Union Dead*," *Agenda*, IV (Summer 1966), 76–78.

609. Davie, Donald. "Low-toned Lowell," Manchester *Guardian Weekly,* March 4, 1965, p. 11.

610. Davis, Douglas M. "In the New Poetry, Lowell's Stature Grows," *National Observer,* January 4, 1965, p. 17.

611. Davison, Peter. "Madness in the New Poetry," *Atlantic,* CCXV (January 1965), 90–93.

612. Dickey, William. "Poetic Language," *Hud R,* XVII (1964–65), 587–596.

613. Doherty, Paul C. "The Poet as Historian: 'For the Union Dead' by Robert Lowell," *Concerning Poetry,* I (Fall 1968), 37–41.

614. Fraser, G. S. "Amid the Horror, A Song of Praise," *NYTBR,* October 4, 1964, p. 1+.

615. Furbank, P. N. "New Poetry," *Listener,* LXXIII (1965), 379.

616. G., D. "Review of *For the Union Dead,*" *Poet Lore,* LX (1965), 188.

617. Gallagher, M. "Review of *For the Union Dead,*" *Studies,* LIV (Summer-Fall 1965), 291.

618. Gullans, Charles. "Edgar Bowers' 'The Astronomers,' and Other New Verse," *Southern Review,* n.s. II (1966), 189–209.

619. Hamilton, Ian. "Robert Lowell," *London Magazine,* V (May 1965), 55–59.

620. Hartman, Geoffrey. "The Eye of the Storm," *PR,* XXXII (1965), 277–280.

630. Hollo, Anselm. "Heard, here," *Ambit,* No. 24 (1965), pp. 41–44.

631. Horgan, Paul. "Review of *For the Union Dead,*" *CSM,* October 15, 1964, p. 11.

632. ———. "Review of *For the Union Dead,*" *Commonweal,* LXXXI (1964), 359.

633. Howard, Richard. "Voice of a Survivor," *Nation,* CIC (1964), 278–280.

634. Jacobsen, Josephine. "Poet of the Particular," *Commonweal,* LXXXI (1964), 349–352.

635. Martz, Louis L. "Recent Poetry: The Elegiac Mode," *YR,* LIV (1965), 285–298.

636. McCall, Dan. "Robert Lowell's 'Hawthorne,'" *NEQ,* XXXIX (1966), 237–239.

637. McCullough, David. "Review of *For the Union Dead,*" *Book-of-the-Month Club News,* December 1964, pp. 10–11.

638. Morse, Samuel French. "Poetry 1964," *WSCL,* VI (1965), 354–367.

639. Offen, Ronald. "Lowell on the Brink," *Literary Times,* November 1964, p. 4.

640. Parkinson, Thomas. "For the Union Dead," *Salmagundi,* I,iv (1966–67), 87–95.

641. Poirier, Richard. "Our Truest Historian," *NYHTWBR,* October 11, 1964, p. 1.

642. Press, John. "Two Poets," *Punch*, CCXLVIII (1965), 486.

643. Pryce-Jones, A. "Review of *For the Union Dead*," New York *Herald Tribune*, October 24, 1964, p. 13.

644. Ramsey, Paul. "In Exasperation and Gratitude," *Se R*, LXXIV (1966), 930–945.

645. Ricks, Christopher. "The Three Lives of Robert Lowell," *New Statesman*, LXIX (1965), 496–497.

646. Rosenthal, M. L. "Poets of the Dangerous Way," *Spectator*, CCXIV (1965), 367.

647. Sealy, Douglas H. "Review of *For the Union Dead*," *The Dublin Magazine*, IV (Autumn/Winter 1965), 114–116.

648. Sergeant, Howard. "Poetry Review," *English*, XVI (1966), 30–32.

649. Smith, John. "Editor's Choice," *The Poetry Review*, LVI (1965), 44.

650. Smith, William Jay. "New Books of Poems," *Harper's*, CCXXXI (August 1955), 106–110.

651. Spector, Robert D. "A Way to Say What a Man Can See," *Sat R*, XLVIII (February 13, 1965), 46–48.

652. Stafford, William. "Poems That Deal a Jolt," *CTBT*, November 15, 1964, p. 11.

653. Stepanchev, Stephen. "American Poets of the '60s," *New Leader*, IL (December 5, 1966), 23–26.

654. Taylor, William E. "The New Poetics or Who Shot Tennyson's Eagle?" *Trace*, No. 57 (Summer 1965), pp. 109–114.

655. Thornhill, Arthur H., Jr., and Victor Neybright. "One That Got Away," *NYTBR*, December 6, 1964, pp. 60, 62.

656. Tripp, John. "Letter," *Spectator*, CCXV (1965), 471.

657. Wain, John. "The New Robert Lowell," *New Republic*, CLI (October 17, 1964), 21–23.

658. Walden, E. H. "Review of *For the Union Dead*," *LJ*, LXXXIX (1964), 3319.

659. Weales, Gerald. "Robert Lowell's Memento Mori," *Reporter*, XXXII (January 28, 1965), 56–57.

660. Woodson, Thomas. "Robert Lowell's 'Hawthorne': Yvor Winters and the American Literary Tradition," *AQ*, XIX (1967), 575–582.

K. *The Old Glory* (1964), (1965), and (1969)

661. "Endecott & the Red Cross," *Time*, XCI (May 10, 1968), 74.

662. "Episcopalians," *Time*, LXXXIV (November 27, 1964), 68.

663. "Pick of the Paperbacks," *Sat R*, IL (November 26, 1966), 40–41.

664. "A Play by Robert Lowell," *Times*, December 31, 1964, p. 4.

665. "Review of *The Old Glory*," *The Booklist*, LXII (1966), 513.

666. "Review of *The Old Glory*," *Choice*, III (1966), 224.

667. "Review of *The Old Glory*," *Quarterly Review*, CCCV (1967), 99.

668. "Triumph Off Broadway," *Newsweek*, LXIV (November 16, 1964), 92.

669. Bannon, Barbara A. "Forecast of Paperbacks," *PW*, CLXXXIX (April 4, 1966), 63–68.

670. Barnes, Clive. "Theatre: 'Endecott and the Red Cross,'" *NYT*, May 7, 1968, p. 50.

671. Benedikt, Michael. "Benito Cereno," *Theatre Experiment*. New York, 1967.

672. Bermel, Albert. "Middleton and Lowell," *New Leader*, XLVII (November 23, 1964), 26–27.

673. Bernard, Sidney. "Manhattan Descants," *Literary Times*, April 1965, p. 3.

674. Brustein, Robert. "Introduction," *The Old Glory*. New York, 1965.

675. ——. "We Are Two Cultural Nations," *New Republic*, CLI (November 21, 1964), 25–30. Reprinted in *Seasons of Discontent*. New York, 1965.

676. Clurman, Harold. "The Old Glory," *Nation*, CIC (1964), 390–391. Reprinted in *The Naked Image*. New York, 1966.

677. Dale, Peter. "Review of *The Old Glory*," *Agenda*, VI (Spring 1968), 95.

678. Elliott, George P. "Writing for the Theater," *NYHTBW*, July 3, 1966, p. 6.

679. Fields, Kenneth. "J.V. Cunningham and Others," *Southern Review*, n.s. V (1969), 573–575.

680. Finn, James. "The Old Glory," *CW*, CC (1965), 323–324.

681. Gardner, Hilary. "A Poet's Plays," *Drama*, n.s. No. 83 (Winter 1966), p. 51.

682. Gates, Gary Paul. "The Beginnings of Salvation," *Holiday*, XL (December 1966), 178–184.

683. Gelpi, Albert J. "He Holds America to Its Ideals," *CSM*, December 16, 1965, p. 11.

684. Gould, Jack. "TV: Robert Lowell of Page and Stage," *NYT*, October 12, 1965, p. 95.

685. Hansen, Harry. "Marketable Excellence," *CTBT*, November 29, 1964, p. 2.

686. Hewes, Henry. "The Teenageling," *Sat R*, XLVII (November 21, 1964), 35.

687. ——. "The Unroyal Hunt," *Sat R*, LI (May 25, 1968), 40.

688. Hochman, Baruch. "Lowell's *The Old Glory*," *TDR*, XI (Summer 1967), 127–138.

689. Howard, Richard. "A Movement Outward," *New Leader*, XLVIII (December 6, 1965), 26–28.

690. Ilson, Robert. *"Benito Cereno* from Melville to Lowell," *Salmagundi*, I, iv (1966–67), 78–86.

691. Jarrell, Randall. "A Masterpiece," *NYT*, November 29, 1964, II, p. 3.

692. Jones, D. A. N. "Revolting Slaves," *New Statesman*, LXXIII (1967), 382–383.

693. Kerr, Walter. "While a Novel Can Roam, A Play Must Stay Home," *NYT*, October 23, 1966, II, p. 1.

694. Kroll, Jack. "Militant Movement," *Newsweek*, LXXI (May 13, 1968), 109–110.

695. Laing, Alexander. "The Knack of Doing Double Duty," *Nation*, CCII (1966), 103–105.

696. Lewis, Theophilus. "Reviewer's Notebook," *America*, CXIX (August 31, 1968), 140–141.

697. Long, Robert E. "Praise for Robert Lowell," *NYT*, November 29, 1964, II, p. 3.

698. Luten, C. J. "Robert Lowell's *Benito Cereno*," *American Record Guide*, XXXI (1965), 806–807.

699. McDonnell, T. "The Old Glory," *The Critic*, XXIV (April-May 1966), 72.

700. Miller, Jonathan. "Delicious Shock," *NYT*, December 6, 1964, II, p. 7+.

701. ———. "Director's Note," *The Old Glory*. New York, 1965.

702. Moon, Samuel. "Master as Servant," *Poetry*, CVIII (1966), 189–190.

703. Morris, Ivan. "Theatre," *Vogue*, CXLV (January 1, 1965), 68.

704. Muggeridge, Malcolm. "Alice, Where Art Thou?" *New Statesman*, LXXI (1966), 933.

705. N., J. R. "The Old Glory," *Literary Times*, February-March 1966, p. 14.

706. Oliver, Edith. "Mr. Lowell and Mr. Haigh," *NY*, XLIV (May 11, 1968), 85–86+.

707. ———. "Off Broadway," *NY*, XL (November 14, 1964), 143–144.

708. Pasolli, Robert. "Review of 'Endecott and the Red Cross,'" *Nation*, CCVI (1968), 710.

709. Porter, Peter. "Lowell's Kinsmen," *Listener*, LXXVI (1966), 359.

710. Press, John. "Old Hands and Appentice Pieces," *Punch*, CCLI (1966), 867.

711. Rosenthal, M.L. "The New Lowell," *Spectator*, CCXV (1965), 699, 702.

712. ———. "Blood and Plunder," *Spectator*, CCXVII (1966), 418.

713. Schevill, James. "The Modern Poets' Terrible Honesty of Imagination," *SFSCTW*, January 31, 1965, pp. 42–43.

714. Schickel, Richard. "New York's Best Theater Group?" *Harper's*, CCXXXIII (November 1966), 92–100.

715. Simon, John. "Strange Devices on the Banner," *NYHTBW*, February 20, 1966, pp. 4, 20.

716. Snodgrass, W. D. "In Praise of Robert Lowell," *NYRB*, III (December 3, 1964), 8, 10.

717. Spector, Robert D. "Other Voices, Other Rhythms," *Sat R*, IL (February 19, 1966), 42–44.

718. Stafford, William. "An Apocalyptic View of History," *CTBT*, November 21, 1965, p. 5.

719. Taubman, Howard. "In Quest of Basic Ideal," *NYT*, November 15, 1964, II, p. 1.

720. ———. "Theatre: Lowell, Poet as Playwright," *NYT*, November 2, 1964, p. 62.

721. Tolan, Michael. "In the Theatre," *New University Thought*, V (Autumn 1967), 30–36.

722. Tomlinson, Charles. "Review of *The Old Glory*," *Critical Quarterly*, IX (Spring 1967), 90–91.

723. Toynbee, Philip. "Poet in the Theatre," London *Observer*, September 11, 1966, p. 26.

724. Wardle, Irving. "Melville's Story Turned to Prose Opera," *Times*, March 9, 1967, p. 10.

725. Weales, Gerald. "Robert Lowell as Dramatist," *Shenandoah*, XX (Autumn 1968), 3–28. Reprinted in *The Jumping-Off Place*. New York, 1969.

726. Worth, Katherine J. "The Poet in the American Theatre," in *American Theatre*, ed. John Russell Brown and Bernard Harris. Stratford-upon-Avon Studies No. 10. London, 1967.

727. Yankowitz, Susan. "Lowell's *Benito Cereno:* An Investigation of American Innocence," *Yale/Theatre*, II (1968), 81–90.

L. *Near the Ocean* (1967)

728. "Open Sores," *TLS*, August 3, 1967, p. 705.

729. "Review of *Near the Ocean*," *The Booklist*, LXIII (1967), 831.

730. "Review of *Near the Ocean*," *Choice*, IV (1967), 984.

731. "Review of *Near the Ocean*," *Christian Century*, LXXXIV (1967), 143.

732. "Review of *Near the Ocean*," *NY*, XLIII (May 20, 1967), 179–180.

733. "Review of *Near the Ocean*," *VQR*, XLIII (Summer 1967), cx.

734. "Twenty For the Top Shelf," Manchester *Guardian Weekly*, December 21, 1967, p. 11.

735. Anthony, Mother Mary. "Review of *Near the Ocean*," *Best Sellers*, XXVI (1966–67), 414–415.

736. Bach, Bert C. "Review of *Near the Ocean*," *Commonweal*, LXXXVI (1967), 238–241.

737. Cushman, Jerome. "Review of *Near the Ocean*," *LJ*, XCII (1967), 125. Reprinted in *The Library Journal Book Review 1967*. New York, 1969.

738. Dale, Peter. "Review of *Near the Ocean*," *Agenda*, VI (Spring 1968), 93–95.

739. Davie, Donald. "A Judgment on America," Manchester *Guardian Weekly*, July 20, 1967, p. 11.

740. Davis, Douglas M. "In the Flow of Poetry, the Ladies Flourish," *National Observer*, February 6, 1967, p. 31.

741. Eulert, Donald. "Robert Lowell and W. C. Williams: Sterility in Central Park," *ELN*, V (1967), 129–135.

742. Feldman, Burton. "Review of *Near the Ocean*," *Denver Quarterly*, I (Winter 1967), 122–124.

743. Fraser, G.S. "Unmonotonous Sublime," *NYTBR*, January 15, 1967, p. 5+.

744. Fuller, John. "Facing the Household Fire," *Review*, No. 18 (April 1968), pp. 62–64.

745. Garrigue, Jean. "A Study of Continuity and Change," *New Leader*, L (March 27, 1967), 23–25.

746. Gilman, Richard. "Securing the Beachead," *NYHTBW*, January 29, 1967, p. 4+.

747. Hoffman, Daniel G. "Robert Lowell's *Near the Ocean:* The Greatness and Horror of Empire," *The Hollins Critic*, IV (February 1967), 1–16.

748. Holloway, John. "Robert Lowell and the Public Dimension," *Encounter*, XXX (April 1968), 73–79.

749. Howard, Richard. "Fuel on the Fire," *Poetry*, CX (1967), 413–415.

750. Kalstone, David. "Two Poets," *PR*, XXXIV (1967), 619–625.

751. Kitching, Jessie. "Forecasts," *PW*, CXC (September 12, 1966), 85–89. The entry on Lowell was revised and reprinted November 28, 1966, pp. 54–58.

752. Link, Hilda. "A Tempered Triumph," *Prairie Schooner*, XLI (1967–68), 439–442.

753. London, Michael. "Wading for Godot," in Robert Lowell: A Portrait of the Artist in His Time, ed. Michael London and Robert Boyers. New York, 1970.

754. Maddocks, Melvin. "A Poet's Dialogue with Himself," *CSM*, January 26, 1967, p. 5.

755. Mahon, Derek. "On Lowell," *Phoenix* (Belfast), No. 2 (Summer 1967), pp. 50–54.

756. Malkoff, Karl. "Review of *Near the Ocean*," NMQ, XXXVII (Spring 1967), 93–96.

757. Martin, Graham. "Wastelanders," *Listener*, LXXVIII (1967), 311–312.

758. Martz. Louis L. "Recent Poetry: Fruits of a Renaissance," *YR*, LVI (1967), 593–603.

759. May, Derwent. "Mid-Sixties Muse," *Times*, July 13, 1967, p. 7.

760. Mazzaro, Jerome. "Lowell after *For the Union Dead*," *Salmagundi*, I,iv (1966–67), 57–68.

761. Parker, Derek. "Lowell, Mead, Macdiarmid," *The Poetry Review*, LVIII (1967), 322–323.

762. Philbrick, Charles. "Debuts and Encores," *Sat R*, L (June 3, 1967), 32–34.

763. Press, John. "New Poetry," *Punch*, CCLIII (1967), 291.

764. Ricks, Christopher. "Authority in Poems," *Southern Review*, n.s. V (1969), 203–208.

765. Rosenthal, M. L. "West of the Park," *Spectator*, CCXIX (1967), 245.

766. Schott, Webster. "The Poet as Folk Hero, Wounded But Game," *Life*, LXII (February 17, 1967), 17.

767. Sheehan, Donald. "Varieties of Technique: Seven Recent Books of American Poetry," *WSCL*, X (Spring 1969), 284–301.

768. Spacks, Patricia M. "From Satire to Description," *YR*, LVIII (1969), 232–248.

769. Stafford, William. "Critical Involvement of the Poet," *CTMB*, February 5, 1967, p. 5.

770. Sullivan, J. P. "Propertius and Juvenal," *Arion*, VII (Autumn 1968), 477–486.

771. Symons, Julian. "Cooked and Raw," *New Statesman*, LXXIV (1967), 87.

772. Taylor, F. H. Griffin. "A Point in Time, a Place in Space," *Se R*, LXXVII (1969), 300–318.

773. Toynbee, Philip. "The Poetic Adventure," London *Observer*, July 2, 1967, p. 20.

774. Vendler, Helen. "Recent American Poetry," *MR*, VIII (1967), 545–560.

775. Zweig, Paul. "A Murderous Solvent," *Nation*, CCIV (1967), 536–538.

M. *Prometheus Bound* (1967)

776. "Yale Will Offer Lowell's Drama," *NYT*, April 4, 1967, p. 39.

777. Bermel, Albert. "Shaky Footholds," *New Leader*, L (June 19, 1967), 27–29.

778. Fergusson, Francis. "Prometheus at Yale," *NYRB*, IX (August 3, 1967), 30–32.

779. Gilman, Richard. "Still Bound," *Newsweek*, LXIX (May 22, 1967), 109.

780. Hewes, Henry. "Idol Conversation," *Sat R*, L (May 27, 1967), 49.

781. Kerr, Walter. "Theatre: 'Prometheus Bound' Performed at Yale," *NYT*, May 11, 1967, p. 52.

782. Lester, Elenore. "Prometheus: Hero for Our Time," *NYT*, May 21, 1967, II, p. 1+.

783. Novick, Julius. "Theatre," *Nation*, CCIV (1967), 829–830.

784. Popkin, Henry. "Lowell's Alternative to Aeschylus," *Times*, June 17, 1967, p. 6.

785. Price, Jonathan. "Fire against Fire," *Works*, I (Autumn 1967), 120–126.

786. ———. "The Making of Lowell's *Prometheus*," *Yale Alumni Magazine*, XXX (June 1967), 30–37.

787. Weales, Gerald. "New Haven Bound," *Reporter*, XXXVI (June 15, 1967), 44–46.

788. Zolotov, Sam. "Yale to Present Aeschylus Play," *NYT*, May 5, 1966, p. 59.

N *Notebook 1967–68* (1969)

789. "The Chameleon Poet," *Time*, XCIII (June 6, 1969), 112, 114.

790. Lask, Thomas. "The Window and the Mirror," *NYT*, June 7, 1969, p. 33.

791. Mazzaro, Jerome. "Sojourner of the Self," *Nation*, CCIX (1969), 22, 24.

792. Meredith, William. "Notebook 1967–68," *NYTBR*, June 15, 1969, pp. 1, 27.

793. Walsh, Chad. "Language Doing What It's Never Done Before," *Book World*, May 11, 1969, pp. 1, 3.

Index

References are to item numbers in the Checklist

Notes on Contributors

WILLIAM ARROWSMITH is the well-known translator of Petronius and of many other volumes. JOHN BAYLEY, the English critic, is author of *The Romantic Survival: A Study In Poetic Evolution* and of a recent book on Tolstoy. BEN BELITT is the distinguished poet and translator who has taught for many years at Bennington. JOSEPH BENNETT is an editor of *Hudson Review* and author of a volume on Baudelaire. MARIUS BEWLEY is author of *The Complex Fate, The Eccentric Design,* and others. The late R. P. BLACKMUR was author of *Language As Gesture* and other classic studies of modernist literature. ROBERT BLY is the fine American poet and editor of *The Sixties.* ROBERT BRUSTEIN is author of two books on modern theatre and Dean of the Yale Drama School. HAYDEN CARRUTH is the well-known poet and critic. RICHARD EBERHART is the distinguished American poet, winner of the Pulitzer Prize for his collected poems several years back. IRVIN EHRENPREIS is author of books on Swift and editor of the volume on American poetry published by Stratford upon Avon Studies in 1965. LESLIE FIEDLER is the American critic and novelist, author of *Love And Death In The American Novel* and other works. GEOFFREY HARTMAN is author of several books including *The Unmediated Vision* and *Wordsworth's Poetry.* RICHARD HOWARD is the American poet, critic, and translator, author of the recent critical volume on American poetry *Alone With America.* The late RANDALL JARRELL was one of the finest poets and critics the U.S. ever produced. Recently his Collected Poems and posthumous criticism have been published.

HERBERT LEIBOWITZ is an editor of *Salmagundi* and author of a recent book on Hart Crane's poetry. He has edited a collection of essays by the late music critic Paul Rosenfeld. NORMAN MAILER is the American novelist and journalist extraordinaire, author of *The Naked And The Dead* and *Armies Of The Night,* among others. JEROME MAZZARO is a poet, translator, and critic, author of *The Poetic Themes of Robert Lowell* and other works. M. L. ROSENTHAL is author of *The Modern Poets* and other volumes on modern poetry, and a widely published poet. FREDERICK SEIDEL is author of the volume of poetry entitled *Final Solutions.* JOHN SIMON is the distinguished critic of films for *The New Leader* and of drama for *The Hudson Review.* His books include the volume *Acid Test.* LOUIS SIMPSON is the American poet, author of *At The End Of The Open Road* and others. ALLEN TATE is the American poet and man of letters. JOHN WAIN is the British poet and novelist. WILLIAM CARLOS WILLIAMS was author of *Paterson* and of many other volumes of poetry, fiction, drama, autobiography, and criticism.